FROM VIETNAM TO 9/11

FROM VIETNAM TO 9/11

ON THE FRONT LINES OF NATIONAL SECURITY

WITH A NEW EPILOGUE ON THE IRAQ WAR

UPDATE 2006

JOHN P. MURTHA with JOHN PLASHAL

THE PENNSYLVANIA STATE UNIVERSITY PRESS ■ UNIVERSITY PARK, PENNSYLVANIA

Library of Congress Cataloging-in-Publication Data
for first paperback edition 2004

Murtha, John P.
From Vietnam to 9/11 : on the front lines of national security /
John P. Murtha ; with John Plashal.
With new epilogue.
p.   cm.
Originally published © 2003.
Includes bibliographical references (p.) and index.
ISBN 0-271-02928-5 (pbk. with update 2006 : alk. paper)
1. Murtha, John P.
2. Legislators—United States—Biography.
3. United States. Congress. House—Biography.
4. United States—Foreign relations—1945–1989.
5. United States—Foreign relations—1989- .
6. Election monitoring—History—20th century.
7. United States—Military relations—Foreign countries.
8. National security—United States—History—20th century.
I. Title: From Vietnam to nine-eleven.
II. Plashal, John.
III. Title.
E840.8 .M83A3 2005
328.73′092—dc22   2004011922

Second paperback edition 2006
The material in Update 2006 is in the public domain.
ISBN 0-271-02928-5 (pbk. with update : alk. paper)

It is the policy of The Pennsylvania State University Press to use acid-free paper for the first printing of all clothbound books. Publications on uncoated stock satisfy the minimum requirements of American National Standard for Information Sciences—Permanence of Paper for Printed Library Materials, ANSI Z39.48–1992.

CONTENTS

To the memory of

FREDERICK MOHRMAN

This book is dedicated to the memory of Frederick Mohrman, who served on the staff of the House Appropriations Committee from 1975 to 1996. He was the staff director for ten years. Fred was a man of integrity who loved Congress and was enormously committed to the institution of the House Appropriations Committee. He put in long hours at his job. Over the years I have always arrived at my office very early in the morning, hours before the actual business of Congress began. No matter how early I phoned Fred to discuss the day's schedule or other issues, he was always at his desk.

Staff plays a key role in facilitating the operations of Congress— writing questions for hearings, writing committee reports, bills, and laws, and advising members on changes to be made to the budget and other legislation submitted by the executive branch. There was no better staffer than Fred Morhman.

Fred served for three years in the Air Force and worked for the federal government in various financial management positions before he began work for the House Appropriations Committee. He was a devoted family man. In addition to raising five children, over the years he and his wife, Jan, took into their home eighty-two foster children who were pre-adoptive or needed protective care.

After retiring from the committee, Fred and Jan moved to Kentucky, where they had bought two hundred acres some years before. There Fred was a gentleman farmer until his untimely death in 2001.

PREFACE

When I arrived in South Vietnam in August 1966, the importance of military and strategic intelligence was not on my mind. I had just volunteered to serve in the Marine Corps and I was not certain what specific duties I would be asked to fulfill when I reported to the 1st Marine Regiment. Then I was assigned to be an intelligence officer for the regiment. It was an education I have never forgotten. When I returned to the States a year later, I brought back with me a plaque given to me by Gunnery Sergeant Wolf that read, "Victory Is Knowing Your Enemy." Those few words were seared into my memory because of my experience in Vietnam. It is a maxim that should be front and center in the minds of every American leader—whether that leader is a 1st sergeant in the military, a general in the Army, a secretary of state, or a president.

History is replete with the lessons of the absolutely vital role of intelligence. One of the major factors in the outcome of World War II was breaking the German Enigma code. However, Stalin ignored intelligence reports that a German attack into Russia was imminent and his country paid dearly. Breaking the Japanese code played a central role in America's success in the war in the Pacific. During the Korean War, one can only guess how things would have changed if General Douglas MacArthur had not dismissed warnings from many of his intelligence officers of a predicted Chinese counterattack when and if UN forces carried the war to North Korea.

It takes brains, experience, intuition, and some luck to put the pieces of the intelligence mosaic together. When I served in South Vietnam, I found out firsthand how difficult it was to put together a clear tactical intelligence picture. The 1st Marine Regiment received innumerable reports about imminent attacks and we seldom knew which were accurate. The same was true in Beirut in the early 1980s, when so many of our soldiers were killed in a terrorist attack. In Somalia, during the deployment of U.S. forces in the early 1990s, the intelligence was totally inadequate. Our military arrived in country knowing next to nothing about the warring clans, the culture, the tradition of the people, and the reasons behind the deep hatred between different factions. We paid a dear price for our lack of understanding. In 1999, the State Department predicted a few days of bombing would bring down the Serbian dictator Slobodan Milošević. In reality it took 23,000 bombs and missiles fired by the United States and its allies and the threat of intervention by a massive ground-force operation before Serbian forces withdrew from Kosovo. Now, in retrospect, it seems apparent that our intelligence agencies failed to link together the scraps of information from hundreds of different sources that would have predicted the catastrophic attack of 9/11.

The way we go about collecting, analyzing, and using intelligence information is one of the most important determinants of our success or failure in world events. Unfortunately, it is a lesson we have had to relearn too often, at a heavy price in American blood and treasure. Throughout this book, I return to the importance of intelligence as I describe my involvement in and perspective on many of America's foreign policy crises in recent decades.

ACKNOWLEDGMENTS

I first met Charles Horner, a veteran of the Vietnam War, many years ago when he was serving as liaison for the Army to the House Defense Appropriations Subcommittee. Charlie was present at many of the events described in these pages. His recollection of events and the meticulous reports he submitted to me after we returned from inspection trips have been very important to me in the writing of this book. I have valued Charlie's advice and counsel over the years.

Numerous people reviewed various portions of the manuscript, including Congressman Nick Rahall (D-W.Va.), one of the most knowledgeable members of Congress on the Middle East; Stephen Solarz, former Democratic congressman from New York, who served on the Foreign Affairs Committee for many years and has a prodigious knowledge of foreign policy; General Anthony Zinni, former CINCENTCOM (commander in chief of the Central Command), who has had a long and distinguished career in the Marine Corps and also served his country as special envoy to the Middle East; Ambassador Steven Bosworth, who has served in several key diplomatic posts over the years; Robert Oakley, who served as U.S. ambassador to Pakistan and special ambassador to Somalia, among his many diplomatic posts; Larry Knisch of the Congressional Research Service, who served on the delegation that monitored the Marcos-Aquino election in the Philippines; and Julie Kim, also of the Congressional Research Service, who has authored numerous papers and studies on the Balkans. Let me quickly add that the fact that these distinguished individuals reviewed portions of the manuscript does not imply that they necessarily agree with my perspective on the events I describe here.

I would also like to thank Dave Morrison and Gabrielle Carruth of the appropriations committee staff for the extensive research they conducted on the war in Iraq and its aftermath. In the Epilogue, I made extensive use of the data they developed.

I also extend thanks to the members of the staff of the Library of Congress who so ably and quickly responded to my many requests for books and source documents, especially Barbu Alim and Marcel Monfort. Thanks also to Andres Plashal, who helped to select some of the photographs, Drew Paulus of FolioGraphics, who did such a professional job in the production and printing of many of the photographs and maps, and the DOD Joint Combat Camera Center and the Defense Visual Information Center, which provided CD-ROMs containing some of the photos that appear in the book. Special thanks go to Barbara Salazar for the exceptional job she did in editing the final manuscript, to Laura Reed-Morrisson for the equally exceptional job in editing the Epilogue, and to Sanford Thatcher and the staff at Penn State University Press for the great job they did in handling the wide range of details involved in the publication of this book.

ACRONYMS AND ABBREVIATIONS

AWACS	Airborne Warning and Control System
CIA	Central Intelligence Agency
CINCSOUTH	commander in chief, Southern Command
CODEL	congressional delegation
COMELEC	Commission on Elections (Philippines)
FLIR	forward-looking infrared radar
GDP	gross domestic product
GNP	gross national product
HEW	Department of Health, Education and Welfare
HUMINT	intelligence gathering by agents and operatives rather than by technological devices
JDAM	Joint Direct Attack Munitions
KLA	Kosovo Liberation Army
LAF	Lebanese Armed Forces
MFO	multinational force and observers
MIA	missing in action
MNF	multinational force
MOS	military occupational specialty
NAMFREL	National Citizen Movement for Free Elections (Philippines)
NATO	North Atlantic Treaty Organization
NCA	National Command Authority
NPA	New People's Army (Philippines)
NSC	National Security Council
OMB	Office of Management and Budget
PDF	Panamanian Defense Force
PLO	Palestine Liberation Organization
ROE	rules of engagement
ROTC	Reserve Officers Training Corps
SDI	Strategic Defense Initiative

Acronyms and Abbreviations

SOUTHCOM	Southern Command
TAOR	tactical area of responsibility
UAV	unmanned aerial vehicle
UNIDO	United National Democratic Party (Philippines)
UNOSOM	United Nations Operation in Somalia
UNPROFOR	United Nations Protection Force
USMNF	United States component, multinational force
USO	United Service Organization

1

SERVICE IN VIETNAM, 1966-1967

My family has had a tradition of military service for several generations. Robert Bell, one of my mother's ancestors, fought in the Revolutionary War. His great-grandson, Abraham Tidball Bell, served in the Union Army during the Civil War. A small wooden box on my desk, where I keep important family documents, contains a letter from him describing his duties: while stationed in Washington, D.C., he guarded the Capitol—the very building I have worked in since 1974. His widow, Mary Bell, lived to be ninety-six. I can remember her telling me when I was a child, "One person can make a difference."

My father's ancestors immigrated from Ireland during the potato famine of the 1840s. The family settled in western Pennsylvania, where my grandfather was involved in coal mining and banking. My father and his three brothers all fought in World War II. I was just eight years old when the United States entered the war. I realized that something of great significance was happening, but I had no concept of the issues involved or the enormity of the war.

A variety of local civic projects were quickly organized to help the war effort. I remember going with my mother to fields just outside town to pick milkweed. The down from this plant was used to fill the linings of life jackets to make them buoyant. We collected aluminum foil (we called it tinfoil) peeled from chewing gum wrappers and Hershey bars and empty packs of cigarettes; wrapped into large balls, the foil became raw material for war plants. Many of the housewives in our town went to work in those plants. By the time the war effort really geared up, more than six million women

joined the workforce and were employed in the production of tanks, personnel carriers, ships, aircraft, and ammunition or served as volunteers for a
variety of agencies and institutions involved in the war effort. Their contribution to the Allies' ultimate victory was enormous. Also, another 350,000
women joined the armed forces.

One of my father's brothers, Regis Murtha, was in the Army Air Corps.
He was shot down over Germany but survived. My father and his three
brothers were overseas during the entire war, but they all returned safely.
Tom Brokaw was indeed right when he called theirs "the greatest generation."

I was twelve when my father and his brothers came home from the war.
I was very curious about what they had experienced, but they had little to
say about it. I was to discover that silence about wartime experiences was
common among World War II veterans. I was never sure if their reticence
stemmed from a sense that a man just had to carry out an obligation to
serve his country and then put it behind him, or if some of their experiences
had been so painful and traumatic that they simply preferred not to talk
about them.

My Decision to Join the Marine Corps

I graduated from high school in 1950, the year North Korea invaded South
Korea. In reaction to the invasion, President Harry S Truman, one of the
most decisive presidents in our history, decided immediately to send American troops to counter the attack under the flag of the United Nations. I
expected it to be a short war. I considered joining the Army, but my mother
and grandfather insisted that I attend college. I enrolled in Washington and
Jefferson College. A casual observer would have thought I was majoring in
football and basketball.

So many young men who ordinarily would have been attending college
were in the service that our football team had only twenty-eight players. I
was in the ROTC (Reserve Officers Training Corps) and planned to go on
active duty as a second lieutenant after I graduated. With so many of my
contemporaries in the service, however, I just didn't feel comfortable sitting
out the war on campus, and I decided to enlist as a private in the Marine
Corps. My mother was furious when I broke the news to her.

I had to wear my civilian clothes for the first two weeks of boot camp.

After completing boot camp at Parris Island in August 1952, I was promoted to private first class and received the American Spirit Medal award.

Uniforms were in such short supply that none were available for me. At the end of boot camp, I received the American Spirit Medal award "for the display of outstanding qualities of leadership best expressing the American Honor, Initiative, Loyalty and High Example to Comrades in Arms." Of the sixteen military awards I've received, I'm proudest of that one.

My first assignment was as drill instructor at Parris Island, South Carolina, molding new recruits into Marines. I took and passed a four-year college equivalency test and was offered a chance to attend the U.S. Naval Academy at Annapolis, Maryland. I declined in favor of the Officer Candidate Screening Course at the Marine Corps base at Quantico, Virginia. There I had an opportunity to become an officer if I successfully completed a vigorous regimen. It was a demanding course, both physically and mentally, designed to eliminate candidates who could not do well under stress. The training involved long marches, familiarization with weapons, being awakened in the middle of the night for surprise training exercises, and constant assessment of initiative under a variety of challenging circumstances. When we gathered on the parade ground on the last day, we were told that each man was to join a group on either the right or the left when his name was called. We knew that one group was graduating and the other was not, but we weren't told which was which. As the names were called, it seemed to me that some of the most capable candidates were told to go to the left. I had been told to go to the group on the right. The presiding officer finally announced that the group on the right had passed and had become second lieutenants. We then took the Officer Basic Training Course, which transformed civilians and enlisted Marines into officers. During the course I gained increased confidence in my leadership skills. Upon graduation, I volunteered to go to Korea and received orders to do so, but the truce ending the war was signed shortly afterward and my orders were canceled.

I still had two years to serve, and during that time I was lucky to have a crusty career Marine—Major Wilson—as my mentor. As a platoon commander and an assistant operations officer stationed at Camp Lejeune, North Carolina, I was involved in a wide variety of training and operations. Major Wilson instilled in me a simple four-word credo that has stuck with me ever since: "Pay attention to details." It is a basic approach that has served me well over the years.

While I was stationed at Camp Lejeune I met Joyce Bell, who lived in the nearby town of Richlands. We started dating, and when I was transferred to the Marine base at Quantico, Virginia, outside of Washington, D.C., Joyce moved to the Washington area with two of her girlfriends. We were married in Alexandria, Virginia, not long afterward. Soon we had three children—twin boys, John and Patrick, and our daughter, Donna. The birth of the twins was a surprise. When Joyce was pregnant, she went to the doctor every month but he never detected any sign of a second child. I remember thinking in the last two months of her pregnancy that this was going to be a big baby. After John was born and scrubbed down, the doctor removed his surgical mask and told the nurses that he was headed for his next appointment. One of the nurses, who had just immigrated from Scotland, said in her Scottish brogue, "Doctor, how aboot the other baby?"

As we began to raise our family, I attended the University of Pittsburgh at Johnstown while working forty hours a week at the car wash and gas station my father had bought. Dad had a long battle with alcoholism, and he was neglecting the business. When it began losing money, I had to take over its operation. My family responsibilities and the long hours I spent running the business forced me to drop out of college. My mother and Joyce were very upset by my decision, but eventually I went back to the University of Pittsburgh part-time, majoring in economics, and received my degree.

During those years of working and attending school, I continued to study military matters and read a lot of military history. I also had an insatiable interest in foreign affairs. In 1954, I followed the news about France's defeat in its effort to regain control of French Indochina, now Vietnam. I read that the Vietnamese had to haul their heavy weapons by hand up the mountains around Dien Bien Phu, where the climatic battle took place. I saw on newsreels the tenacity of the Vietnamese troops and the sacrifices they made. Although the United States provided the French with about $1 billion to assist their war effort in Indochina, President Eisenhower turned down their request for close air support for their embattled forces at Dien Bien Phu. The tide of history was running against colonialism. As I watched those newsreels, I had no idea that twelve years later I would be in Vietnam, fighting against the Viet Cong and North Vietnamese forces. The head of North Vietnam's forces while I served in Vietnam was General Vo Nguyen Giap, the very commander who had defeated the French at Dien Bien Phu.

After I finished my active duty, I joined the Marine Corps Reserves and became the commanding officer of the 34th Rifle Company in Johnstown, Pennsylvania. Serving in the Reserves required one weekend of training a month and two weeks of active duty each year. During those two-week periods I had a variety of assignments, from the jungle warfare school in Panama to a guerrilla warfare school at Camp Pendleton, California. Undergoing this type of training and becoming an expert in those areas seemed especially practical, in view of the victory of Mao Tse-tung's guerrilla forces over Chiang Kai-shek in mainland China, the victory of the Vietnamese in their war against the French, and the ongoing guerrilla wars elsewhere in Asia.

I was promoted steadily and attained the rank of major in the mid-1960s. By that time the United States' commitment to South Vietnam had begun to escalate. At the end of President Kennedy's first year in office, there had been 3,200 American military personnel in Vietnam, primarily as advisers. After Kennedy's assassination and Lyndon Johnson's succession to the presidency, LBJ swamped the Republican candidate, Senator Barry Goldwater of Arizona, in the 1964 presidential race. President Johnson was determined not to be the first American president to lose a war. As our commitment to

South Vietnam escalated, so did the level of our casualties. From January 1961 to July 1965, 503 Americans were killed, 2,270 wounded, and 57 missing or captured. By mid-1965 the scope and stakes of our involvement in Vietnam had begun to change radically. The numbers of North Vietnamese regular troops infiltrating into South Vietnam were increasing significantly, and in July 1965 President Johnson ordered the U.S. forces there increased from 23,000 to 125,000. And for the first time they were to be used in direct combat.

I Return to Active Duty

I decided to volunteer to serve in Vietnam. As a thirty-three-year-old with three children who had previously served on active duty and now was serving in the Reserves, I was not eligible for the draft, but I felt strongly that it was my duty to serve. The family business was doing well by this time and the profits from it plus my Marine Corps pay ensured that Joyce and the children would be taken care of during my absence. My brother Charles ran the business while I was gone. It was an emotional moment when I discussed my decision to return to active duty with Joyce, but she agreed.

When I informed the Marine Corps of my intentions, they sent me a telegram saying I could replace an officer at Camp Lejeune, freeing him to go to Vietnam. I told the Marine Corps my intention was to go to Vietnam myself, not to serve Stateside so that somebody else could go. Soon I received orders for "Ground Forces, Vietnam" and I packed my bags. It was a damp, blustery day when I bade an emotional farewell to my family.

I flew to the Treasure Island Naval Base in San Francisco, filled out some paperwork, and flew on to the island of Okinawa, south of Japan. The officer I reported to said, "We'll keep you here on Okinawa, at least for a while." I protested and showed him my orders: "Ground Forces, Vietnam." After the military and civilian bureaucrats shuffled papers for a day or two, they sent me on to the war zone.

The flight from Okinawa to Vietnam was on a World War II–vintage C-47 transport. I vividly remember the last few minutes of that flight. I was sitting next to a chaplain and we were looking out of the window as we flew over the sea on the approach to Da Nang. The foliage was glistening from a recent rain and the seacoast was a spectacular panorama with the waves breaking on a vast white sandy beach. Everything appeared to be

This photo was taken in August 1966 at the Da Nang air base in northern South Vietnam. Standing next to me is another Marine from Johnstown, Pennsylvania—Gunnery Sergeant Lehmer.

peaceful, exotic, and beautiful. I remember saying to the chaplain, "How could a war be going on in a country of such breathtaking beauty?"

South Vietnam was divided into four military regions and the large air base at Da Nang, where we landed, was the most northern of the four. It was referred to as I Corps, and 41,000 Marines were there in 1966. Two of South Vietnam's largest cities, Hue and Da Nang, were located in the I Corps.

The officer I reported to at division headquarters wanted to transfer to another location in Vietnam and asked me to take over his job. He did administrative work in the G-1 section. I argued with him, pulling out my orders one more time and pointing to the words "Ground Forces, Vietnam." I was getting the feeling that the major obstacle to my serving in the field in Vietnam was the Marine Corps itself.

Colonel Crossfield, the chief administrative officer, heard us arguing and came over to ask what the problem was. When we told him, he decided he did not want to train a reserve officer with no background in administrative work to become his chief administrative assistant. Since I was a senior major by that time, it was difficult to place me because there were few slots for that rank in the First Marine Regiment. Colonel Crossfield decided I should be assigned as the First Marine Regiment's intelligence officer. The regiment had three main missions: destroy the military and supply infrastructure of the Viet Cong guerrillas and their North Vietnamese allies in our tactical area of responsibility (TAOR), protect the Da Nang Air Base from attack, and develop friendly relations with the local Vietnamese people.

I took the intelligence slot with the understanding that if a command position opened up for my rank, I would get it. I was disappointed with the assignment, but within days I realized the vital importance of the position. While our forces had an overwhelming superiority in weaponry, mobility, firepower, and airpower, the Viet Cong had the advantage of knowing every hill, valley, cave, and trail. Clearly a vigorous intelligence effort was needed to optimize our strengths, match the Viet Cong's knowledge of the local terrain, and attempt to exploit their weaknesses.

I started my duties by going into the field every day to learn the terrain and trying to get a feel for the area of our regiment's responsibility. The day-to-day existence in the field was challenging. One misstep on patrol and a poisoned "punji spike" buried in the moist ground would pierce your foot, causing a debilitating injury. Antipersonnel mines, which could maim or kill, were planted by the hundreds of thousands in the ground by the Viet Cong and North Vietnamese. Snipers fired at will.

I studied all the incidents occurring in our regiment's TAOR. There were about seven hundred incidents a month, ranging from casualties from antipersonnel mines and sniper attacks to large-scale ambushes by the Viet Cong and the North Vietnamese who had infiltrated into the country. I read all the operations reports and after-action reports available in an attempt to detect a pattern and determine what steps we could take to counter the incidents and attacks more effectively.

I told the regiment commander, Colonel Mallory, that I wanted a small cadre of the brightest troops who had spent time in the field to assist me in developing a vigorous and effective tactical intelligence capability for the

This grainy photograph was taken at the Marines' regimental headquarters just south of the Da Nang air base in 1966.

regiment. I also argued to keep those troops in their jobs for the remainder of their tour in Vietnam. I had quickly learned that the constant mid-tour transferring of personnel from one kind of job to another was seriously eroding combat effectiveness. Serving in many positions may have been beneficial to one's career, but it definitely detracted from one's ability to do the job at hand. A tour for Americans in Vietnam was one year. When the time it took to learn the details of one's duties, the time granted for well-deserved R&R (rest and relaxation), and the time consumed at the end of the tour for paperwork were factored in, the total time of actual effective performance for many of our troops was probably about eight or nine months. If you add to that the switching from one job to another, it became clear that as far as job effectiveness was concerned, a lot of valuable time was wasted. Besides, the rotation policy was unfair to infantry enlisted personnel, most of whom would spend their entire tour in the field while their leaders frequently switched jobs. I believed strongly that the constant rotation of individuals, rather than whole units, also led to a lack of cohesion and effectiveness. The rotation policy became especially debilitating years later when we scaled back the level of U.S. forces. Rather than rotate units back to the States, the Marine Corps sent back individuals according to their length of time in country. The cohesion of many units collapsed.

General Norman Schwarzkopf, who served two tours in Vietnam as a mid-level officer, was also alarmed about the job rotation policy. Reflecting on his second tour in 1969, he wrote:

> I tried to figure out how the situation had deteriorated so far. Perhaps the answer was ticket punching. In those days all a lieutenant colonel needed to get promoted to colonel was to command a battalion "successfully"—that is, to come back alive with a decent efficiency report. Officers were rotated through battalion command every six months, which enabled the maximum number to punch their battalion-commander ticket, but also meant that many unqualified officers were put in charge of men's lives. . . . Because officers remained in command for such a brief time, they didn't have to suffer the results of their incompetence.[1]

Colonel Mallory agreed with the case I presented to him for expanding the capability of our regiment's intelligence operation. He gave me Marines from each battalion to conduct the operation and also agreed to keep them in that function for the remainder of their tours. We began to work on a system to replace the laborious manual recording of incidents that occurred in our TAOR. The data processing and storage system we used was technologically simple but it did the job we needed done. We divided our TAOR into a grid and collated information about each square. We recorded sixteen factors for each event in each square—time of incident, date, level of illumination, number of enemy, and so on.

With the technical expertise of Captain Bob Olsen (from the S-1 administrative section of the regiment), we used the data processing software to map out the timing, locations, and types of enemy attacks, ambushes, and other incidents encountered by our troops. We were trying to develop recommendations to enhance the protection of our forces and develop a strategy to locate and engage the enemy more effectively. By today's standards this approach was elementary, but it was a lot better than the grease pencils and acetate-covered maps we'd been using before. The United States' tactical intelligence hardware in Vietnam eventually became more sophisticated, but we had none of the high-tech intelligence systems that are now in wide use—satellites that provide quick information on enemy troop and equipment concentrations, UAVs (unmanned aerial vehicles) that provide real-time videos of the enemy's positions, and aircraft that can detect and locate enemy electronic emissions and quickly disseminate that information to troops on the ground. Nevertheless, at the time our modest effort was a technological step forward and it provided valuable intelligence for our unit.

Lessons from Battles

One thing our intelligence team knew for sure was that the Viet Cong and North Vietnamese troops had no vehicles when they deployed to encounter U.S. and South Vietnamese troops. Furthermore, we knew that despite their lack of vehicles, they were able to get to the battle sites within hours and quickly return to their base afterward. They almost always traveled at night. We didn't know where their base was, but by analyzing the data we had compiled, we calculated its likely position. The colonel listened to our recommendation and agreed to send a large number of Marines into that area. We deployed and scoured the surrounding area for two days. We found nothing but a cemetery surrounded by open fields. There was absolutely no action in the area. We concluded that the enemy was probably hiding in a nearby tunnel complex, but we couldn't find it. Then we received agent reports from our regimental headquarters that the Viet Cong base was just five hundred meters to the west of the perimeter we had set up. We still couldn't find it.

The colonel had committed four companies to this mission, and he had said grimly, "This had better succeed." In the course of our search, reports of increased sniping and firefights nearby put pressure on us to abandon our mission and go where the fighting was. The sudden increase in activity to the west of our search area, however, signaled to me that we were in the right place, that the other incidents were intended to draw us away. Finally, after more than two days of uneventful searching, the colonel radioed orders to end the mission. Convinced that our intelligence analysis had been right, I asked him for one more day. He granted it. On the evening of the extra day, a young first lieutenant in our unit said to me, "Sir, the enemy must be hiding in a tunnel structure. They may very well be hurting for food and water by now. While we can't see them, I'm pretty sure they can see us. Why don't we pack up and begin to leave? Then we'll suddenly return to see if our leaving has drawn them out."

Since our efforts had turned up nothing thus far, we decided to take his advice. It was a rainy night. We packed up our gear, broke off the cordon, and began to leave the area, as though we were returning to our respective base camps. All four companies involved in this mission traveled a relatively short distance away from the assumed site of the enemy base camp and then suddenly turned around and rushed back. Sure enough, the Viet Cong and North Vietnamese had come out of their tunnels. All hell broke loose.

An intense battle went on for several hours. Bullets and shells were zinging all over the place. What has been called "the fog of war"—the shouting of orders, the uncertainties, the cries of the wounded, the smoke, the noise and turmoil—can be very disorienting. The discipline and guidelines learned in training are absolutely essential if fighting units are to survive in the chaos of the battlefield and still attain their tactical objectives. We prevailed and the key cadre of the Viet Cong operating in our TAOR was soundly defeated. After the battle, Marine "tunnel rats" went into the tunnels and did their harrowing and dangerous job of flushing out any remaining Viet Cong and then destroying the tunnels.

At the time of this battle we were unaware of the enormous extent of the tunnel systems used by the Viet Cong and their North Vietnamese allies. In many locations in South Vietnam the Viet Cong used these tunnels to hide, rest, reorganize, resupply, and receive medical care. When the *Washington Post* reporter Richard Cohen went to Vietnam in April 2000, twenty-five years after the end of the war, he went into the Cu Chi tunnel complex, north of Saigon. He wrote:

> They started digging them during the war with the French and continued through what they called the American War. By the time they finished, they had three levels, a kind of subway system—miles of tunnels, a maze that led to the river in one direction and under the jungle in another. The Viet Cong had their kitchens in the tunnels, their sleeping quarters, meeting rooms, storage spaces, clinics, operating rooms and, here and there, booby traps for any GIs brave enough to come down. They had wells, a system for disposing of human waste and camouflaged entrances so that they could pop up almost anywhere, engage their enemy and then disappear into the ground.[2]

After we captured many Viet Cong, inflicted heavy casualties on the rest, and destroyed the tunnel infrastructure, the success of the battle near the cemetery was shown dramatically when the incidents against our troops dropped from an average of about 700 a month to 100. The area had largely been pacified.

I learned two important lessons in that battle. The first was that when you have to make a major decision, it is extremely important to listen to those who have a thorough knowledge of an issue, even though they are not necessarily at or near the top of the chain of command. The lieutenant who suggested that we leave and then come back had only recently arrived in Vietnam, yet he had quickly developed a good perspective and realistic assessment of the tactical situation. Whenever I inspect our troops in the field and at bases around the United States, I always meet with junior officers and enlisted personnel to get their views and concerns.

The second lesson was to apply common sense and street smarts to a problem. Our technical research indicated strongly that we had come to the right place to find the enemy, so when we could not find them, logic dictated that we try something else in the same place. The lieutenant's recommendation was elegant in its simplicity and effective in implementation.

Another battle I vividly recall involved a reinforced rifle company of about four hundred Marines under our regiment's operational control but not located at our base. The area this rifle company covered included the highest hill (it looked like a small mountain to me) in the area south of our TAOR. The hill overlooked a route used by the North Vietnamese and the Viet Cong to bring in forces and supplies. Unfortunately, our mode of secure communication with the unit deployed on the hill was somewhat cumbersome. The enemy often monitored our unsecured communications, so to communicate with the rifle company we used a secure radio. Unfortunately, it had a limited range. We had to call to another secure radio midway between our headquarters and the unit on the hill and wait for the call to be retransmitted to its destination.

One day the commanding officer of our regiment was away at a meeting at division headquarters. The regiment's S-3 Major John Andrews, was also absent, so I was in charge. The Marine-reinforced rifle company based on the hill had spotted a contingent of enemy troops moving through the area. They saw that one of the enemy troops was carrying a large radio backpack. A radio of that size was a strong indication that the infiltrating troops were North Vietnamese, because the Viet Cong had no such equipment, at least in our area. The Marines called to our headquarters to tell us they were going to attack. I told them to wait. I was concerned that they had no reserve force and the overcast limited the use of airpower to assist them. By the time they got my message, however, they had already engaged the enemy and were encountering significant counterfire.

Meanwhile the colonel returned to our unit. A large contingent from our regiment went to support the unit under attack. We were led into the battle by one of the finest combat commanders in the Marine Corps, Lieutenant Colonel "Ding Dong" Bell. The weather prevented us from calling in air support of F-4s or other fixed-wing aircraft to bomb the Viet Cong and North Vietnamese troops.

I had been awake more than twenty-four hours by the time we landed. A few hours into the battle, an on-again-off-again event, I could no longer keep my eyes open. I curled up next to a bunker and fell into a deep sleep for about an hour. Even the noise of frequent gunfire didn't wake me up. (One of my fellow officers told me the next morning that when he hadn't seen me for an hour or so, he assumed I was dead.) In addition to our unit, a nearby South Vietnamese ground force arrived and entered the battle. The Viet Cong and North Vietnamese forces faded into the jungle as the forces arrayed against them continued to increase.

Then began the grim task of placing the dead in body bags and evacuating the wounded. One of my responsibilities as an intelligence officer was to write part of the after-action report. These reports provided data and spelled out lessons learned. I argued with the commanding officer about the number of enemy casualties we should report. I insisted we include only bodies we could count. The body count had become our scorecard in our efforts to assess who was winning the war. General Colin Powell, who served two tours in Vietnam early in his career, wrote in his memoirs:

> The Army, under Pentagon pressure to justify the country's invest-ment in lives and billions, desperately needed something to measure. What military objectives could we claim in this week's situation re-port? A hill? A valley? A hamlet? Rarely. Consequently, bodies be-came the measure. Counting bodies became a macabre statistical competition. Companies were measured against companies, battal-ions against battalions, brigades against brigades. The enemy actu-ally was taking horrendous casualties. But it made little difference. As one military analyst put it, divide each side's casualties by the economic cost of producing them. Then multiply by the political cost of sustaining them. As long as your enemy was willing to pay that price, body counts meant nothing.[3]

When the survivors of this battle were debriefed, it became clear what had happened. With their gung-ho attitude, the Marine contingent had vio-lated one of the most basic tenets of tactical warfare: they had gone beyond the range of their mortars and artillery. Without that protection and with-out air support, none of their technological advantage—airpower, mobility, and superior firepower—came into play. They were fighting on the enemy's terms: like the Vietnamese, they had only the weapons they carried.

Those lessons, too, stayed with me. The unit's decision violated basic doctrine. The events that day instilled in me even more strongly my long-held belief that good training is the key to success on the battlefield.

I also acquired an increased awareness of the limitations of airpower. Don't get me wrong. Our airpower in Vietnam, from B-52s bombing large supply depots to helicopters shuttling our troops to and from battles, gave us a tremendous advantage. Fighting the war without those assets would be unthinkable. Furthermore, with smart bombs, smart missiles, and improved aircraft, our air capability has increased dramatically since then. All the same, the reservations I acquired then about reliance on airpower have remained over the years.

My one-year tour of duty in Vietnam ended in late 1967. I was proud of what the First Marine Regiment had accomplished during that year. I was proud of my contribution to that effort. On the flight back to the States, my thoughts went back to the many heroes I had served with during my tour of duty. I especially remembered Captain Bobby Lane. His one-year tour of duty had ended a few months before mine, but he extended it for a month in order to take part in a large operation that had been scheduled against a Viet Cong stronghold. Captain Lane participated in that operation and lost both of his legs when he stepped on a Viet Cong land mine.

At Camp Pendleton, in California, after I received a physical and a discharge, I flew back to Johnstown, Pennsylvania. The reunion with my family was a joyous occasion.

Washington's Misperceptions

During these years, the "Whiz Kids," a group of bright young men whom Secretary of Defense Robert S. McNamara brought to the Pentagon, were his key advisers. Earlier some of them had been on his staff when he headed the Ford Motor Company. Optimistic assessments on the outcome of the war abounded. On October 2, 1963, Secretary McNamara stated: "The major part of the United States' military task can be completed by the end of 1965."[4]

One of Secretary McNamara's methods of gauging progress was to compare the number of villages controlled by the Viet Cong with the number of those under the Saigon government's control and those in an in-between status. Given our military's penchant for optimism and Washington's desire for the best possible outcome, these projections were often very inaccurate. U.S. officials assessing the situation at the local level would exaggerate a village's support for the government. That appraisal would be fed into the system. Those reports were gathered and compiled at higher and higher levels of the bureaucracy. When Secretary McNamara received the reports, he would advise President Johnson to inform the American people that "the tide has turned" and "there is light at the end of the tunnel." Congressman Jamie Whitten (D-Miss.), who served in Congress for over half a century, aptly described these computer projections as GIGO—garbage in, garbage out. I have learned by experience that there is often a wide gap between Washington policy makers' perceptions and reality.

There was some opposition to the war when I returned to the States, but it was relatively low-key. In Congress, for example, only eleven votes were cast against the 1967 Defense Appropriations Bill, which funded the war. The doves in Congress were arguing for a negotiated settlement. While a significant percentage of the American people did eventually turn against the war, it is important to remember just how long U.S. citizens showed strong support for our effort in Vietnam. The massive Tet offensive by the Viet Cong and the North Vietnamese in February 1968 is often cited as the watershed event that caused support for the war effort to decline. Although the Viet Cong and North Vietnamese did not win a single battle in that offensive and suffered enormous casualties, the fact that they were able to carry out such a massive effort after so many years of war and so many optimistic statements from Washington disillusioned many Americans, and public support for the war steadily eroded. Nevertheless, in 1972, seven years after I served in Vietnam, four years after the Tet offensive, and years after the columnists began to write about a "lost cause," the peace candidate for president, Senator George McGovern, carried only one state and the District of Columbia.

In retrospect, however, to a large extent the United States had conducted a war of attrition during its involvement—a most difficult strategy for a democratic society to carry out over such an extended time. I don't recall the name of the commentator who said it, but it was a perceptive observation: "The Viet Cong and North Vietnamese were looking at the calendar. We were looking at the clock."

2

ELECTION TO CONGRESS AND RETURN TO VIETNAM

Ever since I was a young boy, I had two goals in life—I wanted to be a colonel in the Marine Corps and a member of Congress. I'm not sure what instilled those goals in me. My desire to become a Marine colonel probably stemmed from the awe in which I held the World War I and II veterans and my awareness of my family's tradition of service in the military over many generations. My interest in politics started when I was about ten years old and I heard President Roosevelt address the nation. His "fireside chats" were major events in our household, and we would all gather around the radio.

I had no game plan or strategy to enter politics, just a desire to do so. My decision to enter politics was actually a very mundane event. I received a phone call one evening from the chairman of the Democratic Party in Cambria County and he said he wanted to talk to me. When I arrived at his office, he said, "Jack, we need a candidate to run against the incumbent congressman in the Twelfth District and we think you'd be a good candidate." It was that simple.

I accepted the challenge and the next day I was out campaigning. The incumbent was a Republican, John P. Saylor, who had represented the district for over twenty years. I lost the election. I enjoyed the challenge of politics, though, and the interaction with people during the campaign. I decided to run for a seat in Pennsylvania's House of Representatives and won. A few years later Congressman Saylor died in office, and in early 1974 I decided to run for Congress again in the special election held to fill the vacant seat. Saylor had won 68 percent of votes in 1972. My opponent,

Harry M. Fox, had been Saylor's administrative assistant for many years and knew the Twelfth Congressional District very well.

The Watergate scandal was festering at that time. A story about the Republicans' burglary of the Democrats' campaign headquarters at the Watergate complex led the evening news almost every day. The national press covered the Murtha versus Fox campaign in early 1974 because of the implications that the outcome might have for the upcoming November elections for the entire House of Representatives. An article in *Time* magazine stated: "Aware that the race might be seen as a bellwether for November's balloting, both parties trotted out some of their big names to join the campaign—Vice President Gerald Ford for Fox, Senators Henry Jackson, Walter Mondale, Edmund Muskie and Joseph Biden for Murtha."[1] With a total of 120,000 votes cast, I won by 230 votes! Fox demanded a recount and my winning margin was shaved to 122 votes.

My family attended my swearing-in ceremony in an ornate room located between the Speaker's office and the House chamber. The Speaker, Carl Albert of Oklahoma, was out of the country, so Thomas P. O'Neill, the majority leader, administered the oath.

At the time I entered office, new members of Congress seldom spoke during debates on the floor. All the hearings of the Appropriations Committee were held behind closed doors and no citizen or press representative could attend them. The House was run by the seniority system. The chairmen of the various committees wielded enormous power and they attained their chairmanships by only one route—remaining in Congress longer than any other committee member. Congressman George Mahon of Texas was chairman of the Defense Appropriations Subcommittee when it was formed in the 1940s, and he held that position for twenty-seven years. He also became chairman of the full Appropriations Committee. His eventual successor there was Congressman Jamie Whitten of Mississippi, who had served in Congress for thirty-eight years.

In my first year in Congress, I spent a lot of time learning the complex rules of parliamentary procedure as I observed the House in session. I remember asking myself: "How can I make a difference?" I was a member of Congress, but so were 534 others—435 of us in the House and 100 in the Senate—in a system where seniority ruled.

One day I was sitting in the House chamber in the location where the Democratic members from Pennsylvania customarily gathered. Congressman Wilbur Mills came and sat next to me. Before his career ended amid

In 1975, Speaker Carl Albert presented me with a gavel after my first day presiding over the House of Representatives. Joyce was with me at the small ceremony.

personal scandal, he had been one of the most powerful members of Congress as the chairman of the tax-writing Ways and Means Committee. It was said that one of his favorite things to do in the evening was to bring home volumes of the Internal Revenue Service tax codes to study. No one else in the House knew anywhere near as much as he did about tax issues.

When he sat next to me that day in the House, I asked him, "Mr. Chairman, how can I have an impact? What is your advice to a new member?" He replied, "Jack, there are two things you have to do. First, specialize in one area. Second, always keep your word." I have always remembered and followed that advice. Given my military background and my service on a committee involved with military issues, I decided that national security issues would be my area of expertise.

In November 1974, nine months after my victory in the special election, I had to run for office again. The Watergate scandal had made people increasingly disenchanted with politics. In a massive turnover, seventy-four new members of Congress were elected to the House. Another turnover in 1976 moved me rapidly up the seniority ladder and I was appointed to a coveted assignment on the House Appropriations Committee, which provided the discretionary funding for the entire federal government. From that position I was able to carry out my two major political objectives—to provide effective service to my constituents in the Twelfth Congressional District of Pennsylvania and to enhance the United States' national security through service on the Defense Appropriations Subcommittee.

Return to Vietnam

Although I was a new member, my background encouraged the congressional leadership to ask my opinion on Vietnam and other military issues. I returned twice to Vietnam as a congressman, the first time in late February 1975. U.S. forces had withdrawn from Vietnam and the South Vietnamese forces were carrying on the war against the Viet Cong and the North Vietnamese. President Gerald Ford's administration had asked Congress for a supplemental appropriation of $300 million for military aid to South Vietnam and $222 million for Cambodia. In addition to coping with the large numbers of North Vietnamese forces in Cambodia, the country's military forces were fighting a large guerrilla movement led by the despot Pol Pot.

President Ford requested that a bipartisan congressional delegation go to

Vietnam and Cambodia to appraise the situation and report back to him and the congressional leadership. Congressman John Flynt of Georgia led the delegation, which included supporters and opponents of the funding request.

Before our departure President Ford stressed the urgency of U.S. military aid if the Lon Nol government was to survive. Otherwise the Cambodian forces would soon run out of ammunition. The North Vietnamese had an enormous force in South Vietnam and they used Cambodia as a staging base and supply route. The situation was deteriorating rapidly as Pol Pot's forces, the Khmer Rouge, continued to gain ground against Lon Nol's pro-Western forces.

Our first stop was Saigon, where we held a conference with President Thieu and South Vietnamese military leaders. We also held discussions with the U.S. ambassador, Graham A. Martin. All of them stressed the importance of supplemental appropriations for urgently required military equipment. I had never been in Saigon before, having spent my year in Vietnam in the north. I noted that the city was teeming with people going about their everyday business. I became somewhat upbeat about the outlook for U.S. interests and the survival of the government.

I took a quick trip back to Da Nang. Things seemed to have improved militarily in the years I had been gone. I met the South Vietnamese corps commander and drove to the regional capital of Hoi An. In discussions with the local South Vietnamese corps commander and some of the troops, I found morale to be mixed. The South Vietnamese had to reduce their air missions because of a shortage of fuel. They were conducting fewer ground operations, too, because they were short of ammunition, batteries to operate their radios, and other equipment. The corps commander asked me how I thought the "solons," as they called members of Congress, would vote on aid for South Vietnam and Cambodia. I told him I didn't know, but I'd make every effort to ensure that Congress provided the funds they needed to continue their effort to counter the Viet Cong and North Vietnamese forces.

Hoping against hope, and after seeing the thriving economy in Saigon and the apparently improved military situation around Da Nang, I thought there was a possibility that the pending supplemental funding would enable our allies to hold on and ultimately prevail. It was obvious to me that if the funds were not provided, the situation would deteriorate rapidly.

After two days in Vietnam, six of us went on a side trip to Phnom Penh, the capital of Cambodia. We flew on an Air America plane, operated by the CIA. Because of ongoing battles near the airport, the pilot had to keep at a very high altitude until we reached the airfield, then descend in tight circles. After being quickly whisked off the plane, we were taken in bulletproof vans to the residence of the U.S. ambassador, John Gunther Dean. We learned later that shortly after we left the airport, four or five rockets struck the field.

The situation in Cambodia was ominous. From Ambassador Dean we learned that overland supply routes to the Cambodian troops were cut off and the only means to supply them was by air. The government troops in the Phnom Penh region were down to five days of ammunition for some of their weapons.

We met with Lon Nol, the Cambodian premier. His assessment was also grim. I was impressed with his candor when he said he was not indispensable and that under certain circumstances he would be willing to step aside to bring peace.

We had a working lunch with the premier and other top government officials. Actually, it would be more appropriately described as a sumptuous working banquet. We were served an exquisite meal of many courses. It was a very unusual day. Here I was, a strongly pro-defense Vietnam combat veteran, sitting at a huge banquet table across from Congresswoman Bella Abzug of Manhattan, probably the most liberal member of Congress and the most intense opponent of the Vietnam War. While Bella and I argued heatedly about the proposed supplemental appropriation bill between mouthfuls of jumbo shrimp, we were interrupted from time to time by the sound of explosions and gunfire as the Khmer Rouge forces closed their noose around the city. It was a surreal afternoon.

In fact, much about the conflict in Cambodia was surreal. Lewis Sorley has written: "The Cambodians pretended that the North Vietnamese had not taken over the border of their country, the Americans pretended that they were not bombing those enemy sanctuaries, the Cambodians pretended not to notice the bombing, and the North Vietnamese pretended that they weren't there in the first place, the latter stance a decided inconvenience in that it prevented their complaining about the bombing."[2]

Upon our return to the States our delegation met with President Ford and Secretary of State Henry Kissinger. Many of us made the case that approval of aid for Vietnam and Cambodia was essential. At the very least, we said, our allies should continue to be given a chance to succeed. I said it was obvious that if Congress did not provide the funds, the South Vietnamese government would collapse rapidly, because the combat readiness of their troops was being reduced by supply shortages at the very time the North Vietnamese were engaged in a rapid buildup. The Cambodian forces faced the same fate. I testified before the Senate Foreign Relations Committee that the aid should be approved. I also predicted a bloodbath in Cambodia if the Khmer Rouge came to power.

The supplemental appropriation bill to provide funds to our allies was split into two separate bills. The first bill, for Cambodia, passed in the House and was sent to the Senate. History overcame events, however, and before the full Congress could act, the government forces began to collapse. The Khmer Rouge forces soon took over Cambodia and the most degenerate regime since Hitler came to power. The remaining diplomatic mission of the United States left Cambodia on April 12, 1975, about six weeks after our visit. By that time a significant minority of Americans were so opposed to the war that they actually hoped our Vietnamese and Cambodian allies would lose.

Stephen Morris of Johns Hopkins University wrote:

> On April 13, 1975, five days before the Khmer Rouge takeover of Phnom Penh, *New York Times* correspondent Sydney Schanberger wrote that for the "ordinary people of Indochina . . . it is difficult to imagine how their lives could be anything but better with the Americans gone.
>
> Only a few days later, with communist troops emptying the city at gunpoint and Mr. Schanberger in temporary refuge at the French embassy, he began experiencing some doubts. Still, it would take many years—full of undeniable accounts of mass executions, starvation and disease—before Mr. Schanberger and his fellow antiwar journalists, academics and lobbyists would admit that a holocaust had taken place in Cambodia.[3]

Pol Pot's rule in Cambodia is one of the saddest chapters in human history. As Ben Kiernan wrote, "In the first days after Cambodia became Democratic Kampuchea in 1975, all cities were evacuated, hospitals cleared, schools closed, monasteries shut, libraries scattered. For nearly four years freedom of the press, of movement, of worship, of organization, of association, and of dissuasion all completely disappeared. So did everyday family life. A whole nation was kidnapped and then besieged from within."[4]

Photographs of the gruesome results of the despotic Pol Pot regime began to appear in the media; the most common photographs were those of mounds of human skulls stacked about ten high. These mounds appeared throughout the country as the number of victims of the genocidal government continued to grow. The population of Cambodia at the time the Pol Pot forces came to power was about 6 million. According to the Congressional Research Service, the number of Cambodian citizens killed by the Khmer Rouge was variously estimated to be somewhere between 1 and 3 million.[5] The crimes committed against the people of Cambodia were the worst that humanity has suffered since the scourge of Hitler.

The situation also began to unravel quickly in South Vietnam as Viet Cong and North Vietnamese forces closed in on Saigon. By that time President Nixon had resigned in the wake of the Watergate scandal. Vice President Spiro Agnew had resigned earlier because of a tax and bribery scandal. Thus neither of their successors, President Ford and Vice President Nelson Rockefeller, was elected to the office he held and thus had no basis of support that would enable them to react to the massive North Vietnam invasion. I believe the outcome in Vietnam could have been different if the Watergate scandal had not occurred.

A few weeks before the collapse of the pro-Western South Vietnamese government, Joyce and I were invited to a dinner at the South Vietnamese embassy in Washington. On the evening of the dinner we drove to the embassy with Congressman George Mahon and his wife, Helen.

As the invited guests gathered at the embassy, the lead story (actually the only story) on the evening news was the evacuation of the few remaining American diplomats, along with the Marines guarding our embassy. We watched with deep emotion as the dramatic evacuation was carried out and the Viet Cong and North Vietnamese troops seized Saigon and the rest of the country. It was a somber and eerie evening. Congressman Mahon and I had both been strong supporters of the South Vietnamese government. As we observed the evacuation, silence settled over the group. The cause that Mahon had believed in and fought strongly for in Congress, the cause I had fought for in Congress and on the battlefield, was disintegrating before our eyes. Today I am still amazed at the misconceptions that many Americans have about those last days. Many think that our troops were driven out by the North Vietnamese. They have forgotten, if they ever knew, that the last

U.S. combat soldiers had been withdrawn from Vietnam two years before the North Vietnamese and Viet Cong took over.

It is estimated that in the aftermath of the communist victory, a quarter of a million South Vietnamese refugees drowned in the sea as they attempted to escape in small boats that were barely seaworthy. Untold numbers of Vietnamese were sent to "reeducation camps" to learn the "glory of the socialist revolution." A quarter of a century after the communists took over, Vietnam remained in dire poverty while other countries in the region had made dramatic economic progress.

My Last Trip to Vietnam

I revisited Vietnam one more time with a congressional delegation. By the time of our visit in 1978, Vietnam had been united under a communist dictatorship for about three years and Saigon had been renamed Ho Chi Minh City. There I saw some of the villas where American senior officers had lived during the war. Having lived in a tent during my year in Vietnam, I was disturbed by the lavishness of these facilities. Rank has its privileges, of course, but the fact that some of our senior officers had lived in such opulence just didn't seem right.

Our delegation was sent to discuss with the Vietnamese the issue of Americans still listed as missing in action (MIA) and to try to bring back the remains of any Americans that had been found in recent years. We had two meetings on the MIA issue with Vietnam's vice minister of foreign affairs, Phan Hien. He told us of the difficulty of locating the bodies of any American servicemen who had been killed in remote areas. Almost everyone in Vietnam, he said, had a relative who had been killed or wounded during the war, so it was hard to interest them in taking time off from work to conduct a difficult and dangerous search for dead Americans.

Although it was believed that the last Americans had returned from Vietnam years earlier, there had been persistent but unconfirmed reports that some Americans were still being held prisoner. I had very serious doubts about those reports for the simple reason that there was no political advantage for the Vietnamese in holding American prisoners. It seemed to me that if they had wanted to use prisoners as bargaining chips, they would have been only too eager to let us know they had them.

In addition to the two meetings with Vice Minister Phan Hien to discuss MIAS, we met with the mayor of Ho Chi Minh City and with chairmen of

In May 1984, President Reagan, Senator Strom Thurmond, and I presided at a ceremony in the Capitol rotunda honoring the Unknown Soldier from the Vietnam War. The body was exhumed in 1998 and through DNA testing the remains were identified as those of Air Force First Lieutenant Michael Joseph Blassie. The crypt at the Arlington National Cemetery is empty.

several National Assembly committees. The people we encountered in the streets and the officials we met were not at all friendly toward our delegation.

After that hostile reception, I was surprised by the civil, even friendly attitude of our hosts in Hanoi. We stayed in an austere building, furnished with straw mats to sleep on. Through interpreters we held random conversations with a cross section of the North Vietnamese people. Our hosts told us that the remains of eleven American servicemen would be turned over to us for return to the United States. A brief ceremony was held at the airport: we gave flags to the airmen who had flown in on a C-141 and they draped them over the boxes that contained the remains of the eleven victims.

After completing our discussions in Hanoi, we flew to neighboring Laos and met with the acting foreign minister in Vientiane, the capital. He, too, talked about the difficulties of searching for the remains of U.S. airmen whose aircraft had crashed or been shot down in thick rain forest and sparsely populated areas of rugged terrain. Roger Pfump, an American employee of the American Society of Friends (the Quakers), confirmed that it was extremely difficult to find the downed aircraft, especially in thick foliage.

The Laotians did turn over to us the remains of four pilots. Some members of the delegation said the simplest thing would be to take the remains back on our plane. I insisted on the appropriate military honors: the remains should be returned on a military aircraft in boxes covered with flags presented by us as representatives of the American people.

On the morning of the ceremony the sky was a magnificent blue interrupted by a few cumulus clouds. The surrounding hills were a deep green. The notes of taps hung in the air. American flags were draped over the boxes containing the remains and they were carried aboard the military aircraft. It was an emotional moment.

Although the communists had been victorious in Vietnam, by the time of our visit in 1978 tensions had risen between Vietnam and its neighbor to the north, the People's Republic of China. Despite their assumed common geopolitical interests, military skirmishes broke out on the border. I heard from a variety of sources in both Vietnam and Laos that their main concern was a potential threat from China, and that the friendliness of the North Vietnamese was at least partly attributable to their fear of a Chinese invasion. Thus the Vietnamese viewed Americans less as a former enemy than as a counterweight to the Chinese.

I learned that Vietnamese citizens of ethnic Chinese descent, people who had lived in Vietnam for decades or generations, were leaving the country because they, too, believed China was about to invade and feared reprisals. To me, this was important intelligence.

After returning to Washington, I requested an emergency meeting with Secretary of State Cyrus Vance and other administration officials to discuss my findings and impressions. I relayed the concern about a possible Chinese military invasion to Richard Holbrooke, the assistant secretary of state for East Asian Affairs, but he said the U.S. intelligence community had concluded that the Chinese were not going to invade Vietnam.

Months later a large Chinese military force crossed the border into North

Vietnam. Fierce fighting ensued. To me the ultimate irony was that because of the United States' experience in Vietnam, many Americans were cheering on the Chinese. They seemed to forget why the United States got involved in Vietnam in the first place—to block expansion of the political and military influence of the Chinese communists in Southeast Asia. History takes many bizarre turns.

3

TRAGEDY IN LEBANON

Thomas P. "Tip" O'Neill (D-Mass.) was an outstanding member of Congress who served as Speaker of the House of Representatives from 1977 to 1987. Tip was my mentor during my initial years in Congress. I believe he was one of the most effective leaders of the House in the twentieth century. From time to time he asked me to make on-site inspections at a location where a foreign policy crisis was festering, especially if that crisis involved the deployment of U.S. troops.

I have found over the years that an on-site inspection is essential for a realistic assessment of what is actually going on during a foreign crisis and what dangers our troops may encounter. The alternative is to rely on media reports or on recommendations from the executive branch. I have found that the official government reports on foreign crises are often so general or so sanitized that I'm not comfortable relying on them for guidance. The Congress—the people's branch of government—has an obligation to make an independent assessment of key foreign policy issues.

One of the first requests Speaker O'Neill made to me was to go to Lebanon in late 1982. President Reagan had recently deployed a naval task force off the coast of Lebanon and sent a contingent of Marines to Beirut, its capital, because the civil war there might have an adverse impact on the United States' broader interests in the region.

The deployment of our troops to Lebanon had, to put it mildly, a lukewarm reception in Congress. The number of U.S. troops deployed in the country and off its coast was relatively small—about 2,500. All the same, after our experience in Vietnam, the Congress and the American public

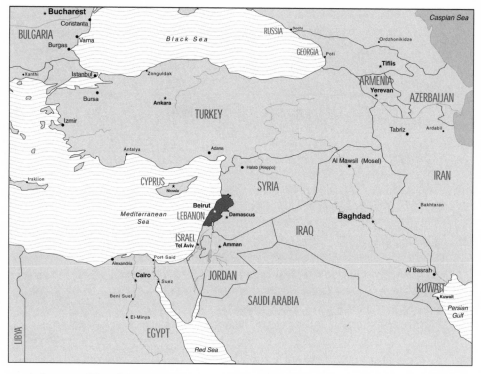

Lebanon and its neighbors

greeted any deployment of U.S. troops into a potential combat environment with wariness and concern.

The Background

With the exception of Israel, Lebanon was the most developed country in the Middle East. Beirut, a beautiful city, was known as the Paris of the Middle East. It's a small country, about the size of Connecticut. In 1982, when the U.S. troops were sent there, it had a population of about three million.

The social, religious, and political fabric of Lebanon is very complex. The Muslims and Christians are divided into a variety of sects. A Muslim may be a Shia, a Sunni, a Druze, an Ismaili, or an Alawi. A Christian may be Maronite, Greek Orthodox, Greek Catholic, Roman Catholic, Jacobite,

Armenian Orthodox, Assyrian, or any of several Protestant denominations. All told, seventeen religious bodies are officially recognized. So integral is this religious and ethnic diversity to the country's political life that Lebanon's constitution requires government jobs and appointments to be allocated on the basis of religion. In accordance with an unwritten covenant of 1943, the president is always a Maronite, the prime minister is a Sunni Muslim, and the Speaker of the Chamber of Deputies is a Shiite.[1] In *Lebanon: Death of a Nation*, Sandra Mackey wrote, "Lebanese society, often spoken of as 'pluralistic,' actually was a mosaic of many groups, none of them committed to the common good of Lebanon; rather, each looked solely to its own special interests in a rigidly hierarchical political and economic structure."[2]

The violence engulfing Lebanon was not confined to its domestic struggles; numerous other factors were causing tremendous strain on the country's social fabric. Complicating the religious and ethnic strife were hundreds of thousands of Palestinian refugees. Guerrillas of the Palestine Liberation Organization (PLO) periodically launched attacks against Israel from bases in southern Lebanon. Finally, Lebanon's military weakness vis-à-vis its neighbors made it a pawn in the geopolitics of the region. At the request of Lebanon's president, Syrian forces entered Lebanon in June 1976 to help maintain peace; more than 25,000 Syrian troops were now in Lebanon's Bekaa valley. Add to this complex mix more than twenty extralegal militias and the Israeli troops that had invaded Lebanon months before the deployment of U.S. forces, and it was no wonder that Lebanon was a volatile and explosive corner of the world.

Sandra Mackey noted one other important factor:

> Lebanon is cursed by its size. Its population of disparate identities, each harboring conflicting aspirations and fears, is trapped within the country's four thousand square miles. As a result, the intensity with which each group senses its own interests is magnified by the close proximity of its rivals. . . . Consequently, the civil war in Lebanon, unlike most modern conflicts, is fought not with armies facing each other over battle areas ranging many square miles but by armed militias engaged in combat from urban block to urban block.[3]

A violent civil war engulfed Lebanon beginning in 1975. Although a cease-fire was soon announced, conflicts went on intermittently for years. It is estimated that more than 100,000 people were killed between 1975 and 1983. To put that figure in perspective, 58,000 Americans died in Vietnam and our population was about eighty times larger than Lebanon's.

In view of the enormous economic and social progress that has been made in so many areas of the world in the last half of the twentieth century, it is hard to understand why other regions with widely diverse religious and ethnic populations that had long lived at peace were suddenly engulfed in massive violence: not only Lebanon but Cambodia, Somalia, Bosnia, Rwanda, Burundi, Kosovo—the list goes on.

American Troops Deploy to Lebanon

On July 15, 1958, at the request of the president of Lebanon, President Eisenhower had ordered 14,000 Marines and some Army forces into Lebanon. My brother Jim, who was a Marine, served in that task force. The deployment lasted three months; our troops suffered one death from sniper fire and two from accidental drowning.

A quarter of a century later, on June 6, 1982, Israel invaded Lebanon to drive out Palestinian guerrillas. Eight days later the Israelis linked up with the Lebanese Christian forces in East Beirut.[4] On August 20, about ten weeks later, 800 U.S. Marines, along with French and Italian troops, became part of a multinational force (MNF) deployed to Lebanon. The Marines assisted in evacuating thousands of PLO members and Syrian forces from Beirut. This rapid evacuation, welcomed by all Lebanese, was over by September 1. By September 14 the Marines withdrew, having suffered four casualties: a Marine was killed while defusing a cluster bomb at the airport and three were wounded.

Less than two weeks later, President Reagan announced that once again U.S. troops were being sent to Beirut as part of an international force to quell violence. He said it would be "for a limited amount of time." The president-elect had been assassinated and Phalangist forces had killed more than 700 Palestinian and Lebanese civilians. According to Congressman Nick Rahall (D-W.Va.), a Lebanese American and very knowledgeable about the Middle East, the decision to deploy our troops came at the request of the new president of Lebanon, Amin Gemayel, the Phalangist leader and brother of the assassinated president-elect, Bashir Gemayel. The deployment began on September 29, 1982. The mission of our forces, the State

In November 1982, I met with Egyptian President Hosni Mubarak during an inspection trip to the Middle East. Congressman Nick Rahall (D-W.Va.) is on Mubarak's right and Congressman Bob Livingston (R-La.) is on my left. John Plashal, of the committee staff, is third from the left of Congressman Livingston.

Department said, was "to provide an interpositional force . . . and thereby provide the multinational presence requested by the Lebanese government." The Marines provided security at the Beirut International Airport and engaged in other operational missions nearby. British, French, and Italian troops were assigned to other locations in metropolitan Beirut.

Inspection Trip to Beirut

At Speaker O'Neill's request, I set out for Lebanon in early November 1982, accompanied by Nick Rahall, whom the Speaker had appointed three months earlier to lead a congressional delegation to several countries in the Middle East; Bob Livingston (R-La.), a relatively new member of Congress, who later became chairman of the House Appropriations Committee; and

Al Barry, assistant secretary of defense for congressional relations. In five days we visited Lebanon, conferred with President Hosni Mubarak in Cairo, and inspected the U.S. troops deployed in the Sinai Desert as part of a multinational force and observers (MFO) charged with maintaining a truce in the area.

On the first leg of the flight from Andrews Air Force Base, outside of Washington, D.C., we flew on a regularly scheduled flight of an Air Force C5-A cargo plane. The C5-A is an awesome aircraft. These behemoth planes have been used extensively over the years for military and humanitarian missions. They are so tall that taking off and landing in one are kind of surrealistic. At twenty-five feet above the runway, one never feels in contact with it. On the two flights I have made on one of those planes, I sat in the jump seat during the landing, right behind the two pilots, and had a panoramic view. When are we going to finally set down? I wondered, and then realized that we *were* down.

After arriving in England, we switched to a small aircraft for the final leg of the flight. As we flew into Beirut and I looked over the terrain, my first thought was that our troops at the airport were in potential danger. The Beirut International Airport is bounded by the Mediterranean to the west and by uplands on the other three sides. My experience in Vietnam had made me sensitive to the topography of an area where our troops are located. The Marines at the Beirut airport were based in a partial valley and they didn't control the high ground. It didn't take unique insight to observe that they would be vulnerable if the situation deteriorated.

I also didn't like to see Marines remaining at a fixed site, in a defensive position. Marines are trained as a highly mobile "close and destroy" force: they are expected to identify the target and destroy the enemy rather than provide a static defense. Eric Hammel has expressed it well: "The Marine Corps found itself facing in Beirut a mission that was early proving to be antithetical to its stated doctrine, which is active rather than passive, aggressive rather than defensive. Marines have always been trained to shoot to kill, to wreak havoc upon an opposing force, and to defend only where attack is obviated."[5]

We were met at the airport by the Marines' commanding officer, Colonel Tom Stokes. Colonel Stokes "had made his mark in 1960 when, as a young captain, he had been the only American to parachute with Belgian commandos at Stanleyville in the heroic, tragic rescue of European civilian hostages during the Congolese civil war."[6] I had served with him sixteen years earlier in Vietnam. He had never mentioned that dramatic mission in Africa. I didn't learn of his heroic action at Stanleyville until I read about it in Eric Hammel's book.

A special bond develops among those who have served together under combat conditions, and that bond lasts a lifetime. We briefly reminisced about some of the more memorable moments of our year in Vietnam before he gave me an overview of the situation in Beirut. After his briefing, we went on an inspection tour of the areas where Marines were conducting their missions, including the areas surrounding the airport and the American International University in Beirut.

The local population was very friendly to us as we drove through the streets. Beirut was bustling with people, and children would come up to our jeep whenever it stopped and shake our hands. It seemed to me that the disparate elements of Lebanon took a similar view: that "the Americans have arrived and everything's going to be fine."

When I conduct these inspections, I always ask very specific questions of our troops. What is their understanding of the mission? Are there any deficiencies or shortages of the equipment they need to carry out their mission? Do they think the goals of their mission are achievable? How is morale? Are they getting their mail on time? The advice Major Wilson gave me all those years ago at Camp Lejeune, "Pay attention to details," is never more pertinent than when it comes to assessing the challenges faced by our deployed troops and ensuring that they get what they need to make their living conditions tolerable and their mission successful. Too often there is an enormous gap between the policy decision to deploy troops and the day-to-day situation those troops encounter in the field.

I asked the enlisted Marines about the rules of engagement (ROE). Whenever U.S. troops are sent to any hot spot around the world, the Defense Department issues detailed instructions on how the troops are to perform their mission and how they should react to various potential situations.

Here are some of the key rules of engagement for our forces in Beirut:

- When on post, mobile or foot patrol, keep loaded magazine in weapon, bolt closed, weapon on safe, no round in the chamber.
- Do not chamber a round unless told to do so by a commissioned officer unless you must act in immediate self-defense where deadly force is authorized.
- Keep ammo for crew-served weapons readily available but not loaded.

- Call local forces to assist in self-defense effort.
- Use only a minimum degree of force to accomplish the mission.

Colonel Stokes told Eric Hammel that he was concerned about the "potential for mayhem that could result from even an innocuous exchange of fire between his Marines and the factional militias that appeared to be returning to the relatively lawless environs of the Beirut International Airport."[7]

In the back of my mind, however, I had an uneasy feeling about the ROEs. Granted, the friendly attitude of the local people was reassuring and the immediate environment of the airport was not hostile at the time of my inspection. Still, the violence was not over and more was threatened. From my perspective, the ROEs did not offer sufficient protection to our troops if the relatively benign situation should change. I was also concerned that they emphasized the avoidance of incidents to the detriment of the safety of our forces. Yet the troops I talked to were not concerned.

I had left Washington with an open mind about the deployment, but within hours of my arrival I had serious reservations about the wisdom of the mission. The unfavorable topography, with our troops in a valley, the defensive posture set forth in the rules of engagement, and the incredible complexity and historic strife among the various sects of Lebanon all contributed to my concern. Also, it appeared to me there was a mismatch between the level of the forces deployed and the policy objectives the administration hoped to attain by their deployment. In a letter to Congress, President Reagan wrote that the deployment of our troops

> will improve the prospects for realizing our objectives in Lebanon:
>
> - A permanent cessation of hostilities;
> - Establishment of a strong, representative central government;
> - Withdrawal of all foreign forces;
> - Restoration of control by the Lebanese Government throughout the country; and
> - Establishment of conditions under which Lebanon will no longer be used as a launching point against Israel.

These were all worthy goals, but the question was whether this limited deployment of U.S. and other forces had the military muscle to attain them.

Another question was whether the countries that deployed those forces had the political will to carry out operations that would lead to a successful conclusion.

Upon my return to Washington, I told Speaker O'Neill of my reservations about the administration's policy, including the lack of clear mission goals, and my concern about the Defense Department's rules of engagement. O'Neill talked to President Reagan about my findings but the discussion had no effect on his policy.

I felt it was important to express my misgivings to the Defense Department. I had been serving on the House Defense Appropriations Subcommittee for a few years by that time, so I went to see Secretary of Defense Caspar Weinberger to inform him of my views. He was well aware that I was a Vietnam combat veteran and strongly pro-defense. When we met in his office at the Pentagon and I explained my impressions, Weinberger said he was very sympathetic to my concerns, but as a loyal member of the Reagan administration he supported its policy. Although I was unaware of it before the meeting, Weinberger had lost out in the internal debate on the decision to deploy our troops to Lebanon. It is a fact of life in Washington that government officials who disagree with a specific policy proposal support that policy after those higher in the chain of command have decided to adopt it.

The National Security Council (NSC) is charged with taking into consideration the views and recommendations of all the executive branch departments and agencies involved in carrying out U.S. foreign policy—the State Department, the Defense Department, the CIA, the Defense Intelligence Agency, the U.S. ambassador to the country involved, and foreign policy experts. After sifting through all this information, the NSC provides the president with options and recommendations on a particular issue. The NSC was especially aggressive in arguing for the deployment of troops to Lebanon. Its head at the time was Judge William Clark, President Reagan's former personal attorney. Clark's chief deputy on the Lebanon issue was a former Marine colonel, Bud McFarlane.

Many people assume that when an administration is formulating a policy on a specific foreign crisis and is considering deploying U.S. forces, the Defense Department favors that option. That is not necessarily the case; it certainly wasn't in regard to Lebanon. In his book *Fighting for Peace,* Weinberger noted: "Bud McFarlane's demands for another Multinational

Force (MNF), supported by the State Department, became more petulant. I still objected, of course, very strongly, because the MNF would not have any mission that could be defined."[8]

I eventually learned that not only was Secretary Weinberger opposed to the deployment, but so were the Joint Chiefs of Staff and the commandant of the Marine Corps, General Robert Barrow. He was the commanding officer of the service responsible for the ground deployment and a holder of the Army's Distinguished Service Cross, as well as the Navy Cross. Despite the Defense Department's opposition, the National Security Council and the State Department had continued to push for the deployment of our troops to Lebanon, and their position prevailed.

In his autobiography, *My American Journey,* General Colin Powell wrote:

> The Marines had been deployed around the Beirut airport as what State Department euphemists called an "interpositional force." Translation: the Marines were to remain between two powder kegs, the Lebanese army and Syrian-backed Shiite units fighting it out in the Shouf mountains. . . . I was developing a strong distaste for the antiseptic phrases coined by State Department officials for foreign interventions which usually had bloody consequences for the military, words like "presence," "symbol," "signal," "option on the table," "establishment of credibility." Their use was fine if beneath them lay a solid mission. But too often these words were used to give the appearance of clarity to mud.[9]

Increasing Violence and Congressional Reaction

For some months after my inspection trip, events in Beirut proceeded fairly smoothly. The Marines and the multinational force continued to conduct their day-to-day routine operations and the deployment seemed to fade from the public's interest. Some rumblings were heard in Congress, but no serious efforts were made to pass legislation limiting the duration or the size of the deployment.

After about six months, however, the relative calm that prevailed in Beirut after the arrival of the multinational force began to fade and violence broke out again. On January 29, 1983, a French soldier was wounded by a grenade; three days later two French soldiers were wounded by gunfire; in March eight Italian soldiers were wounded by gunfire and five U.S. Marines were wounded by a grenade.

On April 18, 1983, terrorists bombed the U.S. embassy in Beirut and killed 63 people, including 17 Americans. Another 100 people were wounded, 40 of them Americans. About four months later two Marines were killed by artillery fire and two others were killed a week later. In response our troops increased the firepower they used to protect themselves and sent up Cobra helicopter gunships for defensive operations.

The situation for the deployed Marines underwent a dramatic change in September 1983. A major battle was in progress between the Lebanese Armed Forces (LAF) and Shiite and Druze militias in Suq-al-Gharb, a village overlooking the city. On September 12 the U.S. National Command Authority (NCA) determined that the success of the Lebanese defenders was essential to the safety of the Marines. A week later the White House announced that U.S. ships would fire to defend the LAF at Suq-al-Gharb.[10]

Of course, using whatever firepower is required to protect our troops is always necessary and justified, but the firing of U.S. battleships was a classic case of "mission creep." Our original mission had been significantly expanded. What had started as an "interpositional" force to provide "presence" and "stability" had been drawn into constant exchange of gunfire and artillery with various combatants and ultimately had chosen sides in a civil conflict. The Marines who had been sent to bring peace to a country with which we had long had friendly relations were now hunkered down at the airport under fire from the surrounding hills. A study prepared by the Federal Research Division of the Library of Congress found "deep and ominous divisions" in Lebanese society. "Many observers claim that these divisive forces have origins at least centuries old; others believe that the sources of these forces can be traced back even further, perhaps as long ago as ancient times."[11]

Clearly, events were now evolving rapidly, and the increase in the level of violence was a matter of deep concern. I discussed the crisis with Speaker O'Neill and he thought I should go back to Beirut. This time we were given helmets and flak jackets when we arrived. No children waved to us as we traveled around the city by jeep. In fact, we saw hardly any people in the streets at all. To my dismay, despite the dramatically changed environment and the warlike atmosphere, our basic rules of engagement had not changed.

The report of the Defense Department commission that analyzed the events in Beirut after our troops withdrew read in part:

> The inability of the Government of Lebanon to develop a political consensus, and the resultant outbreak of hostilities between the LAF and the armed militias supported by Syria, effectively precluded the possibility of a successful peacekeeping mission. It is abundantly clear that by late summer 1983, the environment in Lebanon changed to the extent that the conditions upon which the U.S. mission was initially premised no longer existed. The Commission believes that appropriate guidance and modification of tasking should have been provided to the USMNF (the U.S. component of the multinational force) to enable it to cope effectively with the increasingly hostile environment. The Commission could find no evidence that such guidance was, in fact, provided.[12]

If you strip away the bureaucratic language, the report was saying that despite the rapidly deteriorating and increasingly dangerous situation, our troops were still under orders to keep "weapon on safe, no round in the chamber"; not to "chamber a round unless told to do so by a commissioned officer"; to "keep ammo for crew-served weapons readily available but not loaded"; to "call local forces [the ones under fire at Suq-al-Gharb?] to assist in self-defense effort"; and to "use only a minimum degree of force."

After this whirlwind inspection trip, I returned to Washington and briefed Speaker O'Neill and the majority leader, Jim Wright. In his book *Balance of Power,* Jim Wright, who later became Speaker, wrote: "Murtha . . . described what he saw as a dangerous vulnerability of the Marine detachment, which was bivouacked in a building at one edge of the international airport. Sitting beneath a range of mountains from which artillery shells could be fired without warning, that Marine base seemed an invitation to terrorist attacks. Murtha argued for physical dispersal of the troops over a wider area."[13]

With the increase in violence and casualties, Lebanon moved onto the front burner in Congress. A House joint resolution was introduced that "called upon the President to submit within 48 hours a report under Section 4(a) (1) of the War Powers Act stating that U.S. forces in Lebanon were in hostilities, and that the 60-day time period for congressional approval under the War Powers Act . . . for the Marines' continued stay in Lebanon would begin with the President's report." Senator Robert C. Byrd (D-W.Va.) and Senator Charles Mathias (R-Md.) introduced separate but similar legislation in the Senate.

Realistically, there were no politically viable and achievable options for members of Congress who wanted to withdraw our forces from Beirut. While technically it would have been possible to include a provision in a defense appropriations bill that prohibited the use of funds for the continued operations of our deployed troops, that option was never feasible. For such an amendment to become law, it would have had to be included in legislation approved by the House and Senate. Such an amendment would never have received a simple majority in either chamber, much less the two-thirds majority needed to override Reagan's inevitable veto. Pressure to support an administration is intense once it has deployed our armed forces, even if the policy is controversial. The only time Congress cut off funds for a military operation that I can recall was when it prohibited the use of funds for the bombing of Cambodia near the end of our involvement in the Vietnam War.

As the debate in Congress on the deployment of our troops to Lebanon heated up, the issue centered on the implementation of a provision in the War Powers Act that would have required congressional approval for the deployment. The legislation that eventually passed was a joint resolution, referred to as the Multilateral Force in Lebanon Resolution, which approved an eighteen-month presence of our forces in Beirut, with the provision that Congress could change its mind and vote out a joint resolution calling for the immediate withdrawal of our troops.

Voting on the Multilateral Force in Lebanon Resolution was a painful exercise. I have always instinctively wanted to support the president on foreign policy, regardless of party. But when the time came to vote to extend the Marines' stay in Lebanon, I faced a dilemma. On the basis of my findings, I had argued in private for their withdrawal. Yet the resolution was sponsored in the House by the Democratic chairman of the Foreign Affairs Committee, Clem Zablocki of Wisconsin, and the Speaker was concerned that withdrawing the troops would cause other nations to lose faith in the United States as a peacemaker. O'Neill had received the president's personal assurance that our troops would be safe, so he was supportive of the resolution. Since I had been his emissary in Lebanon, he said, I would embarrass him if I voted against the resolution.

Also weighing heavily on my mind was the negative impact of failure to pass the resolution. In effect, we would be saying that Congress did not support our troops. Obviously, that would have had a detrimental effect on their morale and would have been a setback to the administration's objectives in the Middle East. Another factor was the Soviets' support of the Syrian troops in Lebanon. I was worried about the geopolitical implications of a failed U.S. policy.

Finally, the very escalation of violence made it all the more difficult to oppose the deployment of our troops, given the international environment at that time. Once our troops were there, to have precipitously withdrawn them after they and our embassy had been attacked would have sent the wrong message to our current and potential future adversaries.

Ultimately, I decided to support the president, the Speaker, and the Foreign Affairs Committee. The House passed the resolution by a large majority.

Terrorist Attack

After the car-bombing of our embassy in Beirut and the increased number of sniper, mortar, and artillery attacks on U.S. forces, reports warning of another terrorist attack streamed into our intelligence-gathering operations. Unfortunately, as is almost always the case, the reports were vague, giving no specific information about how or when such an attack would be carried out. When such reports are numerous, it's difficult to determine which are serious and which are diversionary or mischievous. Furthermore, after troops have been warned repeatedly but no attack has come, they tend to disregard the warnings.

On October 23, 1983, a truck loaded with explosives slowly approached the building that housed the Marine contingent at the Beirut airport. The truck made it through the security perimeter and up to the building. There the driver detonated the explosives. A total of 241 U.S. troops died—220 Marines, 18 sailors, and 3 from the Army. Many more were wounded.

When I saw the report on television, the first thing I thought of was those rules of engagement. When a soldier is constantly reminded that his weapon is to have no round in the chamber and that he is not to load unless he has been ordered to do so, it is easy to understand how the Marine at the gate did not fire his weapon.

The day after the terrorist attack I returned to Lebanon with the new

Marines searching for survivors after the terrorist attack against the Marine headquarters in Beirut, Lebanon, in October 1983.

commandant of the Marine Corps, General "P. X." Kelley. On the way there we stopped at an Army hospital in Frankfurt, Germany, where many of the wounded had been evacuated. One of the wounded soldiers said that shots had been fired at the attacking truck. General Kelley announced to the media that security plans had been correctly in place. His comments made me uneasy. It seemed premature to make such an announcement before a thorough investigation had been conducted.

In Beirut the devastation of the building was total and the remains of dead Marines were still being pulled from the rubble when we arrived. I decided that rather than hold discussions with the commanding officers, I should talk to surviving Marines who had served on sentry duty. I asked them if the sentry on duty had fired at the truck that fateful morning and they replied, "No, sir."

President Reagan had said recently that the Marines had fired at the truck. I related my findings to Speaker O'Neill. When Tip called Vice President Bush, who had just returned from Lebanon, I was on an extension. I told the vice president why I believed no shots had been fired at the truck. Bush insisted I was wrong: the sentry had fired at the truck. Two days later, on a Saturday evening, I was at my home in Johnstown when the phone rang. The vice president was calling from Texas to tell me that my version of events on that fatal day was correct.

Entrance Rationale, Not Exit Strategy

When U.S. troops are deployed for combat, the goals should be clear, the mission understandable, tactics developed and refined, battle plans executed effectively, and the soldiers, sailors, airmen, and Marines know precisely their specific role. Since the early 1980s, however, our troops have at times been deployed in places (Lebanon, Somalia, Haiti, Bosnia, Kosovo, no-fly zones over northern and southern Iraq) and missions (drug interdiction) in which combat is not the primary purpose. Each of these deployments was unique and each had its own rules of engagement. One of the major tragic lessons of Lebanon is never to send a small force into a potential or actual combat situation under rules of engagement that do not provide optimal protection on a mission that is not clear or essential to our national interests.

As General Colin Powell wrote in his memoirs: "There are times when

American lives must be risked and lost. Foreign policy cannot be paralyzed by the prospect of casualties. But lives must not be risked until we can face a parent or a spouse or a child with a clear answer to the question of why a member of that family had to die. To provide a 'symbol' or a 'presence' is not good enough."[14]

The buzzword of many foreign policy experts in recent years is "exit strategy." The idea is that before we deploy our troops we should have decided under what conditions or within what time frame we will withdraw them. (In the interest of full disclosure, I must admit I have used the term favorably a few times myself.) In a perceptive article in *Foreign Affairs* Gideon Rose wrote that "the term became part of the vernacular . . . during the withdrawal from Somalia. . . . In the past, policy makers often gave little thought to the specific objectives and potential endings of their foreign adventures, with chaotic results. But the idea of a formal exit strategy, with its anti-interventionist bias and stress on rigid public planning, is misguided in theory and unhelpful in practice. . . . The key question is not how we get out, but why we are getting in."[15]

In the congressional debate on Lebanon in 1983, Congressman Bill Young of Florida (who later became chairman of the Appropriations Committee) quoted from a speech he had given years earlier, during the debate on the War Powers Act. His words should be heeded by everyone involved in deciding whether American troops should be deployed in an international crisis: "The lessons of history have taught us that we cannot commit troops in a conflict and then arbitrarily withdraw them without damaging our national interest and jeopardizing the safety of the troops themselves. Once the commitment is made, the tendency is to continue on the deadly course of conflict."

4

THE SOVIET UNION'S DEFEAT IN AFGHANISTAN

The Soviet Union's invasion of Afghanistan, the United States' opposition to that invasion, and the central role played by Congress in developing that policy were watershed events that contributed significantly to the breakup of the Soviet Union and the end of the Cold War. On Christmas Eve, 1979, massive numbers of Soviet military aircraft filled with troops and equipment landed in Kabul, the capital of Afghanistan. Within seventy-two hours the Soviet troops had seized communications stations, Afghan leftists had assassinated the president and his family, resistance in the city had ended, and the Soviets had installed their own puppet as president. Within a week, 30,000 Soviet troops had poured over the border into Afghanistan, a landlocked, Texas-sized country in south-central Asia with a largely rural population of about 15 million. With this decisive stroke, the Soviet Union boldly marched into its own Vietnam nightmare, an event so traumatic that it helped seal the doom of the Soviet empire.

For many years, the Reagan administration's response to the Soviet invasion was tepid. Ultimately the House Defense Appropriations Subcommittee and one member in particular, Congressman Charlie Wilson of Texas, made a key contribution to the outcome of the war in Afghanistan.

The Background

Although Afghanistan is a landlocked, poverty-stricken country with very limited natural resources, it has been the site of numerous military campaigns and wars over the centuries. As Milton Bearden wrote:

Alexander the Great sent his supply trains through the Khyber Pass, then skirted northward with his army to the Konar Valley on his campaign in 327 B.C. There he ran into fierce resistance and, struck by an Afghan archer's arrow, barely made it to the Indus River with his life. Genghis Khan and the great Mughad emperors began passing through the Khyber a millennium later and ultimately established the greatest of empires—but only after reaching painful accommodations with the Afghans.[1]

In the nineteenth century, the Russians and the British vied to incorporate Afghanistan in their empires. In the twentieth century it became the last battleground in the Cold War. Fifteen years after the Soviets withdrew, Afghanistan became the battlefield of the first major war of the twenty-first century.

Afghanistan had been a monarchy from 1747 until 1973, when it was overthrown in a coup led by Muhammad Daoud Khan. He established a one-party Communist state and worked to establish economic and military relations with the Soviets. But Daoud was a nationalist as well as a Communist. In Sandy Gall's words, he "began to get cold feet about the extent of his dependence on Moscow and started to reverse the policy."[2] The party broke into factions, and a fundamentalist Muslim group started an insurrection. In 1978 leftists in the military overthrew Daoud and murdered him and his family.

The Communist factions combined as the People's Democratic Party of Afghanistan under Nur Muhammad Taraki as secretary general, president of the Revolutionary Council, and premier of the country. The new rulers' programs—land reform, equal rights for women, a ban on usury—"challenged both traditional Afghan values and well-established power structures in the rural areas."[3] Opposition to the Taraki regime was especially strong in the countryside. The government's repression of the Islamic clerical hierarchy, which had always played a quasi-political role in Afghanistan, fueled the insurgency that had started under Daoud. To the applause of the village elders, the mullahs called for a jihad (holy war) against the presumed infidels. Within a year, writes Sandy Gall, the mujahedin (holy warriors) "were gaining the upper hand," and it was clear that "it was only a matter of time before they . . . installed their own Islamic government in Kabul. This the Russians were determined to prevent—not least because it would torpedo the Brezhnev doctrine, which laid down that a Communist takeover (in any country) was irreversible."[4]

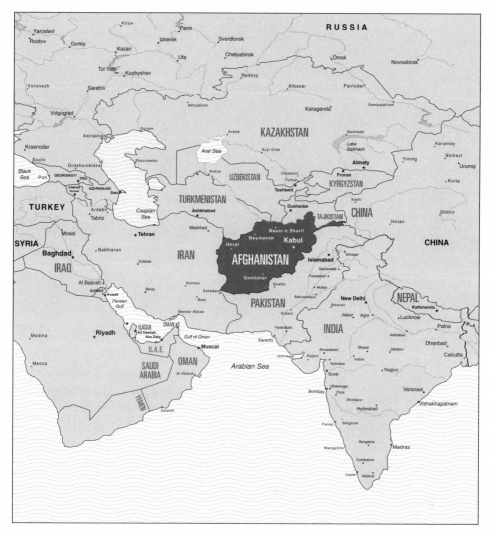

Afghanistan and its neighbors

The Soviets decided to invade and install their own client state to ensure that Afghanistan would remain in the Soviet orbit. Two Soviet officers, Major General Oleg Sarin and Colonel Lev Dovoretsky, later wrote:

> The intervention decision was made in defiance of the Constitution of the USSR (clause 73, paragraph 8). . . . The Supreme Soviet of the USSR and its Presidium did not have a chance to consider the question

of sending the troops to Afghanistan. The decision was made by a narrow circle of persons. The Politburo of the Communist party did not even bring its complete membership together to discuss the question and to approve the decision.

The names of those who made the decision are: Leonid Brezhnev, . . . the general secretary of the CC [Central Committee] of the CPSU [Communist Party of the Soviet Union]. . . ; the former minister of defense of the USSR, Dmitri Ustinov; the chairman of the Committee of State Security of the USSR [KGB], Yuri Andropov; and the minister of foreign affairs of the USSR, Andrei Gromyko.[5]

Because Afghanistan shares a long border with the Soviet Union, supplying their troops was greatly simplified. The Soviet invasion force soon grew to over 100,000, supported by another 50,000 troops just across the border. In addition, the Soviet-supported Afghan government had 40,000 of its own troops fighting the Islamic guerrillas. The Afghan government forces, however, were an ineffective fighting force and suffered from widespread desertions. Many deserters joined the guerrillas.

The world's second largest military force (numerically China's was larger), in alliance with its client state's military, was locked in a contest with fractured guerrilla movements that had only rudimentary weapons. Afghanistan was one of the poorest countries in the world, with per capita income of $214 per year, a life expectancy of fewer than thirty-eight years, and a literacy rate between 10 and 20 percent. At the time, most observers viewed the outcome of the war as a foregone conclusion: the Soviets would score a quick victory.

Despite these overwhelming odds, the Afghans have never been under the rule of a colonial power. As the authors of *Afghanistan: A Country Study* wrote, "The peoples of the region had always resisted government control of any kind, and they had contested with particular vigor invasions by non-Muslim aliens. In the nineteenth century the British-Indian government sought on two occasions to establish a government in Kabul that would be amenable to British guidance, but in neither instance was it successful." The ferocity with which the Afghan people fought in these wars over the centuries was epitomized in the first Anglo-Afghan war, when the British military garrison retreated in humiliation in 1842 after a lengthy war. "Although a Dr. W. Brydon is often cited as the only survivor [out of

15,000 who undertook the retreat], in fact a few more survived as prisoners and hostages."[6]

Through the sheer size and firepower of their invasion force, the Soviets inflicted enormous casualties on the Afghan resistance forces. The Soviets' main firepower consisted of tanks, HIND helicopter gunships, SU-25 fighter-bombers, and artillery barrages. About 5 million Afghans, a third of the population of the country, were made refugees in Pakistan and Iran.[7] An estimated 1.3 million people were killed in the war.

Especially devastating to the resistance forces was the withering gunfire from the armored Soviet HIND helicopters and the bombing attacks from the SU-25 tactical fighter-bombers. The HIND helicopter has eight tube-launched guided missiles and twin 23-millimeter cannon turrets. Much of the terrain of Afghanistan is mountainous and treeless. Thus whenever Soviet pilots spotted Afghan guerrillas, the HIND helicopters decimated them. For years the guerrillas countered this massive onslaught with World War II–vintage anti-aircraft weaponry.

America's Reaction

Although reporters and television journalists made occasional forays into Afghanistan, their access was so limited that the Western media could not adequately portray the terrible suffering caused by the war, so it did not register with the vast majority of Americans. The war was not a major political issue in the United States.

In reaction to the Soviet invasion, President Jimmy Carter's administration initiated a small covert program that provided some communications gear and old weapons to Afghan guerrillas. The weapons supplied were Soviet, so that the United States could plausibly deny assisting the mujahedin. President Carter imposed a grain embargo against the Soviets and boycotted the summer Olympics in Moscow so that the United States would not be perceived as turning a blind eye while the Soviets were massacring civilians in Afghanistan. These measures were imposed more for moral and political purposes than to inflict punishment, and their actual impact was minimal. The Carter administration had no intention of confronting the Soviets in Afghanistan and creating a world crisis over a remote country in which the United States seemingly had no vital interests at a time when those interests were more clearly being challenged elsewhere. In Teheran,

Iran, fifty-two Americans (one of them a constituent of mine, Staff Sergeant Regis Ragan) were being held hostage in the U.S. embassy by militant followers of the Ayatollah Khomeini. Tragically, our attempt to rescue them ended in failure. The Marxist Sandinistas had just come to power in Nicaragua. Numerous other countries had become Communist or pro-communist in recent years—South Vietnam, Laos, Cambodia, Ethiopia, and South Yemen.

Increasing my concern about these numerous setbacks to the United States' geopolitical situation was the fact that our military was in its post-Vietnam doldrums, suffering from low morale, low budgets, low prestige, drug use, aging equipment, and inability to attract high-quality troops. Spare parts were in such short supply that a large percentage of our combat aircraft were unable to fly. So many recruits were not high school graduates that it was increasingly difficult to train them for the operation and maintenance of complex weapons systems. The situation was so serious that the maintenance manuals for M-1 tanks were published in comic book form.

Ten months after the Soviets invaded Afghanistan, Ronald Reagan defeated President Carter in an Electoral College landslide, 489 to 49. By that time I had been in Congress almost seven years. I was determined to do whatever I could to help improve the quality of our armed forces, enhance their readiness, and upgrade their equipment. As a member of the Defense Appropriations Subcommittee, which annually provides funds for the Defense Department, I was in the right place to work toward these goals.

Another new member of the Defense Appropriations Subcommittee was Congressman Charlie Wilson, a Democrat from Texas. Charlie was a graduate of the U.S. Naval Academy and had a remarkable propensity for making outrageous comments without suffering political damage in his congressional district. He was a flamboyant, bigger-than-life, hard-drinking, politically astute playboy who was enormously popular in his district and in Congress, and he was extremely good at getting what he wanted included in legislation. He stated his intentions very succinctly: "Force the [expletive deleted] Soviets out of Afghanistan." He pursued that mission with perseverance, effectiveness in the halls of Congress, and physical courage on his excursions into the war zone in Afghanistan.

In a conversation I held with former congressman Steve Solarz in November 1999, he told me, "If I were to rank those who made the most important contributions to end the Cold War, the top three would include President Ronald Reagan, President Mikhail Gorbachev, and Pope John Paul II. I'm not sure where I would rank Congressman Charlie Wilson, but he would definitely be in the top ten."

Congressman Wilson and the CIA's Afghan Program

Put succinctly, to address the United States' deteriorating position in the global arena, President Reagan had a two-pronged national security policy: propose massive increases in the defense budget requests submitted to Congress and oppose communist expansion wherever it appeared. As part of this strategy, the CIA continued covertly supplying arms to the Afghan mujahedin, but this effort was having little effect. Many Reagan administration officials, as the *New York Times* reported, "were initially reluctant to provide vigorous support for the Afghans, fearing that it might unrealistically raise their hopes for a military victory or provoke Soviet reprisals against Pakistan, the main conduit to the rebels." The covert program "provided the guerrillas with weapons designed and manufactured by the Soviet Union or other East Bloc countries so they could deny that the United States was supplying such assistance. They could maintain that the guerrillas had captured these weapons from the Afghan government or from Soviet troops in Afghanistan." The undersecretary of defense, Fred C. Ikle, was quoted as saying that in the first three or four years of the Reagan administration "there was a general shyness and hesitation, a reluctance to make a more concerted effort to provide more instruments and tactics to freedom fighters in Afghanistan."[8]

The war dragged on and the Afghan guerrillas fought courageously, but the Soviets were inflicting tremendous suffering, death, and destruction on them. The Afghans appeared to have no hope of victory. Congress passed a resolution in late 1984 that "it would be indefensible to provide the Afghan freedom fighters with only enough aid to fight and die, but not enough to advance their cause of freedom." Congressional resolutions can influence policy and their importance should not be underestimated, but resolutions do not win wars.

Congressman Wilson became the leading advocate in Congress for a more aggressive Afghan covert program. He was not the chairman of any committee or subcommittee, but he had great powers of persuasion, was knowledgeable about military matters and weapons, and knew more about Afghanistan than anyone else in Congress. This was a classic case of a member of Congress being so focused and knowledgeable about an issue that seniority and position on a committee were not important.

Legislation originating in the House Permanent Select Committee on Intelligence and the Senate Select Committee on Intelligence authorizes funds for the CIA. The legislation begins with the words "There is hereby authorized to be appropriated . . ." In other words, an authorization bill does not provide funds for the executive branch agencies. The actual money is provided in the annual defense appropriations bill. That bill was the legislative vehicle Congressman Wilson used to increase the funds for equipment for the mujahedin.

During his travels to Pakistan and into Afghanistan, Charlie had met with the leaders and fighters of the guerrilla factions to discuss their military equipment requirements. The tactics he employed to help the Afghan resistance forces defeat their enemy were clearly focused: add funds in Congress to provide the mujahedin with more advanced military equipment, especially Stinger anti-air weapons, and pressure the Reagan administration to procure and deploy those weapons.

Acting on a recommendation from Bob Seraphin of the committee staff, the House Defense Appropriations Subcommittee funded a program to render the Stingers missiles useless if they fell into the wrong hands. The Stingers would be equipped with "lock-out chips," and an individual code for each weapon would be disseminated by a separate channel. Any weapon that was stolen or otherwise diverted would be useless without the code. "This program," the committee report read, "will provide the capability to render the weapon inoperable without entry of a predetermined code, and is therefore of great importance in addressing the threat of potential terrorist use of Stingers." We added funds for the program twice but the Pentagon continued to resist spending the money. Once again we were reminded of the iron rule of so many bureaucrats: If we didn't think of it, we're not doing it.

The Reagan administration argued that the Afghans did not have the technical proficiency to operate sophisticated weapons. Despite the administration's position, I deferred to Charlie's judgment on this issue. He had been in the Afghan war zone and knew the forces involved. His case was more convincing to me than the arguments made by Washington policy makers who never left their desks.

In 1983 the House and Senate passed their respective defense appropriations bills and the two defense appropriations subcommittees met in conference to iron out the differences between the two bills. After the conference committee reached a consensus, the agreement would be passed in the House and Senate and then be sent to the White House for the president's signature. Toward the end of the conference we cleared the room of all but members and a few staffers who had the appropriate clearances to discuss intelligence conference issues. The House and Senate participants began deliberating on the amount of money to be provided for the specific programs within the budget of the intelligence community. As planned, Congressman Wilson proposed adding funds for modern anti-aircraft equipment for the Afghan guerrillas. Charlie eloquently described how the Afghans were being decimated by the HIND helicopters and ended his brief comments with a statement that it was time to act.

This was a historic moment. The actual discussion leading up to the decision to provide the additional funds for the Stinger anti-air missiles took just a few minutes. There were no long philosophical debates on geopolitical issues. We simply talked briefly about Charlie's proposal and added the funds. Years earlier a few Soviet leaders meeting in the Kremlin decided to launch the Afghan war. Now a few members of Congress meeting in the Capitol decided to counter that decision aggressively. Our decision launched the United States on a course that changed the outcome of the Afghan war and the global East-West struggle.

The moment was ironic as well as historic. During the Reagan years, the congressional committees responsible for oversight of the CIA and funding its budget constantly strove to restrain covert programs proposed or carried out by the administration, especially those involving Central America. In the case of Afghanistan, the Congress was recommending and legislating a more aggressive foreign policy through covert action and being resisted by the administration.

The Hunters Become the Hunted

It took painfully long for the congressional add-on of funds for the Stinger anti-air missile to work its way through the system. The administration put many bureaucratic hurdles in the way of the program and Charlie Wilson became increasingly frustrated.

Most folks probably assume that once funds are included in an appropriations bill passed by Congress and signed into law by the president, those funds are soon committed to expenditure. The reality is that it is often a lengthy struggle—sometimes years—before the appropriated funds are actually spent. Part of the problem is that any administration tends to resist congressional spending initiatives—the "not invented here" syndrome. Bureaucratic inertia comes into play, too. Then when the funds are finally released and the program involves the procurement of defense hardware, there is a lengthy bidding process to determine which corporation will actually be awarded the contract to proceed with the program. Even after a contract is awarded, often a losing corporation will challenge the government's decision and appeal the contract.

Charlie continued to pressure the administration to proceed with the program. He even threatened to try to reduce expenditures for other intelligence programs that the executive branch strongly supported. I don't know what specific event or series of events triggered the release of the funds for the modern weapons for the guerrillas, but since Congress ultimately controls the purse strings and the administration desperately wanted congressional support for other initiatives, it finally relented and began to execute the program. After the money was released, the Stinger missiles had to be procured, shipped to Pakistan, and transshipped to the Afghan guerrillas. Finally, in September 1986, about six and a half years after the Soviet invasion began and about three years after the Congress had provided the funds for them, the Stinger missiles were deployed to the mujahedin.

The Stinger is a highly accurate, heat-seeking, supersonic, shoulder-fired, fire-and-forget ground-to-air missile. It will quickly ruin the day of a HIND helicopter or fighter-bomber pilot. The case for the ability of the Stinger anti-air missile to level the playing field in the Afghan war was compelling. Soviet ground troops and tanks were not effective outside the cities and garrisons because the terrain was mountainous and the Afghan guerrillas knew every inch of it. When the Soviet troops traveled from one city or base to another, their convoys were frequently attacked and ambushed by the mujahedin and suffered heavy casualties. The Soviets beefed up their air cover and punished the guerrillas by strafing and bombing their villages. This tactic was proving to be very effective, as the Afghans had no effective weapons to counter these attacks.

The Stinger anti-air missiles in the hands of the Afghan resistance fighters were an incredibly effective marriage between American high-tech weaponry and illiterate but skilled guerrillas. The Stingers dramatically changed the direction of the war. The HIND helicopters were so vulnerable to the Stingers that their importance and role in the war declined precipitously.

After the introduction of the Stingers, the Soviet helicopter pilots had to adjust their flight plans. When the HIND helicopters flew from a support base to a forward base, they would climb in a circular pattern until they reached an altitude beyond Stinger range and then fly to the forward base. When they reached their destination they had to repeat this circular flight pattern to land. Since the forward base was smaller than the support base, however, so was the circle. With a tighter target area, the guerrillas were often able to shoot the landing HINDs out of the sky.

The subsequent impotence of the Soviet HIND helicopters totally changed the dynamics of the war. The morale of the Soviet forces collapsed. As the *Boston Globe* stated, "When the CIA delivered the Stingers, the hunters became the hunted."[9] The *Washington Post* reported that "Afghan rebels . . . have inflicted heavy losses on Soviet and Afghan [government] aircraft in the past three months, shooting them down about one a day, the State Department said yesterday."[10] Two years after these weapons were delivered to the war zone, the world's largest country with the second largest Army in the world was humiliatingly defeated by a politically divided but determined guerrilla force.

The Funeral of President Zia

Pakistan was the United States' key ally in carrying out the program to support the Afghans fighting the Soviet invaders. On August 17, 1988, the president of Pakistan, General Mohammad Zia ul-Haq, was killed when his plane crashed shortly after take-off from a base in Pakistan. The American ambassador to Pakistan, Arnold Rayfield, and the head of the U.S. military mission to Pakistan were also killed. President Zia had been an unwavering supporter of the U.S. program to provide assistance to the Afghan guerrillas.

Secretary of State George Shultz asked me to accompany him as part of an official U.S. delegation to the state funeral. Congressman Wilson was also a part of the delegation, as was Robert Oakley, who had been nominated to be our next ambassador to Pakistan. (I worked with Ambassador

Oakley years later during the Somalia crisis. He is one of the finest and most talented civil servants I have ever known.)

During the flight, Shultz asked me to meet with the mujahedin leaders while we were in Pakistan and to emphasize two points: first, that there was continued strong support in both the Congress and the administration for their effort to drive the Soviets out of their country; second, that the guerrillas should not attack the Soviet forces as they withdrew from Afghanistan.

Within hours of our arrival in Pakistan we were at President Zia's funeral. It was a very emotional ceremony. About a half-million people massed in a funeral procession in Islamabad, the Pakistani capital. The temperature was over 100°F and the humidity was almost as high. Medical personnel were kept busy attending to people who collapsed from heat exhaustion. Sirens wailed as ambulances inched their way through the masses of people in an attempt to rescue the stricken. Thirty heads of state and thousands of other dignitaries and invited guests sat under a massive outdoor canopy to watch the procession. When Zia's casket passed in front of us, it was rather unceremoniously juggled about. There was an outpouring of grief from the teaming mass of humanity lining the streets as the casket passed.

The day after the funeral, Congressman Wilson and I met with thirteen Afghan guerrilla leaders, each from a different faction. Although these leaders had their cultural and political differences, they were united in their determination to drive the Soviets out of their country. The gathered mujahedin leaders had their rifles in their hands, ammunition belts crisscrossed their chest, and long curved knives rested in scabbards on their belts. Their skin was wrinkled and leathery from long exposure to the sun. They exuded courage, toughness, and tenacity.

A State Department interpreter stood beside me as I addressed the guerrilla leaders. I began by telling them some of my experiences in Vietnam and that I understood the dangers and stress of combat. I praised them for their resilience in fighting the Soviet invaders so courageously over the years and told them their valiant effort was having a major impact on the course of world events. I also praised Charlie Wilson and mentioned that he was the key person in Congress responsible for the United States' assistance to them. They all knew Charlie from his previous visits and they were very deferential to him.

I spoke for about ten minutes and concluded my comments by making Secretary Shultz's two points. I assured them that Congress continued to support them and that funds and equipment would continue to flow to them. They cheered and pumped their rifles up and down in enthusiasm. Then I made the point that since the Soviets were withdrawing from their country, their troops should hold their fire and let them go.

A senior leader of the guerrillas rose to respond. Through an interpreter he thanked our delegation for all the assistance the United States had provided over the years. In an emotional and steadily rising tone he concluded by saying, "No Soviet soldiers will ever be safe in Afghanistan. We will not allow them to march out of Afghanistan with their heads held high, their bands playing, and their flags waving. We will continue to attack and kill them until every single Soviet has left Afghanistan." The gathered guerrillas rose to their feet and loudly cheered and waved their rifles in the air. I had carried out my mission, but my effort at diplomacy had failed.

On February 15, 1989, Lieutenant General Boris Gromov, the commander of the Soviet forces in Afghanistan, was the last Soviet soldier to leave as he crossed a bridge linking the two remote locations of Heiratan in Afghanistan and Termez in the Soviet Union.

End of the Cold War

The term "Cold War" is to a large extent a misnomer. As Gabriel Schoenfeld wrote in *Commentary*, the Cold War was

> a conflict that, for well over four decades, had divided the world into two hostile camps. In the course of those decades, wherever Marxism-Leninism had been planted by force of arms, millions of people were deliberately murdered or spent their best years in prison camps. Those not imprisoned lived constricted, fear-filled lives. In hot wars involving the superpowers in remote corners of the world, from Angola to Afghanistan to Nicaragua, the human toll was great on both sides. More than 54,000 Americans died in the Korean war; another 58,000 died defending South Vietnam.[11]

Historians continue to analyze the central factors that contributed to the collapse of the Soviet empire and the end of the Cold War. The United States' tenacious commitment to NATO and other military alliances throughout the last half of the twentieth century, our shouldering of the burden of the Korean and Vietnam wars, and the greatly expanded capability of our armed forces in the 1980s were all key factors in containing the expansion of the Soviets or their surrogates.

I have no way of proving it, but I believe that the Strategic Defense Initiative (SDI) —the "Star Wars" program—also was an important factor. I recall a visit I made to Moscow with Speaker Tip O'Neill and other members of Congress in the mid-1980s. We met with President Gromyko and other top Soviet civilian and military leaders. What stands out in my mind about the discussions we held with the Soviet leaders was a meeting with the Soviet ministers of defense and foreign affairs. Congress had recently funded the SDI, and the issue came up. The emotion with which the Soviets voiced their opposition to the program was very revealing to me. The intensity of their responses, their raised voices, and their body language all indicated that Star Wars was an issue they felt very strongly about. In retrospect, they probably realized SDI was a program they could never hope to challenge either fiscally or technologically.

Beyond the military factors, the ethnic diversity and sheer size of the USSR contributed to its breakup. (How does a nation with more than a hundred ethnic groups and eleven time zones stay united?) The inherent strength and dynamism of the United States' private enterprise system in contrast to the stagnant command economy of the Soviet system may very well have been the most important factor in the collapse of the Soviet empire. The disparity of living standards between East and West was just too great for the Soviets to hide. The technology and information revolutions in the West clearly made an important contribution to the historic shift in favor of the West in the East-West struggle.

Finally, the defeat of the Soviets in Afghanistan was clearly another large factor in the collapse of the Union of Soviet Socialist Republics. On November 10, 1989, just 265 days after the Soviet withdrawal, the House Defense Appropriations Subcommittee was negotiating with the Senate on the fiscal year 1990 defense budget. During a break in the negotiations, Congressman Joe McDade, the ranking Republican on the subcommittee, and I were strategizing on developing a compromise position on some outstanding issues that had not been resolved between the House and Senate. Also in the room were Don Richbourg, the subcommittee's staff director; John Plashal, of the subcommittee staff; and Kevin Roper, who worked for Joe McDade. A television set was on the table behind us. Joe, looking over my shoulder at the TV, asked John to turn up the sound. We turned to look at the screen. We saw a lot of people sitting on top of a wall and others striking at the wall with a variety of tools and implements. In a festive mood, thousands of German citizens were chipping away at the Berlin Wall with hammers, crowbars, and anything else they could get their hands on. The wall came tumbling down, chip by chip, section by section. "Hammer and sickle emblems came crashing to the ground from Warsaw to Bucharest. Military defeat in Afghanistan meant not just the end of the Soviet empire, but the public disgrace of the command economy in Russia."[12] One of the prized possessions in my office is a chunk of the Berlin Wall.

In terms of geographical reach, the Soviet empire reached its zenith when its troops occupied Afghanistan. The Soviet system had required its citizens to make decades of personal sacrifices in order to build a huge and expensive military machine. Yet after all those years of sacrifice, a guerrilla force in a country on the Soviets' border defeated them militarily. Today the capability of Russia's conventional military forces has declined dramatically.

An interesting perspective on this important chapter in history is the testament it provides to the strength and brilliance of the United States' constitutional system of government. The checks and balances built into our system over 200 years ago still function admirably today. The Constitution reads: "No funds shall be withdrawn from the Treasury, other than in consequence of appropriations made in law." Congress, reviewing and questioning the recommendations and budgets submitted by the executive branch, funded programs that changed the outcome of the war in Afghanistan and contributed greatly to the collapse of the Soviet empire.

In a parliamentary system of government, the national budget developed by the executive branch is automatically rubber-stamped by the majority in the parliament. England's parliament has virtually no staff, since there is no need for the legislators to draft questions for budgetary hearings, investigate the inadequacies of the executive branch, or draft legislation different from that proposed by the executive branch. If we had a parliamentary system, or even weak congressional leadership that chose not to take political risks, the geopolitical situation today might have been less favorable to the United States' global interests.

Granted, our system of governing is complex, cumbersome, and often vitriolic and accusatory. But despite those shortcomings, it is a magnificent system in which one member of Congress—Charlie Wilson of Texas—by perseverance, commitment, personality, and courage, almost single-hand-edly forced a policy that changed the course of history in favor of freedom and led us into a much less dangerous international environment.

As the authors of *The Great Reckoning*, James Dale Davidson and Lord William Rees-Mogg, wrote:

> The Communist system was brought down by a crucial megapolitical event—the microchip. It would have died anyway of its many defi-ciencies and functional contradictions. But it died sooner and more suddenly because there was no way for the lumbering command economy to accommodate the decentralizing impact of micro tech-nology—the new growth sector of the world economy.
>
> It became ever more difficult for Communist authorities to dam the flow of information reaching their people. And no item of infor-mation was as crucial to the revolution of 1989 as news from Af-ghanistan that the Soviet military had been defeated. Illiterate Afghan peasants had harnessed the microchip, in the form of the deadly new Stinger missiles, to effectively immobilize Soviet air power. Moscow could no longer impose its will by military edict, even on its own borders.[13]

The Aftermath

Tragically, in the wake of the Soviet withdrawal from Afghanistan, civil war raged for years among the country's tribal and ethnic factions, and U.S. foreign policy paid almost no attention to it. One of the relatively obscure factions in the civil war was the Taliban. About a decade after the Soviet defeat, the medieval Taliban controlled much of the country and governed as one of the most reactionary regimes in the world. They ruthlessly con-trolled the population and offered safe haven to Osama bin Laden and the international terrorists trained at his bases. Women were forbidden to work; girls could not go to school. The Taliban ordered that all religious artifacts be destroyed.

Just as the microchip in the form of Stinger missiles had played a central role in defeating the Soviets in the 1980s, the silicon chip in the form of smart weapons fifteen years later enabled the United States, in concert with the Northern Alliance and other Afghans opposed to the regime, to defeat the Taliban.

How strange that events in obscure, landlocked, desolate, and poverty-stricken Afghanistan, which has so few natural resources, have played a central role in the end of the Cold War and the first war of the twenty-first century.

5

HIGH-DRAMA ELECTION IN THE PHILIPPINES

In February 1986 President Reagan appointed Senator Richard Lugar (R-Ind.) and me as the co-chairmen of a delegation to monitor the voting of a presidential election in the Philippines. The election pitted President Ferdinand Marcos, who had been in power over twenty years, against Mrs. Corazón Aquino, the widow of an assassinated political opponent of Marcos. It was a historic election that transformed the political system of the Philippines and had an impact on world affairs.

The Background

In 1898, during the Spanish-American War, Commodore George Dewey, under orders from Theodore Roosevelt, then acting secretary of the Navy, sailed to the Philippines and destroyed the Spanish fleet anchored in Manila Bay. In the final settlement of the war between the United States and Spain, Cuba gained independence but the Philippines, Guam, and Puerto Rico were ceded to the United States. After the war the relationship began badly when the United States suppressed a Filipino insurgency aimed at gaining independence. Violence was widespread and many lives were lost.

Despite this inauspicious beginning, a "special relationship" between the Philippines and the United States evolved and became especially close during World War II. The Japanese invaded the Philippines the day after their attack on Pearl Harbor. A massive U.S. counterinvasion eventually drove out the Japanese. By the end of the war, over a million Filipinos had been killed in the conflict. Some 18,000 American soldiers are buried in a cemetery outside Manila.

The Philippines became an independent nation on July 4, 1946. The diplomatic relationship between the United States and the Philippines became increasingly intertwined after China became Communist in 1949. Our foreign policy toward Asia became reliant on the presence of U.S. armed forces at military facilities in Asia, including two massive bases in the Philippines. The Seventh Fleet used the Subic Bay Naval Base for resupply and repair of our naval forces throughout Asia. The primary mission of Clark Air Force Base was to provide logistics for the U.S. Thirteenth Air Force throughout the region. About 15,000 military personnel were stationed at these two facilities. They were an important link in a forward-based strategy that had worked well over the years. A close strategic and political relationship between our two countries lasted for decades.

Ferdinand Marcos came to power in 1965 and ran the country with his wife, Imelda. He was a close ally of the United States and over the years enjoyed the support of numerous administrations of both parties, even though his rule became increasingly repressive. Seven years after he came to power, Marcos declared martial law, shut down opposition newspapers, and exercised tight control of the mass media. By 1981, military compounds run by the army and the Philippine constabulary held 30,000 detainees.

Key Marcos loyalists were rewarded with the profits from huge monopolies subsidized by the government. The Marcoses accumulated enormous wealth. Their lifestyle was lavish and their personal holdings included Swiss bank accounts, commercial high-rise buildings in Manhattan, and enormous land and stock holdings.

The Philippines was often described as a "staunch democratic ally" of the United States, as our military presence and cordial diplomatic relations furthered our geopolitical goals in Asia. As one pundit described it, however, under Marcos the Philippines was more of a "kleptocracy than a democracy." Ferdinand and Imelda Marcos had the rather dubious distinction of being in the Guinness *Book of World Records* as the wealthiest thieves in the world. As so often during the Cold War, U.S. policy makers usually overlooked these factors because of our strategic goals. Stanley Karnow wrote:

> Successive administrations in Washington, primarily focused on the future of the Philippine bases, had flinched at exerting pressure on

Marcos that might complicate new negotiations. Their concern was realistic. Fourth of July rhetoric notwithstanding, morality has never been the test for America's diplomatic ties to other nations, and to hold Marcos to American standards of behavior would be tantamount to breaking relations with the Russians unless they shut down the Gulag. . . .

But U.S. foreign policy experts also perceived that the longer Marcos's excesses continued, the faster the Communist insurgency would spread, and increasingly threaten the bases. So his profligacy, corruption and repression represented a potential danger to America's strategic interests.[1]

A combination of corruption, widespread poverty, a deteriorating economy, frequent student protests, and a burgeoning Communist guerrilla movement led to a steady decline in the popularity and international stature of Ferdinand and Imelda Marcos. In this deteriorating environment, the military wing of the Communist Party in the Philippines, the NPA (New People's Army), grew steadily until it numbered 26,000 in the mid-1980s.

As Marcos's political position continued to decline, analysts predicted that if the trends in the Philippines continued, the Communists would probably come to power. The evolving situation was a classic case of enormous wealth being accumulated by a few while the vast majority of the citizens remained mired in poverty. It seemed to me that unless democratic forces came to power, the Philippines might well end up like Iran, where our continued support for the Shah, despite his repressive rule, led to a revolution and produced a regime that was detrimental to our security interests.

President Marcos versus the Housewife

Despite his declining political status, on November 3, 1985, Marcos called for a presidential election, though legally an election was not scheduled to be held for another year. Marcos made the announcement while he was being interviewed on *This Week with David Brinkley*. A victory, he said, would give him a "fresh mandate." On December 2 the Batasang, the Philippine legislature, obligingly passed a bill that made it legal to hold such an election, and it was then scheduled for February 7, 1986—just nine weeks later.

The leading opposition candidate soon became Corazón Aquino. Mrs. Aquino had graduated from the College of Mount St. Vincent in New York, where she majored in mathematics and French. She was from a prominent and wealthy family, but she was a novice at politics. Her campaign literature listed her previous occupation as housewife. She had been married to a prominent Filipino, Benigno "Ninoy" Aquino, who had been the leading political foe of Marcos. After spending eight years in prison in the Philippines, he went into a prolonged exile in the United States. Upon his return to Manila on August 21, 1983, Ninoy Aquino was murdered at the airport as he left his airplane. A large detachment of the Philippine Army was there to "protect" him. There was widespread speculation that the Marcos regime had ordered the assassination. Almost two million Filipinos participated in a ten-hour procession at Aquino's funeral.

In the aftermath of the assassination, Mrs. Aquino appeared at many rallies and became known throughout the country. In *Four Days of Courage,* Bryan Johnson, wrote:

> Passionate demonstrations and inflammatory statements raged for months following the opposition leader's brutal assassination. And though his widow, Corazón, did not lead the protests, she played a crucial role at every major rally. After the politicians had rent the air with clenched fists and epithets, Cory would step forward for a few gentle remarks about her husband. Day after day she ended the rallies with a solemn recital of the same quotation.
>
> "Ninoy always said that courage and cowardice had one thing in common. They are both contagious. We can all be cowards, or we can all be heroes together."[2]

Time wrote:

> In the weeks and months that followed [the assassination], street vendors and socialites, businessmen and radicals all awoke from years of resignation to cry out their rage. Yet the official opposition to Marcos remained fatally factious, divided into more than a dozen self-seeking groups, each of them tainted either by extremist positions, associations with the government or long years of failure.
>
> It soon became obvious that the only person far enough above the

political differences to unite the opposition was the martyr's widow. She was also, by no coincidence, the only one who did not seek the role.[3]

One million Filipinos signed petitions asking her to run for the presidency. Although she was shy about speaking in public, Mrs. Aquino gave speech after speech. Her campaign steadily gained momentum. As the election approached, a million Filipinos attended a rally for her in Manila.

The election that pitted a housewife against an entrenched politico became a major international event. An election held just nine weeks after it was called obviously gave an enormous advantage to the incumbent. The Marcos regime owned and operated Channel 4, which, as an international observer group wrote, was "the only station available in many parts of the country. The remaining stations, while nominally independent, were owned by friends of Marcos."[4]

But Cory Aquino had her own strengths. She was able to buy air time on radio stations, which gave her an advantage in rural areas where no TV signals were received. More important were her moral stature, her inner strength, and her willingness to counter Marcos's attacks vigorously. Lewis Simons wrote, "Marcos started attacking her for being inexperienced. Her response was a masterful speech, probably the most damaging of her counterassaults: 'I concede that I cannot match Mr. Marcos when it comes to experience. I admit that I have no experience in cheating, stealing, lying, or assassinating political opponents.'"[5]

She was also strengthened by running as the head of the United National Democratic Party (UNIDO), whose president, Salvador Laurel, agreed to run as her vice president. The Catholic Church issued pastoral letters urging the faithful to be vigilant against attempts at intimidation and vote-buying. An emotional and committed grass-roots movement rapidly emerged in support of the Aquino ticket as she rallied voters across the nation.

The election had all the elements of a high-stakes international political drama. An aging, increasingly repressive and corrupt national leader was being challenged by a political novice. All across the nation, massive numbers of citizens volunteered to work at the polls and in the vote-counting process to try to ensure that the election was honest. Media personnel from around the world arrived in droves to cover the proceedings.

Because evidence of widespread fraud and corruption in previous elections was so compelling, numerous countries and international organizations sent delegates to monitor the balloting. President Reagan appointed Senator Lugar and me to chair the American team. I had monitored previous elections abroad. Senator Lugar was the highly respected chairman of the Senate Foreign Relations Committee and a wise and reasoned expert on foreign affairs. His committee had just held hearings on the situation in the Philippines. Having co-chairmen of the delegation from the two major American political parties added the important element of bipartisanship to our mission. We flew out of Andrews Air Force Base on February 5, 1986, and arrived in the Philippines the following day.

Our delegation had eighteen other members: Senator Thad Cochran (R-Miss.); Senator John Kerry (D-Mass.); Senator Frank Murkowski (R-Alaska); Congressman Bernard Dwyer (D-N.J.); Congressman Jerry Lewis (R-Cal.); Congressman Robert Livingston (R-La.); Congressman Samuel Stratton (D-N.Y.); Fred Fielding, counsel to the president; Admiral R. L. J. Long, USN (ret.); Jack Brier, secretary of state of Kansas; Natalie Meyer, secretary of state of Colorado; Norma Paulus, former secretary of state of Oregon; Bishop Adam Mida, Green Bay, Wisconsin; Larry Knisch, of the Congressional Research Service; Van Smith, former president of the U.S. Chamber of Commerce; Ben Wattenberg, co-editor of *Public Opinion*; Mortimer Zuckerman, chairman of *U.S. News & World Report*; and Allen Weinstein, president of the Center for Democracy. The delegation was a mix of seasoned elected officials, technically oriented individuals who had been involved in the electoral process for years, and a few journalists. Our mission was especially challenging because of the size of the Philippines: it had 20 million eligible voters, some 85,000 polling sites, and 91 provincial counting centers. When a country is relatively small and a significant number of its citizens live in one city, as in Panama and El Salvador, monitoring the balloting is obviously a more manageable and precise operation.

It probably appears rather presumptuous for a handful of people from one country to go to another for a few days and decide whether an election is honest and democratic. But I have headed and participated in a number of vote-monitoring delegations to various countries and I can tell you it's quite surprising how well a delegation can develop a clear picture of the fairness of an election.

For one thing, the delegates need street smarts when they talk to officials and voters at the polls. Knowing which questions to ask is important; so is a feel for the sincerity of the answers. The complexity of the registration process and the number of people at the polling sites who complain about irregularities or that their names are missing from the voting lists, even though they have registered, are other indicators of the fairness of the electoral process.

Delegates must have detailed knowledge of the mechanics of the vote-counting process. Who controls the ballot boxes? Does each political party have people to monitor them after they leave the polling site? What opportunities are there for fraud during the transportation and tabulation of the votes after the polls close?

In addition to the U.S. delegation, an international observer delegation consisting of forty-four delegates from nineteen countries was there to monitor the election. It included members of national parliaments, election experts, and scholars who specialized in the Philippines. This very prestigious group was led by my friend John Hume, a member of the British and European parliaments (years later he won a Nobel Prize), and Co-Chairman Misael Pastrana, a former president of Colombia.

Of course, even the sixty-four of us on our two delegations could monitor only a small percentage of the polling sites, but our presence was important to the Philippine people. In addition to our primary monitoring mission, we bolstered the commitment of the massive numbers of Philippine citizens involved in attempting to ensure a fair election.

After arriving at the airport in Manila, our delegation went immediately to the U.S. embassy to be briefed by Ambassador Steven Bosworth and the embassy staff. Steve Bosworth, a career State Department official, is an individual of outstanding ability and integrity. At our initial meeting he gave a very balanced presentation that provided a candid assessment of the challenges we faced.

He also described an elaborate and complex system being set up by the Philippine government to administer the election and verify the vote count. A parallel entity was set up by private citizens to monitor and verify the vote. The nine commissioners of the government entity, COMELEC (Commission on Elections), appointed by Marcos, exercised broad authority over the media, campaign activities and finance, voter registration, preparation of ballots, Election Day activities, and counting of votes. The nongovernmental entity, called NAMFREL (National Citizen Movement for Free Elections), organized and trained volunteers to monitor the electoral process. Hundreds of thousands of citizens volunteered.

When Ambassador Bosworth described to us the great number, enthusiasm, and dedication of the volunteers, it was obvious that a very significant portion of Filipino citizens did not trust the government to conduct a fair election. I approached my duties on Election Day with an open mind, but past Filipino elections and the enormous commitment of Filipinos to try to ensure a fair election suggested that this election still had to be watched closely.

Ambassador Bosworth advised us that none of us should wear anything yellow when we monitored the election. Mrs. Aquino always wore a yellow dress, so if any of our delegation wore yellow, we might be considered prejudiced in favor of the Aquino ticket. Ironically, the colors of the posters for Marcos's party were red, white, and blue.

Election Day

On Election Day, our delegation split into subgroups to monitor voting sites across the nation. The Filipino people received us warmly. As Paul D. Wolfowitz, assistant secretary, Bureau of East Asian and Pacific Affairs, Department of State, said on the *MacNeill-Lehrer News Hour,* "One of the things that really struck our presidential observer delegation that was sent there was the incredible warmth with which they were greeted everywhere they went. . . . There was just an outpouring of pro-American feeling."

One of the delegation's subgroups went to the province of Cebu, in the northern Philippines. Larry Knisch, one of the official delegates, was walking toward a voting booth in northern Cebu when a peasant woman stepped out of the voting line and motioned to him. She simply said, "We're happy that you are here." By itself, that little encounter was inconsequential. But it was typical of the atmosphere throughout the vast archipelago—so many citizens voiced support for our presence that it was clear that many Filipinos had little confidence in the integrity of the government.

Senator Lugar and I monitored votes in the metropolitan Manila area and in the city of Concepción in Tarlac province. We were followed everywhere by the media, as were other members of the delegation. In *Letters to the Next President,* Senator Lugar wrote about how the Marcos people exploited one comment he made early on Election Day. In describing a brief exchange with a correspondent from the TV station run by the government, Lugar wrote,

I stated that we had witnessed many courageous people who wanted to vote participating in a reasonably smooth election. When asked if I had sighted fraud personally, I said that I had not.

That interview proved to be a misstep in what had been a reasonably adept tightrope act to that point. While I was preparing for the NBC *Today* program, Marcos was appearing on the same program stating that the official observer team sent by President Reagan was convinced that the elections were "free, honest and clean." Channel 4 played my . . . interview throughout the evening as supporting testimony for the Marcos statement.[6]

A correspondent from *The Economist* captured the essence and drama of the day when he wrote that the election

> was exceptionally bloody—more than 40 people were killed on election day. But it was also remarkable in a way that lifted the spirit. More than a million Filipinos mounted vigil over the ballot boxes to ensure that the votes were protected. Polling stations were surrounded day and night by human chains to protect the ballots from being stolen or destroyed by local warlords and their thugs. When the boxes of votes were transferred to towns and from towns to cities, thousands of people, many in their bare feet, trudged alongside.[7]

In a press conference after the election, John Hume, the co-chairman of the other large vote-observation delegation, said, "For anybody watching those volunteers in action, and watching Filipino women protecting ballot boxes, and the determination and the commitment to the sacredness of the fundamental democratic act—the casting of a vote—is an expression of a deep sense of what democracy should be."[8]

Bryan Johnson wrote, "The so-called 'NAMFREL Marines' were organized as a crack trouble-shooting unit: a SWAT team dispatched to scenes of violence and intimidation. The 'Marines' were made up of six hundred of the tiniest, meekest and holiest-looking nuns that Joe Conception [the founder of NAMFREL] could find. One of the volunteers told Johnson, 'We don't fight fire with fire. NAMFREL fights fire with God.'"[9]

The vote-monitoring subgroups returned to Manila that evening. Some of them arrived quite late, since they had been monitoring the voting far from the capital city. Someone from the Cebu subgroup mentioned that a lot of thugs had tried to intimidate voters in that province, where the leadership was strongly pro-Marcos. Soldiers and others with rifles were at many of the polling booths. The subgroup met with Ramón Durano Sr., the head of the wealthiest and politically most powerful family in northern Cebu, although he had no official governmental position. Durano said, "Many of my critics refer to me as a warlord. I reject the 'war' component of that title. However, I freely accept the 'lord' part of this description."

The delegates held no formal meeting that evening, since it had been a very long day and some of the delegates did not return until about ten in the evening. A lot of the delegates exchanged stories of the day's events. The next morning we all gathered with Ambassador Bosworth around a large conference table in the U.S. embassy and gave our perspectives on what we had observed. It was a historic moment, and the eloquence of each delegate was most impressive. The give-and-take of the discussion as we strove to reach a consensus was itself an example of democracy in action. It was a very tense meeting, ably presided over by Ambassador Bosworth. Although many delegates had observed instances of vote fraud, at the end we did not have a consensus as to its extent or whether the delegation should declare the voting too flawed to be considered legitimate. Everyone remained open-minded, however. Since the vote-counting process at the NAMFREL and COMELEC was in its early stages, we decided to extend our stay briefly and make further observations. Events later that evening and the next day brought a consensus.

In addition to the potential for fraud at the actual polling sites, there is an even greater potential for malfeasance in the process of gathering the ballot boxes and tallying the votes. The government's voting infrastructure (COMELEC) and the citizens' volunteer group (NAMFREL) agreed to conduct a "parallel and coordinated operation," referred to as "Quick Count," to determine the results of the election and get the news to the public. Quick Count, despite its name, turned out to be a rather elaborate procedure in which both NAMFREL and COMELEC officials stationed throughout the Philippine archipelago would take various administrative steps in counting and verifying the votes. These officials would then transmit the voting results to the two separate Quick Count headquarters in Manila. Because of the importance of the Quick Count process to the integrity of the overall election, we decided to monitor events for another day or so before returning to Washington.

The evening after Election Day I went to the government's Quick Count center, which was set up in a cavernous room full of technicians sitting at computers entering the election results as they came in. As the results from the precincts were fed into the computers, the cumulative vote totals appeared on a large screen.

As I observed this process, I was struck by the fact that although more than twenty-four hours had passed since the last vote had been cast, there was an almost total lack of activity at the government's Quick Count center. Indeed, at times there were intervals of fifteen or twenty minutes when the numbers on the electronic board that posted the total vote tabulation did not change. This struck me as passing strange. By this time, a full day after the election, vote totals from the precincts should have been pouring in.

My immediate assumption was that Marcos's people realized that their guy was losing, so they were slowing the vote-counting process until they could determine what they had to do to ensure a Marcos "victory." Indeed, I eventually found out that forty-eight hours after the election, the results tallied by the two "parallel" Quick Count centers were far apart. The government's center had tabulated results from 28 percent of the precincts, while the citizens' volunteer center had tabulated results from 46 percent of the precincts. According to the COMELEC count, Marcos was leading by 150,000 votes, while NAMFREL reported Cory Aquino leading by 750,000 votes.

Our delegation was scheduled to leave the next morning. We had not made any formal statement, but the evidence was growing that significant fraud was being committed by the Marcos political machine. On the evening before our departure, a number of computer technicians walked out of the government's Quick Count center and held a predawn press conference to report that COMELEC officials were manipulating the voting data. Congressman Bob Livingston (R-La.) was there. Livingston told the *New Orleans Times-Picayune and States-Item* that until that point he had been cynical. But then he saw the vote counters gathered in the sacristy of a church for an hour, watched them pray together for five minutes, and saw them come out holding on to one another, obviously scared out of their wits. He said, "These young folks were taking their lives, and the lives of their families, in hand. . . . I saw this and I was moved. Tears came to my eyes. I totally believed what they had to say." Senator John Kerry (D-Mass.) also observed the press conference. When the conservative Republican from Louisiana and the liberal Democrat from Massachusetts reported back to the delegation on what they had observed, we knew we had our smoking gun. The election was fraudulent.

The Delegation's Departing Statement

The night before our departure, a draft of the delegation's departing statement, which was to be delivered to the media the next morning, was being written by Allen Weinstein of the Boston-based Center for Democracy; Graeme Bannerman, the staff director of the Senate Foreign Relations Committee; and John Plashal, of the House Appropriations Committee staff. As they worked on the statement that night, various members of the delegation returned to the hotel where we were staying. On the way they observed increasingly violent and repressive activities by the Filipino police and troops, including the beating of civilians. As the delegates returned during the evening, they told the staff to strengthen the statement condemning Marcos and the unfairness of the election. The drafters revised the statement and added tougher accusations in stronger language.

I went to bed about midnight and, as is my lifelong habit, got up about five in the morning. The staff had been up all night putting the final touches to the proposed draft of a departing statement, which the delegation was to review to ensure there was a consensus. The statement was to be read to the thousand media folks who would be gathered in an auditorium in the Manila Hotel to hear it.

When I read the draft statement, my immediate reaction was that it was too strong in its condemnation of Marcos and the election. Everything in the draft statement was true, and I fully agreed with the facts it contained. I was convinced that the Marcos forces had engaged in massive fraud and I had been in favor of a strong statement. My political instincts, however, told me that if we produced such a harsh statement, Marcos, like Claude Raines in *Casablanca,* would say he was "shocked, shocked!" that such goings-on could have occurred. He would then declare the election invalid and announce that a future election would be held (again) under "democratic" conditions. Meanwhile he would stay in power.

Frantic efforts were made to redraft the statement. Senator Lugar and I and the rest of the delegates agreed with the final draft, and later that morning Lugar made the following statement to the media representatives gathered in the Manila Hotel:

From northern Luzon to southern Mindanao, we have observed dedicated people, inspired and motivated by their faith in democracy. Moreover, we have seen concrete examples, both in voting and counting ballots, of success in the administration of the electoral process.

Sadly, however, we have witnessed and heard disturbing reports of efforts to undermine the integrity of that process, during both the voting and vote-counting process, which is still under way. Even within the last twenty-four hours, serious charges have been made in regard to the tabulation system.

The count is at a critical moment. We share the concern, expressed to us by both government election officials and citizen monitors, that the remainder of the COMELEC and NAMFREL Quick Count operations proceed to a credible conclusion without further delay. We join all Filipinos of goodwill in deploring all incidents of election-related violence and intimidation.

The process of counting and certifying the results of this election continues. Our mission as observers also continues.

We leave the Philippines today to deliver an interim report to President Reagan. Our final report will include information provided by those who will continue to observe on our behalf the remainder of the current electoral process. It is our hope that, in the days ahead, the current divergence between the two electoral Quick Count tallies will give way to a uniform electoral result that is broadly accepted by the Filipino people.

Each of us takes back to the United States individual memories and a common prayer. Our memories are those meetings with many Filipinos, meetings which have evidenced the strong and historic bonds of friendship between our two peoples. Our prayer is that this election process will end soon with the people of the Philippines reconciled through the triumph of the democratic process.

The press, which had been actively covering every aspect of the events of the last few days, had questions for our delegation after the statement. Members of the delegation answered the press inquiries for about forty-five minutes.

An interesting aspect of this fascinating chapter in history was the impact of the global media on events as they unfolded. Media coverage of the

United States' involvement abroad has, of course, existed since our nation was established, but the role played by the press in shaping events in this election was unprecedented.

In *Turmoil and Triumph: My Years as Secretary of State,* former Secretary of State George Shultz wrote of this phenomenon:

> Yet another development of the "information age" came to the fore: Cable Network News (CNN). Via CNN millions followed the Philippine drama as it was occurring. The American networks and press were all over Manila, reporting constantly, first on the voting and the atmosphere at the polling places and then on the counting. The Filipino media, in turn, were simultaneously rebroadcasting the American coverage back to the Philippines. So the Filipino people were watching themselves and hearing themselves analyzed primarily through American eyes.[10]

The global communications and information revolution of the last decades of the twentieth century has had an enormous impact on our foreign policy. When the century began, the United States' ambassadors would send occasional telegrams and reports back to Washington informing the State Department of the situations in the countries where they were stationed; the public was frequently uninformed of events. By the end of the century, people around the world received twenty-four-hour coverage of important events as they were unfolding, and many of them were sending faxes and Internet messages to one another, giving their perspectives on the situation.

At the conclusion of the press conference we departed by bus for the airport. A hostile, placard-waving pro-Marcos crowd outside the hotel demonstrated against our delegation. As we flew back to the States, we decided to send back a small delegation to the Philippines to continue monitoring events. Allan Weinstein, of the Center for Democracy, led that group.

After arriving in Washington, we went to the White House to report to President Reagan and administration officials. A number of the delegates spoke briefly about what they had observed. The preponderance of the discussion was about the group's serious misgivings about the honesty and openness of the pro-Marcos forces.

Unfortunately, the president later made a comment to the press that it was possible that fraud in the Philippine election "was occurring on both sides." He mentioned something about ballots from a pro-Marcos area having been found tossed into a ditch on the side of a road.

When I heard that comment reported in the media, I immediately thought back to the evening before our departure from the Philippines. I was in the lobby of the Manila Hotel talking to some other members of the delegation when I overheard some people talking next to us. Someone said, "You know there was cheating on both sides. I heard that ballots for a pro-Marcos area had been found on the side of a rural road." I thought that was a strange comment, because no one in our delegation had observed fraud by the Aquino forces. Granted, it is possible that isolated cases of such fraud occurred, but we observed no indication of it. I asked the people I was talking with who the guy was who made the comment about the discarded ballots. They said, "He's employed by the lobbying firm of Black, Manafort, and Stone, in D.C. The Marcos government is one of their big clients."

Obviously this lobbying firm had significant access to the White House. Someone from the firm had mentioned this story to the president or one of his top advisers. According to *Time,* "Reagan first made the accusation [of fraud on both sides] during a practice question-and-answer session with his staff. . . . The President was corrected, but, says a Reagan aide, "he had it in his mental computer, and it couldn't be erased."[11] When Senator Lugar was asked about the comment, he replied that the president was "not well informed."

George Shultz wrote: "I was quite aware that President Reagan wanted Marcos to change, not leave. However bad the Philippine situation might be, Ronald Reagan felt that Marcos had been a friend and ally of the United States, and Reagan stood up for people when the going was tough."[12]

The Marcos Regime Implodes

In the ensuing days, pressure against the Marcos regime rapidly built in Congress. The Senate Republican leader, Bob Dole, introduced a bill to have the Pentagon study alternative sites in the Asian region where the U.S. military bases in the Philippines could be relocated. Dante Fascell (D-Fla.), chairman of the Foreign Relations Committee, wrote President Reagan : "I urge you to consider immediate suspension of all military and economic assistance to the Philippines pending a full executive branch review of U.S. policy." He also said, "An aid suspension is a prudent and necessary step in light of the inevitable damage the United States will suffer if it fails to distance itself from a regime that has obviously decided to stay in power regardless of the consequences of thwarting the democratic process and the will of the people."[13]

The Asian subcommittee of the Foreign Affairs Committee, headed by Congressman Stephen Solarz, voted unanimously to cut off all military aid to the Philippines. Over the years Solarz had held several congressional hearings that raised serious questions about the legitimacy and ethics of the rule of Ferdinand and Imelda Marcos. These hearings did not result in legislation, but they were a method of keeping pressure on the Marcos regime to clean up its act, since the United States was a major source of financial and military assistance to the Philippines.

Meanwhile, back in the Philippines, the National Assembly reported final voting totals five days after our delegation's departure. Marcos was declared the winner. In an Orwellian comment, Marcos said his victory "would protect and save the democracy of our republic." The official totals actually verified the extent of the fraud that had been committed. You might say that Marcos did pretty well in certain areas of the country. In Ilocos Norte there were 197,983 registered voters, and according to the government's figures 96 percent of them voted. Marcos received 189,897 of those votes, as opposed to Mrs. Aquino's 718. Now I've heard of some very enthusiastic voter turnouts and landslides before, but 96 percent of the eligible voters showing up at the polls and the victor winning by 99.62 percent of the vote? In the city of Los Baños, the government had Marcos winning by 57,225 to 342. The government's figures showed 100 percent of the vote going to Marcos at some polling sites. The poll-watching clerks for the Aquino ticket who had voted at those sites had a legitimate question: "What happened to my vote?"

In less than a week after we left Manila, the 103-member Catholic Bishops Conference of the Philippines issued a statement read in churches throughout the nation on February 16. It stated in part: "In our considered judgment, the polls were unparalleled in the fraudulence of their conduct. A government that assumes or retains power through fraudulent means has no moral basis. Such an access to power is tantamount to a forcible seizure and cannot command the allegiance of the citizenry."[14]

Events unfolded rapidly as pressure against Marcos built up in the Philippines and the United States. Defense Minister Juan Ponce Enrile and the deputy chief of the armed forces, Lieutenant General Fidel V. Ramos, announced they were no longer supporting Marcos and that Mrs. Aquino had won the election. Ponce announced at a press conference that Marcos had stolen the election and was "no longer fit to rule." Ramos said that the "military had become practically the servants of political power in our society rather than the servants of the people."

Once again the Filipino people played a key role as events unfolded. Ponce and Ramos, with just 300 loyal troops, waited for an attack on their garrison. At that point, the pro-Marcos military forces could have easily overwhelmed the small rebellion. Marcos hesitated, however, and Defense Minister Ponce telephoned Cardinal Jaime Sin, who had the church-owned Radio Veritas urge the people to come out and defend the rebellion. The *Los Angeles Times* reported: "Priests, nuns and seminarians flooded out of their churches and monasteries. . . . Their cause became a national cause. By sunrise Sunday, the entire eight-lane width of Efran de Los Santos Street was choked with humanity. By the afternoon . . . the civilian crowd summoned by Radio Veritas' 'People Power' campaign had grown to nearly 100,000 and stretched for miles down the street."[15]

Marcos belatedly ordered an armored column to go to an army camp near the rebel stronghold. From that position they could have shelled it. The armored column never reached its destination. Tens of thousands of citizens put their lives at risk to block Marcos's military forces. *Time* reported that "Marcos' tanks rolled toward the crowds, only to be stopped by nuns kneeling in their path, saying the rosary. . . . Little girls offered their flowers to hardened combat veterans. In the face of such quiet heroism, thousands of Marcos loyalists defected."[16] The armored column returned to its barracks. The Reagan administration sent a message to Marcos saying that if he attacked the rebel stronghold, the United States would cut off military aid.

As his political situation became increasingly untenable, Marcos made a telephone call to Senator Paul Laxalt (R-Nev.). The first time Senator Laxalt had been in the Philippines was during World War II, in October 1944. As a young Army medic, he had spent harrowing months with the U.S. division that liberated the island of Leyte. Years later, after he had become a U.S. senator, Laxalt revisited the Philippines, and his war experience led to a friendship with Marcos.

Senator Laxalt was also a close confidant of President Reagan, so it was logical for Marcos to communicate with him when his own situation deteriorated. President Reagan sent Laxalt to the Philippines to deliver a letter outlining Reagan's concerns. After returning to Washington, the senator received a phone call from Marcos. In an emotional discussion, Marcos asked "what Laxalt thought he should do. Laxalt told Marcos that he personally thought that the time had come for Marcos to make a clean break, to leave the Philippines. Marcos replied, 'I am so very, very disappointed.'"[17]

On February 25, 1986, eighteen days after the election and just ten days after the Philippine Congress had declared Ferdinand Marcos the victor, Ferdinand and Imelda Marcos, along with an entourage of thirty, were flown by four U.S. H-3 helicopters from the grounds of the Malacanang Palace to Clark Air Force Base. There they were joined by another sixty Marcos loyalists who had arrived by ground transportation. Marcos went onto a hospital aircraft and the rest of the entourage went on a C-141 transport aircraft. The planes flew to Guam and then on to Hawaii.

In the aftermath of their departure, crowds poured onto the grounds of the abandoned Malacanang Palace. As they went from room to room, they observed the incredibly lavish lifestyle of Ferdinand and Imelda Marcos. Fox Butterfield of the *New York Times* reported: "A renowned Filipino art collector helping the new Government sort through the possessions that Ferdinand Marcos and his wife, Imelda, left behind at Malacanang Palace said today she was flabbergasted by her findings. The art collector, Beatrice Zobel, . . . said 'Imelda would buy a million dollars in jewelry at one store in the morning and then turn around and buy $2 million worth from an antique store in the afternoon.'" Imelda had 3,000 pairs of shoes on racks in the basement of the palace. Fox Butterfield quoted Congressman Steve Solarz (D-N.Y.), who had just gone on a tour of the palace: "'Compared to Imelda, Marie Antoinette was a bag lady.'" "On the intercom system, Mr. Marcos's bedroom was labeled 'King's Room' and Mrs. Marcos's 'Queen's Room.'"[18]

In a perceptive and eloquent reflection on the Marcos legacy, Lewis M. Simons wrote:

> Their abandoned palace yielded . . . racks hung with more dresses than are displayed in many department stores, gallon jugs of perfumes that sell for a hundred dollars an ounce, tasteless trinkets, and boxes full of receipts for the most extravagant of indulgences. More importantly, they left behind a plundered economy, where once there had been the greatest promise for prosperity in Southeast Asia; a disheartened and politicized military force, where once there had

been professional soldiers committed to a constitution and flag; and an increasingly threatening Communist insurgency, where once there had been little more than a defeated gang of ideologues. In the end, Marcos was just one more dictator, turning to America for protection in return for two decades of favors, running away from the nation he had driven into penury.[19]

When Cory Aquino ascended to the presidency, she maintained some official offices at the Malacanang Palace, but refused to live there. This was an important symbolic act. The communist movement, which had refused to participate in the election, rapidly lost strength and stature, and the Philippines became a functioning democracy.

President Aquino Addresses U.S. Congress

After her dramatic ascension to power, President Aquino came to Washington to meet with President Reagan, deliver a speech before Congress, and make other appearances. An invitation to speak to a joint session of Congress is usually extended only a few times a year. The chamber of the House of Representatives is large enough to accommodate not only the 435 representatives but also the 100 senators, the Cabinet, the Supreme Court, and the Joint Chiefs of Staff.

She delivered a blockbuster speech. Speaker Tip O'Neill called it the finest speech he had heard in the thirty-four years he had served in Congress. Stanley Karnow eloquently captured the magic of the moment of President Aquino's address to the joint session of Congress when he wrote:

> But the climax of her Washington visit . . . would be her appearance before a joint session of Congress—where the money was. . . . She wore a tailored yellow suit, and the packed chamber was a dazzle of yellow. Senators and Congressmen, cabinet members, diplomats and spectators reveled in yellow shirts, blouses, ties, handkerchiefs. The House majority leader, Jim Wright, had shipped in two hundred yellow roses from his home state of Texas, the flowers bedecking her path as she walked down the aisle to the podium—the chant of "Cory, Cory, Cory" rising in cadence to the rhythm of her steps.[20]

Speaker "Tip" O'Neill and I met with President Cory Aquino of the Philippines shortly before she gave a blockbuster speech to a joint session of Congress.

She spoke for about a half hour and was frequently interrupted by applause. She referred to her husband's assassination as the moment that began her country's "resurrection." She said that the killing of her husband "began the revolution that has brought me to democracy's most famous home, the Congress of the United States." Near the end of her speech she spoke of the will of the poor people of the Philippines who so strongly backed her effort to defeat Marcos at the ballot box:

> Slum or impoverished village, they came to me with one cry: Democracy! Not food, though they clearly needed it, not work, though they clearly wanted it—but Democracy. . . . Has there been a greater test of national commitment to the ideals you hold dear than what my people have gone through? You have spent many lives and much treasure to bring freedom to many lands that were reluctant to receive it. And here you have a people who won it by themselves and need only help to preserve it.

A volcanic ovation erupted. Engulfing Cory as she descended from the podium, legislators cheered, applauded, and jostled one another as they reached to grasp her hand. The chamber again chanted, "Cory, Cory, Cory" as she walked up the aisle, escorted by Senator Robert Dole, the leader of the Republican majority. "You hit a home run," he remarked to her—to which she snapped back without hesitation, "I hope the bases were loaded."[21]

Senator Frank Murkowski (R-Alaska) put these dramatic events in perspective when he said:

> Space does not permit an account of the tumultuous days surrounding the February 7 election and the coming to power of Cory Aquino as the result of blatant election fraud carried out by the Marcos regime. That final indignity caused millions of Filipinos to rise up in democratic wrath and declare Marcos' adversary . . . their leader. These historic events and the role of the Presidential Observer Delegation, led astutely and courageously by Senator Richard Lugar and Representative John Murtha, were voluminously reported by the American media. . . . I doubt that any similar American observer group will ever again play such an important role in support of the democratic process.[22]

It was very satisfying to serve as co-chairman of the delegation. Twenty American citizens from disparate backgrounds came together for a brief moment in time, traveled to a distant land to monitor an election, carried out their duties with deep commitment and professionalism, resolved their differences in a democratic forum, and successfully carried out a mission that had important ramifications. Democracy expanded in Asia.

The United States eventually unwillingly withdrew its forces from Clark Air Force Base and the naval base at Subic Bay. Yet the Philippines remains a staunch ally and close friend of America. The extent to which democracy in the Philippines took hold under Cory Aquino was dramatically shown some years later, after Joseph Estrada became president. In the wake of widespread corruption, he was removed from office after pressure from the citizens of the Philippines.

6

A STOLEN ELECTION AND U.S. INTERVENTION IN PANAMA

The United States and the Republic of Panama have had a unique relationship since Panama became a nation early in the twentieth century. Diplomatic relations between the two countries reached a low point when General Manuel Noriega and his cronies attempted to steal a presidential election in 1989. President George H. Bush appointed me chairman of a delegation to monitor that election.

The Background

The interests of the United States and Panama have been intertwined since the founding of the Republic of Panama in 1903. Although it is one of the smallest countries in the world, its strategic importance has been enormous because of the role of the Panama Canal in world trade and the link it provides to enable our navy to navigate quickly between two oceans.

For centuries people had envisioned the construction of a canal across the isthmus of Central America. A ship traveling from New York to San Francisco through the canal cuts off 8,000 miles from a 13,000-mile voyage. The economic impact of increased trade and lower shipping costs is obvious.

The engineering and financial challenge of a construction project of this magnitude was indeed daunting. The French attempted to build a canal across Panama in 1882. They failed, and 20,000 people lost their lives, mainly to disease.[1]

When the irrepressible Theodore Roosevelt became president, construction of a canal by the United States became a priority. In *The Path Between the Seas,* David McCullough wrote: "The building of the Panama Canal was one of the most grandiose, dramatic, and sweeping adventures of all time. Spanning nearly half a century, from its beginning by France in pursuit of glory to its completion by the Untied States on the eve of World War I, it enlisted men, nations, and money on a scale never before seen in all of history. Apart from the great wars, it was the largest, costliest single effort ever mounted anywhere on earth."[2]

So massive was the excavation of earth that the waterway was, in the words of the historian Walter LaFeber, "equal to a channel dug ten feet deep and fifty-five feet wide from Maine to Oregon." The water required to lift each ship through the canal's series of locks is "fifty-two million gallons, about the amount used each day by a city of a half million people."[3] It was truly an engineering marvel that attests to both America's engineering ingenuity and the vision and leadership of Teddy Roosevelt.

The major event defining U.S.-Panama relations was the 1978 treaty transferring ownership of the canal to Panama. The debate in the Senate was contentious and emotional, but President Jimmy Carter's proposed legislation prevailed. The transfer occurred in gradual increments over many years; the final transfer took place as scheduled on January 1, 2000.

When the Reagan administration came to power in 1981, it was eager for allies in Central America to support its opposition to the Marxist Sandinista regime in Nicaragua. One of the supportive countries was Panama, led by its dictator, Manuel Noriega. As so often in the past, the support of a despicable dictator was considered necessary to achieve a broader geopolitical goal. Walter LaFeber describes the dilemma: "If Washington got tough [against Noriega], it would alienate the same military force that was helping the U.S. overthrow the Sandinistas, that was supposed to help protect the canal. . . . If, however, Reagan did not get tough, he would continue to be linked to Noriega's corrupt, violent, drug-trafficking officer corps."[4]

Granted, foreign policy should be based on a realistic assessment of the United States' strategic needs and a practical analysis of any alternatives. But relying on dictatorial governments to protect our interests can be like building a foundation on sand.

The Rise of Manuel Noriega

Manuel Noriega was born in a slum of Panama City. His ticket out of it was a scholarship to a military school in Peru. After graduating he joined

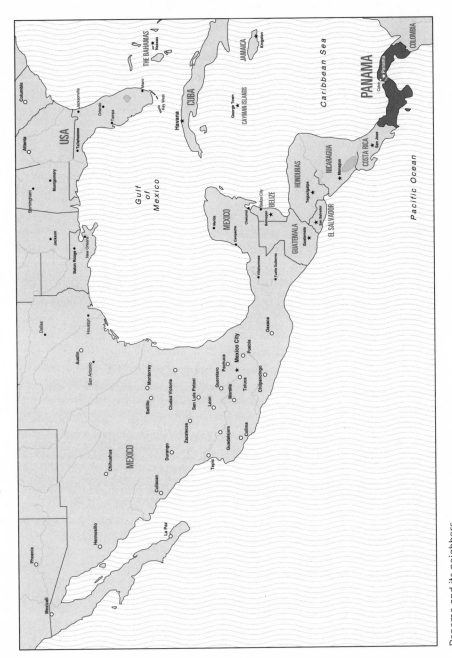

Panama and its neighbors

Panama's Guardia Nacional. A street-smart man, he worked his way up to become head of the intelligence unit of the Guardia Nacional. The intelligence unit was responsible for the external and internal intelligence of the entire Panama government. In that job, Noriega began to receive payments from the CIA for information on international drug trafficking. There were persistent rumors that he was receiving funds from international drug traffickers at the same time for assisting their operations. These rumors were accurate; playing both sides of the street came quite easily to this chameleon. Moreover, as the head of domestic intelligence, he had access to the files of many important Panamanian citizens. The intelligence apparatus of the Guardia Nacional was extensive throughout the country.

In July 1981, the head of the Guardia Nacional, General Omar Torrijos, died in a military plane crash. In 1983, after a power struggle, Noriega emerged as Torrijos's successor and the de facto leader of Panama. He merged the military and police into a single Panamanian Defense Force (PDF) and its size grew to 15,000.

The PDF controlled extensive sectors of the Panamanian economy and made lucrative profits in the drug trade, money laundering, and legitimate businesses set up with illegally obtained funds. Noriega built up a fortune of hundreds of millions of dollars and had luxurious homes and massive bank accounts in many locations around the world. The PDF was also the central player in Panamanian politics. Although presidential elections were held every four years, the civilian who was elected president was only a figurehead; the real power remained in military hands.

Manuel Noriega became increasingly controversial. Negative articles about him appeared in the press and Senator Kerry of Massachusetts conducted hearings on the alleged involvement of Noriega and his cronies in drug trafficking and money laundering. A grand jury in Miami indicted him for drug trafficking. Noriega deposed the sitting president, Nicholas Ardito-Baretta, and his successor, Eric Arturo Delvalle, went into hiding.

After damage was inflicted on the U.S. embassy in June 1987, the United States suspended economic and military aid. Noriega declared a state of emergency and suspended constitutional rights. The media were censored. The economy deteriorated and peaceful demonstrations were brutally broken up by both the PDF and civilian goon squads euphemistically called "dignity battalions." Panama became increasingly isolated and scorned.

Despite the erosion of his political position, all that mattered to Manuel Noriega was holding on to power. He was determined to remain as head of the Panamanian Defense Force and to have his handpicked candidate "win" the 1989 presidential election.

The Election Is Stolen

In May 1989, the newly elected president George H. Bush named me as chairman of the U.S. delegation to observe the presidential election in Panama. There were also vote-monitoring delegations from other countries and international organizations. The most notable of them was led by former president Jimmy Carter and included former president Gerald Ford. U.S.-Panama relations were very strained at this point and Noriega warned that our delegation would not be allowed into Panama. I mentioned this at a brief news conference before we took off from Andrews Air Force Base. The delegation included Senators John McCain III (R-Ariz.), Bob Graham (D-Fla.), and Connie Mack III (R-Fla.), Representatives Lawrence Coughlin (R-Pa.), Alan Mollohan (D-W.Va.), Dan Glickman (D-Kans.), Robert Lagomarsino (R-Calif.), and Lawrence Smith (D-Fla.). Other officials in the delegation were Mayor Xavier Suarez of Miami, former U.S. senator Richard Stone (D-Fla.), former ambassador to Panama Jack Vaughn, Andrew Gibson of the Panama Canal Commission, and Michael Kozack, acting assistant secretary of state for inter-American affairs.

After landing at Howard Airfield, I delivered a brief statement to the press:

> The members of the delegation are pleased to be in Panama as representatives of President Bush and the people of the United States of America to observe tomorrow's important political event.
>
> In the last ten years, Latin America, responding to the sacrifices and desires of its people, has become an example to the rest of the world as fertile ground for the growth and restoration of democracy. The United States has supported this process, and the respect for human and political rights that is the hallmark of any country that calls itself democratic. It is that spirit that motivates our visit here.
>
> In recent years, the people of Panama have manifested clearly their desire to join the worldwide movement to freedom and democracy. The May 7 election offers an opportunity for the will of the people to be peacefully expressed and to be respected in their choice of political

leadership through a fair political process. These elections offer an opportunity for the resolution of Panama's political and economic crisis. That is what we hope to witness here. President Bush has asked us to observe, without preconception or prejudgment. We will draw our conclusions and make our report to the President based on what we see and hear in Panama over the next three days.

The people of Panama have our best wishes for an honest election, free of fear and intimidation, that will accurately reflect the will of the Panamanian electorate.

We immediately went to be briefed by the U.S. ambassador, Arthur Davis, and the embassy staff. As we heard the details of the procedures to be followed in the pending election, it became clear that the potential for fraud was there. The registration procedures, for example, allowed members of the Panamanian Defense Force to vote at any voting booth in the country (vote early and vote often) and go to the head of the line at any polling site. The rest of the citizens had to vote in their neighborhood or village, and of course wait in line.

The delegation spent the rest of the evening planning our next-day election-monitoring activities. As in the Philippines, we divided into subgroups so we could monitor the election throughout the country. Several delegates spoke Spanish, and the embassy provided interpreters for those of us who didn't.

It was clear that the Panamanian people were enthusiastic about the election. Voters turned out in significant numbers throughout the country in both urban and rural areas. State Department spokeswoman Margaret Tutwiler stated that the Panamanian government's electoral tribunal had released figures showing that more than 1.18 million people were registered to vote, an increase of more than 160 percent over the votes cast in the previous election.

Noriega's handpicked candidate, Carlos Duque, was the owner of a company that had been skimming money for the PDF for years. There had been fraud in past Panamanian elections, and in view of the enormous amount of illegal funds flowing to Noriega and his inner circle, it was only logical to assume that they would attempt to steal the election if they felt they might lose otherwise. Polls revealed that Noriega's candidate was running far behind the challenger, Guillermo Endara. Nevertheless, I kept an open mind.

The morning of the election, the component of the delegation that I headed drove from the Canal Zone into Panama City without incident. We had no specific schedule or timetable, and I asked the driver to pull over at the first polling site we saw. There we saw three young women in military uniforms voting. Their uniforms and boots were brand-new and must have just been issued. Their fingernails were long and meticulously manicured. I had no proof that they weren't actually PDF soldiers, but let's say it looked suspicious. Wearing military uniforms, they could go from polling site to polling site throughout the city—indeed, throughout the country—and vote at all of them. At many of the polling sites I monitored I heard numerous vociferous complaints about inaccuracies in the registration lists and an absence of ballots.

The delegation's subgroups monitored polling sites from the border with Costa Rica to the province of Darién, on the border with Colombia. At the end of the day the subgroups returned to the Canal Zone and in a lengthy meeting we described the events we had observed. The consensus was that fraud had been widespread. Repeated voting by members of the PDF was at the top of the list. Some members of the delegation actually followed PDF personnel as they brazenly traveled from polling site to polling site, voting at each one. The delegation saw people whose names were not on voting lists being given credentials allowing them to vote; an absence of opposition ballots at some voting precincts; registration lists that contained the names of dead people lacked the names of people who had voted in the past and insisted they were registered.

Although we were convinced that fraud was widespread, I wanted to make a broader assessment before composing a draft departure statement for review by the rest of the delegation. Early the next morning I went to the home of Archbishop Marcos McGrath in Panama City. He was the leading cleric in the country, very influential, and a Panamanian nationalist who had long advocated that control of the canal be turned over to Panama. Under his leadership the Catholic churches had monitors at polling sites throughout the country, and they stayed at their posts the entire day. The archbishop told me the church's monitors found considerable evidence of abuse and fraud everywhere. They also noted that the PDF was in charge of collecting the ballot boxes and bringing them to central locations to "verify" the vote count—an open invitation to further electoral abuse.

The combination of actual fraud observed by our delegation and the international delegation headed by President Carter and the widespread voting violations observed by the church monitors convinced me the election was fraudulent. I phoned Bishop McGrath to get an update on his information and then read the following brief statement to the gathered media people:

> President Bush sent this delegation of members of Congress and private citizens to Panama to observe the Panamanian national election. The delegation was tasked by the President to determine whether, in its judgment, the election in Panama was open and fair.
>
> We observed the voting process at selected polling places where the majority of the Panamanian people live. We met with the leaders of various political parties and discussed the election with them. We met with the leaders of the Catholic Church in Panama and discussed the church's plan to monitor the election at over 400 polling places representing 10 percent of the election.
>
> I just talked to the archbishop of Panama a few minutes ago. According to him, he has information on 125 to 130 precincts and the results are overwhelmingly in favor of the opposition by 70 to 30 percent.
>
> In summary, the delegation received a wide range of information through both direct observation and contact with local officials and citizens of Panama. We agree that, in our view, the mechanics of the election process were so flawed that there were continuous and widespread opportunities for the manipulation of the voting results by the incumbent regime.
>
> Furthermore, individual members of the delegation observed numerous irregularities and instances of actual fraud. The delegation cannot certify that this was a fair and free election.

An interpreter translated my announcement into Spanish. A TV station in the Canal Zone broadcast the announcement and the question-and-answer session live throughout the country. I don't remember the name of the interpreter, but she did a magnificent job, especially during the question-and-answer session. She had not been taking notes but she repeated in rapid Spanish the lengthy comments of delegation members. She was one of the many skilled and knowledgeable people working at U.S. embassies throughout the world. The television station carrying the news conference continued to rerun my address and the question-and-answer session until Noriega ordered the signal jammed.

On the flight back to Washington I reflected on the events of the last two days. When our delegation had left Washington it was not certain we could even get into Panama. We not only had gotten into the country but had monitored the election, determined it was manipulated by Noriega's forces, and then, through an interpreter on national TV, declared in Spanish to the people of Panama that the election was fraudulent. An intense forty-eight hours!

After the Election

Three days later the Panamanian government announced that the election had been annulled and claimed interference by the United States and fraud by the opposition. Noriega's reign became increasingly repressive. He used his "dignity battalions" to break up peaceful demonstrations with baseball bats and tire irons. One of the two opposition vice presidential candidates, Billy Ford (who many years later became Panama's ambassador to the United States), was beaten up badly during a peaceful demonstration against the fraudulent election. His bloodied face appeared on the cover of *Time*.

In the months after the stolen election the Panamanian economy progressively deteriorated. Various heads of state pressured Noriega to go into exile. He resisted these pressures and things appeared to return to normal. Noriega hinted through various channels that he might leave the country. A State Department official told me, "Noriega is at his best making promises and stalling for time."

At the suggestion of Ambassador Davis, who had been recalled to the United States, I went to Panama in September 1989 to attempt to drive a wedge between Noriega and the Panamanian Defense Force. I held a news conference at the airport and said that from the United States' perspective the problem between our two countries was the rule of Manuel Noriega and not the PDF. President Bush had made similar comments. A clandestine meeting was arranged so I could talk to the political leaders from whom Noriega had stolen the election—Guillermo Endara, Ricardo Calderón, and Billy Ford. They asked me, "What more can we do?" They had generated demonstrations of up to 200,000 protesters. Think of that number for a moment. All of Panama City had approximately one million people. Thus, at this particular opposition rally, a crowd equal to one of every five citizens of Panama City marched in opposition to the Noriega regime.

A month later, on October 7–8, 1989, two developments drew me back to Panama. The Bush administration had replaced General Fred Woerner, CINCSOUTH (commander in chief, SOUTHCOM, or Southern Command) and an expert on the region, because he had failed to comply with an order to evacuate American dependents from Panama. The administration was becoming frustrated by the apparent failure of economic sanctions and diplomacy against Noriega and wanted to pursue a more aggressive strategy. General Woerner had disagreed with this approach. Senator John McCain, who had been a member of the vote-monitoring delegation earlier in the year, had recommended that he be replaced.

The new CINCSOUTH was General Max Thurman, a no-nonsense bachelor who was married to the Army. He had done an outstanding job in the early 1980s as the chief of Army recruiting and later as the Army's vice chief of staff. The recruiting program he implemented had helped transform the Army from the lows of the late 1970s to the high-quality force it had become in the late 1980s. He was also the architect of the slogan "Be all that you can be."

The second development was an attempted coup against Noriega that ended in tragedy. Since I had asked the Panamanian people to rise up against Noriega and the situation was deteriorating rapidly, I felt that an on-site assessment was necessary.

I conferred with John Maisto, the chargé d'affaires at the embassy, and other members of the embassy staff. I learned that Adela Bonilla de Giroldi, wife of Major Moisés Giroldi of the PDF and an employee of the U.S. embassy, had secretly notified our embassy that a coup was going forward. Her husband, she said, intended to initiate it. Major Giroldi was the commander of the Urraca Battalion, whose primary mission was to guard the PDF headquarters in Panama City.

In *The Commanders*, Bob Woodward wrote: "As a major, one of the senior ranks within the PDF, Giroldi was in a position to carry out a successful coup. But they [the CIA] had discovered that he had helped Noriega crush a coup only 18 months earlier, in March, 1988. Giroldi had turned in the coup participants, and Noriega had them jailed and tortured."[5]

Major Giroldi's intentions were to lead a coup with no casualties, which would force Noriega to retire. (A fascinating aspect of this episode came to light when I talked to the CIA's mission chief in Panama. He said that if Major Giroldi had told him a coup was going to be tried against Noriega, and that the participants intended to kill Noriega, under the CIA's rules the agency would have had to notify Noriega of an impending coup. When I returned to Washington, I called Brent Scowcroft, the national security adviser, and told him of my conversation with the CIA agent. He didn't believe me. About three weeks later I noticed an article in the *Washington Post* that read in part, "U.S. law reveals that we must inform dictators of threats on their life.") Noriega was held in the PDF headquarters as the coup unfolded. The rebels occupied the building just before dawn.

Giroldi's officers began polling other units to see if they would support the takeover. Unfortunately, Noriega had been left alone in a room where a telephone was available. He called his political allies, who alerted troops loyal to Noriega, and they immediately came to his rescue.[6] In the wake of the failed coup, there were rumors that Noriega himself killed Major Giroldi.

General Thurman had assumed command of SOUTHCOM just a day before the attempted coup and General Colin Powell had become chairman of the Joint Chiefs of Staff only a few days earlier. Although U.S. forces had been deployed to block two roads after the coup began, they did not actively intervene to assist the coup attempt, nor did Major Giroldi ask them to. Both General Thurman and General Powell were concerned that a trap was being set, and that U.S. soldiers might be taken hostage if American forces intervened.

The next morning I went to Southern Command headquarters to confer with General Thurman and was briefed on the sequence of events of the previous week. I was immediately struck by the fact that in addition to the new commander, all of the key staff (chief of staff, G-2, and G-3) were also newly assigned to Panama. In fact, the entire leadership had rotated during the past seven weeks. The military continued to adhere to normal rotational policies despite the fact that the practice left limited "institutional memory" for dealing with a potentially explosive situation.

It increasingly looked as if a popular uprising against Noriega would not succeed because of his brutal response to demonstrations. It also appeared that a coup by the PDF was not going to be a viable option. Most of the top soldiers around Noriega were also corrupt and relied on the entrenched system for their economic well-being. I concluded that a military intervention by the United States was the only feasible option. The situation began to look ominous and President Bush ordered a buildup of U.S. forces in the Canal Zone. Many U.S. citizens left Panama City and others withdrew into the Canal Zone.

I also visited Bishop McGrath, who had given our vote-monitoring delegation valuable advice months earlier. He was a graduate of the University of Notre Dame, and at the time of my visit to his residence a Notre Dame football game was being broadcast on television. It was soon obvious that his primary interest at the moment was that football game. I asked him if he thought we should invade. He said yes, his eyes still on the screen.

Our group—John Plashal of the committee staff, Charlie Horner of the Pentagon, Enrique Perez of the State Department, and I—arranged to meet again clandestinely with the three candidates who had actually won the election. The presidential candidate, Guillermo Endara, was a friendly bear of a man who related well to the working people and farmers of Panama. Ricardo Arias Calderón, one of the vice presidential candidates, had a Ph.D., and in the limited time I conferred with him he seemed very intense and focused. The second vice presidential candidate, Billy Ford, was an outgoing, back-slapping man who had an engaging laugh and spoke English with no trace of an accent.

From my perspective, these leaders needed to request U.S. military intervention. I believed that such a request would legitimize intervention because they really were the democratically elected leaders of the country and they would be requesting intervention on behalf of the Panamanian people, who had expressed their collective will in the election.

I pressed this point with them, and the decision was obviously painful for them to make. They were nationalists who loved their country. They asked me how I, as a member of Congress, could ensure that U.S. troops would come if they did request them. I told them I could not guarantee that the United States would act, but I would take their request back to the Bush administration, where the decision would have to be made.

I repeated my view that the situation had evolved to a point where only U.S. intervention could bring a legitimate government to their country. The three of them huddled in a corner of the room for a few minutes, then turned to me and said they agreed and asked me to relay the message to the Bush administration. Upon returning to Washington I requested a meeting with Brent Scowcroft and relayed the message to him, along with my view that we should invade.

On December 16 four off-duty U.S. officers were stopped at a roadblock

I met with Guillermo Endara, whose victory at the polls was stolen by the dictator Manuel Noriega. I led the vote-monitoring delegation that concluded that the election was not honest. Endara became president after intervention by U.S. forces.

near PDF headquarters as they were returning to the Canal Zone from Panama City. "There was no way to avoid the roadblock. When the PDF soldiers spotted the Impala, they ostentatiously snapped back the cocking levers of their AK-47s and leveled the weapons at the car," wrote Malcolm McConnell. When the car sped away, they fired their weapons. Lieutenant Robert Paz was killed. The shooting was observed by a U.S. Navy lieutenant and his wife, Adam and Bonnie Curtis. They were interrogated for hours. He was beaten into unconsciousness and the PDF threatened to rape his wife.[7] They were released five hours later. U.S.-Panama relations had reached a new low. Four days later the invasion was launched.

The Invasion of Panama

The invasion, called Operation Just Cause, began in the first minutes of December 20, 1989. Just before the invasion Endara, Calderón, and Ford were sworn in as the leaders of Panama at a secret ceremony.

Operation Just Cause involved simultaneous nighttime attacks on numerous installations and the capture of facilities. Two battalions were primarily instrumental in the invasion, one from the 75th Ranger Regiment of Fort Stewart, Georgia, and the other from the 82nd Airborne Division of Fort Bragg, North Carolina. Elements of the 82nd as well as the 5th and 7th Divisions had been positioned in Panama earlier, supposedly to provide increased security or to conduct jungle training. Panama had been the home of the Jungle Warfare School for decades, so it wasn't unusual for American forces in the Canal Zone to conduct training exercises there. Surprise was an important element of the invasion plans. A total of 428 airlift missions were flown by C-5A, C-141, and C-130 aircraft carrying 14,000 troops and 12,500 tons of cargo. In addition, 172 tanker missions refueled 274 airborne aircraft. A wide variety of missions were simultaneously undertaken—commando units liberated American prisoners and Panamanian political prisoners; Navy Seal teams attacked and secured a small airport in Panama City that Noriega might have used to escape; Rangers attacked and secured the large commercial airport at Panama City and the Río Hato barracks, where Noriega loyalists were stationed; and artillery, tanks, and airborne gunships attacked the PDF headquarters in Panama City.

Overall, the invasion was carried out almost as planned, but some snags are inevitable in any operation. Malcolm McConnell wrote about one glitch in the execution:

> The Rangers were right on schedule. But a full brigade of the 82d Airborne Division—the combat muscle of Task Force Pacific—was hopelessly delayed. One of the worst ice storms in recent years was sweeping across the southern United States, and had struck with disastrous effect at Pope Air Force Base, adjacent to Fort Bragg, North Carolina. Almost 3,000 82d Airborne troops were rigged out, ready to board their C-141 Starlifters. But the airlift was stalled on the ground due to limited deicing equipment; only a few planes at a time could be deiced for takeoff.[8]

I'm sure that an ice storm at Pope Air Force Base is such a rare event that the bean counters responsible for budget matters would have rejected a request for additional deicing equipment. One of Murphy's Laws of Combat—when an operation begins, the weather turns bad—was in full operation that night. An underappreciated fact is that much of the equipment vital to combat success seemingly has little to do with combat.

An important aspect of Operation Just Cause was the effort to minimize casualties, since our differences were with Noriega, not with the Panamanian people or most of the Panamanian Defense Force. Thus various aspects of the operation relied on the element of surprise, with the use of weapons to frighten and disorient opponents. Psychological warfare techniques were also used. In several instances our troops used bullhorns to inform the PDF that no shots would be fired if they surrendered.

The invasion force soon overwhelmed the resistance forces. Noriega, however, escaped and ended up in the Vatican's embassy in Panama City. Negotiations with him continued intermittently over the next ten days. In a psychological ploy to harass him, U.S. soldiers played rock and country-western music at high decibel levels through massive speakers outside the Vatican embassy. They also blared news broadcasts reporting that Noriega's troops had stopped fighting after he abandoned them and that U.S. officials were moving to freeze funds he had sent abroad. The music stopped after three days when the papal nuncio, Monsignor José Sebastián Laboa, complained that he couldn't get any sleep. A radio station in the Canal Zone that broadcast for the American troops reported that the song most frequently requested while Noriega was in the Vatican embassy was "Nowhere to Run—Nowhere to Hide" by Martha and the Vandellas.

Monsignor Laboa let Noriega know that he had signed a letter authorizing the U.S. Army to storm the building if a hostage situation arose.[9] Pressure against Noriega intensified when crowds of angry Panamanians massed outside the embassy, shouting "Assassin!" and "Murderer!" Monsignor Laboa said that he warned Noriega "of the danger he could be lynched, like Mussolini, and posed to public derision in a square." In a classic understatement, Monsignor Laboa told Noriega that "such an event would be quite undignified."[10]

About 9 P.M. on January 3, 1990, Manuel Noriega donned a clean, pressed uniform with four general's stars, walked through the embassy's iron gates, and surrendered to General Maxwell Thurman, commander of SOUTHCOM.

I made my final inspection trip to Panama about one week after the invasion. Sonny Montgomery, one of Congress's leading advocates of a strong national defense, accompanied me. Lieutenant General Stiner, commander of the Joint Taskforce South, gave us an overview of the operation. He mentioned that the intensity of the fighting and the vast amounts of weapons uncovered throughout the country surprised him. A total of 49,652 weapons were captured.

The major deficiency in the operation, he said, was the lack of solid intelligence. "We can tell where every Soviet submarine is under the oceans around the world but I couldn't find out where the dignity battalions were in Panama City or what they would do to counter our intervention." His criticism of the lack of HUMINT (human intelligence, the gathering of intelligence through agents and operatives as opposed to the use of technology) has been a recurring theme over the years. We have taken various steps in Congress to improve HUMINT but it still has a long way to go before we achieve our full national security capabilities.

We went to Noriega's personal quarters at various government facilities. The guy definitely had a thing for hats and ceramic frogs. Baseball caps, safari hats, military hats were everywhere. An elaborate Native American headdress was at one of his offices. Ceramic frogs of all sizes were on display in cabinets and on tables.

An interesting aspect of the postinvasion inspection trip was a side trip to Renacer prison, on the banks of the canal. The prison had been under the control of the PDF although it was within the Canal Zone. Many political prisoners had been incarcerated at the Renacer prison, and liberating them was a high priority. In a daring raid, two UH-60 Blackhawk helicopters landed in a courtyard at the center of the prison compound at night. The courtyard was barely larger than the Blackhawks. Other units invaded from the perimeter of the prison.

As we were escorted around the prison by Captain Johnson of the 82nd Airborne Division, he mentioned that his unit had deployed to Panama earlier in December. They had conducted a training exercise right at the perimeter of the prison three days before the attack on it. Over the years as an active-duty Marine and as a Marine Reservist I have trained often under conditions that closely resembled actual combat conditions, but this training exercise may have been the first time in history that a military force practiced an attack on a target that it actually attacked a few days later. Pretty clever!

The F-117 stealth aircraft, which had been secretly funded in the defense budget for a number of years, was first used to attack the barracks at Río Hato, a base striding the Pan American Highway well outside Panama City. The plan was for the bombs to hit near the barracks at Río Hato to sow confusion and avoid casualties among the Panamanian troops asleep inside the barracks and the patients in a dispensary next to the barracks. U.S. Rangers were to parachute in and secure the area as soon as the bombs were dropped.

Weeks later I was at the Wolford Hospital at Lackland Air Force Base, where one of the Rangers who had parachuted into the Río Hato base was a patient. He told me he had parachuted in from just 500 feet. That's equal to leaping from a fifty-story building and activating the chute in time for a safe landing. The jump was so close to the ground that if the primary parachute did not activate, a Ranger had only a quarter of a second to open the backup chute. During the attack one of his legs was so badly shot up that it had to be amputated.

He had been told that they would see a flash, feel a concussion, and then would immediately jump. Actually he hadn't seen any flash, but he did feel the concussion. He hit the ground amid a hail of bullets. The Rangers got behind a berm and used it and the 120 pounds of gear that each was carrying as protection against the fire from the Panamanian forces. There were explosives in their gear, and he shouted to the squad leader that everyone should remove them. As they were digging out the explosives, an American AH-64 helicopter mistook his unit for the enemy and fired at them. He said he had been lucky to have been shot only in the leg. The squad leader had been killed instantly. Despite the loss of his leg, he was upbeat. He said about three times that he couldn't wait to get back to his unit.

In his autobiography Colin Powell wrote: "A CBS poll conducted soon after the installation of President Endara showed that nine out of ten Panamanians favored the U.S. intervention. . . . The lessons I absorbed from Panama confirmed all my convictions over the preceding twenty years, since the days of doubt over Vietnam. Have a clear political objective and stick to it. Use all of the force necessary, and do not apologize for going in big if that is what it takes. Decisive force ends wars quickly and in the long run saves lives."[11] Seven months after the intervention in Panama, Saddam Hussein's forces invaded Kuwait. The lessons learned in the invasion of Panama, as Powell articulated them, were about to be applied on a much larger scale.

The process of political reform, economic reform, and reform of the Panamanian Defense Force began immediately after President Endara assumed office. Manuel Noriega remains in prison.

7

Operations Desert Shield and Desert Storm

The Iraqi dictator Saddam Hussein is one of the vilest despots who ever ruled a country. As Mortimer Zuckerman of *U.S. News & World Report* wrote:

> Someone who should know Saddam Hussein, Syria's dictator Hafesz Assad, said that Saddam is like a chain smoker, lighting another cigarette before he has finished the first. But Saddam's addiction is not nicotine; it is bloodshed. . . . Here is a man who used poison gas on Iranians and nerve gas on his own people. He invaded Iran in 1980; he began the gulf tanker war in 1984; the next year he bombed and rocketed Iran's cities; he stopped firing at Iran in 1988 but hardly paused for breath before invading Kuwait in 1990; he suppressed the postwar popular uprising in his own country; he resumed the slaughter of the Kurds; the list goes on and on.[1]

In *Unholy Babylon*, Adel Darwish and Gregory Alexander wrote of Saddam's early years in a family overly familiar with domestic violence. He committed his first murder when he was sixteen and his second at age twenty. Saddam became a member of the Regional Command Council of the Ba'ath party. "He was put in charge of the special force responsible for terror and assassination and was an interrogator and torturer in the Qasr as-Nihayyat (the Palace of the End). . . . He designed new instruments of torture and then experimented with them on his victims. . . . Saddam had a macabre and sadistic habit of presenting victims with a list from which they had to select the method by which they would 'prefer' being tortured."[2]

After working his way up through the Ba'ath political party, Saddam declared himself president in July 1979. The violence he has inflicted on his own people continues to this day. In April 1998, the former foreign minister of the Netherlands, Max van der Stoel, in a report presented to the United Nations Human Rights Commission, concluded that 1,500 Iraqis had been executed in the previous year, most of them for political reasons. According to a description of the report in the *New York Times*, "Most of the deaths occurred during a 'prison cleansing campaign.' . . ordered by Mr. Hussein's younger son, Qusay. He directs Iraq's Special Security Organization, one of a number of armed intelligence agencies that sustain an atmosphere of terror in Iraq." The report says that after Qusay Hussein's visit to one prison, Abu Garib, large numbers of prisoners condemned to death or to sentences of fifteen years or more were shot, hanged, or electrocuted. The families of those shot were forced to pay for the bullets that killed them before they could claim the bodies.[3]

Building up his armed forces and developing weapons of mass destruction were Saddam's major objectives as president of Iraq. Numerous Western companies, the Soviets, and the Chinese sold him weapons systems. Iraq also purchased capital equipment from Western companies for research or production of nuclear, chemical, biological, and other weapons of mass destruction.

The Background

In 1980 Iraq invaded its neighbor Iran. An estimated one million people died in the eight-year war that followed. Saddam ordered his forces to use chemical weapons against the Iranians. This was a war fought with the tactics of World War I: troops in trenches a few miles apart would launch a human-wave attack and gain a few miles of ground, only to lose it soon to a counterattack.

Because of their fear of Iran, various Middle Eastern countries, including Kuwait and Saudi Arabia, made enormous loans to Iraq during the war, and by the end of the conflict Iraq was in debt by over $70 billion, whereas it had had $30 billion in cash available when it started the war. According to Judith Miller and Laurie Mylroie, "Saddam and all the Arabs knew that this debt would never be repaid. Saudi Arabia no longer even bothered to keep the loans on its books. . . . But Kuwait had repeatedly raised the debt issue as a bargaining chip whenever Iraq reiterated demands for territory or more money after the war's end."[4]

Within about a year after the end of the war there were significant indications that Iraq was again becoming warlike. An article in *The Economist* noted: "Between February and April [1990], Mr. Hussein had demanded the withdrawal of the American Navy from the Gulf, called on fellow Arabs to reactivate the oil weapon, and threatened not just to attack Israel . . . but to burn it with chemical weapons. Add Iraq's challenge to Syria in Lebanon, plus a relentless arms buildup, and the evidence was plain: the bad old . . . Iraq was back again."[5]

Numerous articles have appeared about two meetings between Saddam Hussein and American officials in 1990, which probably reassured him that the United States would not act if Iraq invaded Kuwait. In April he met with a group of U.S. senators, who reportedly told him that a commentator for the Voice of America who had attacked Saddam's policies had been relieved and that they "assumed" President Bush would oppose the trade sanctions against Iraq that the Congress was considering imposing.

The other meeting, on July 25, 1990, was between Saddam Hussein and the U.S. ambassador to Iraq, April Glaspie, who reportedly told him, "We have no opinion on the Arab-Arab conflicts, like your border disagreement with Kuwait." *The Economist* put this meeting in perspective when it wrote:

> Some of the State Department's critics now say Ms. Glaspie's interview with President Hussein was the final, fatal sign of American weakness that tempted him over the brink. Maybe . . . but it is too simple to pin the blame on one interview, let alone one ambassador.
>
> For five months, from his speech in Amman in February until he marched into Kuwait in August, . . . [Saddam] would do or say something outrageous. Western experts would warn their governments not to overreact. The underreaction was then construed in Baghdad as weakness. "In Saddam's world, when you issue a threat you expect to get a counter threat," says professor Amatzia Baram, of Haifa University. "If you don't, it means weakness, appeasement and eventually retreat."[6]

Iraq Attacks Kuwait

On August 2, 1990, massive numbers of Iraqi troops and equipment conducted a blitzkrieg attack into Kuwait. The small Kuwaiti military was overwhelmed, and soon hundreds of thousands of Iraqi troops plundered, raped, and pillaged the country.

Within days after the invasion, President George H. Bush sent Secretary of Defense Dick Cheney to Saudi Arabia to meet with King Fahd, who agreed to the deployment of U.S. fighter aircraft and troops to his country to deter the Iraqi forces. The Army's 82nd Airborne and Air Force F-15 fighters were immediately deployed.

It was obvious that the world's stakes in this unfolding crisis were enormous. The first question was the shape of the "new world order" that would emerge in the post–Cold War era. The Berlin Wall had come down just eleven months earlier; the Warsaw Pact and the Soviet Union had not yet imploded.

Miller and Mylroie wrote:

> After the sudden collapse of repressive East bloc regions in 1989, analysts in Washington hoped that the end of the bipolar world would mark the beginning of a less fractious one, of a more stable order. But now it seemed the opposite was true . . . without the restraining hand of the superpowers upon their shoulders, former client states felt more free to meddle in their neighbors' affairs. . . .
> If Saddam Hussein's annexation of Kuwait was permitted to stand, Washington reasoned, wholesale disavowals of old colonial borders and land grabs throughout the Middle East and the Third World might become commonplace. . . . The rule was straightforward: big countries should not be permitted to gobble up small ones. . . . But there was a larger issue . . . national boundaries, increasingly fragile in a world of shifting allegiances, had to be respected.[7]

Beyond the form the architecture of the international community would take was the issue of oil. Despite its size (slightly smaller than the state of New Jersey), Kuwait had enormous reserves of oil. Furthermore, the fabled oil fields of Saudi Arabia were not far south of the Iraqi troops who had invaded Kuwait. At the time of the invasion, 32 percent of the world's oil output—over half of all the petroleum being shipped in trade on the global market—was from the Middle East and North Africa; another 25 percent was in the Soviet Union and China. If Saddam Hussein's troops had proceeded unchallenged into Saudi Arabia, he would have had over 40 percent of the world's then known oil reserves under his control.

In the aftermath of the war, various analysts have written that Saddam did not intend to invade Saudi Arabia. Others, including General H. Norman Schwarzkopf, believed he intended to proceed beyond Kuwait. He told interviewers that the enormous amount of Iraqi supplies stored in Kuwait were far above any level needed to attack only Kuwait. Thus he believed the evidence was strong that Hussein planned further military action.

Even without invading Saudi Arabia, Saddam, through sheer intimidation of his neighbors and with Kuwaiti oil integrated into his empire, would have had enormous influence over the supply and price of oil and ample financial resources to develop weapons of mass destruction and become the preeminent power in the Middle East.

President George H. Bush Meets with Congressional Leaders

As the U.S. military buildup of our troops in Saudi Arabia steadily increased, the question arose as to what, if any, congressional authorization should be approved for conducting military operations. President Bush was in constant communication with the leaders of other members of the international coalition that were deploying troops to the Persian Gulf. The president also met with congressional leaders and key members of Congress to keep them apprised of unfolding events and to ask for their support.

On September 21, 1990, about a month after his initial order to deploy U.S. troops, the president invited a small group of members of Congress to the White House to discuss the crisis. We met in the president's private dining room. In most such gatherings at the White House the company engages in small talk and banter before discussing the issue at hand. This time there was no small talk. We got right down to business.

The president, Secretary of State James Baker, and Brent Scowcroft, director of the National Security Council, were the only people present from the executive branch. Those present from the legislative branch were senior members of national security or foreign affairs committees. The meeting was interrupted twice when the president answered phone calls from heads of states that were involved in the deployment.

President Bush began the meeting by explaining why he felt it necessary to order the deployment of our troops and saying that he hoped each of us would support him. While most of the members present were supportive of the actions taken thus far, there were many words of caution about taking military action. The president asked how long we thought our troops could remain in Saudi Arabia and retain the support of the American people. Some members thought our troops could remain for an extended period of time. I said I believed it would be only about six months before the morale of the deployed troops and the support of the American people would significantly erode. My reason was quite simple. Our troops would be in one of the most hostile physical environments on earth. If no conflict occurred and the policy was to wait until the economic boycott toppled Hussein, our forces would inevitably think, "If we're not going to do anything but sit here, what are we doing here?" They would express their frustration in letters and telephone calls to their families and friends back in the States, and public support would rapidly decline. Although the polls indicated strong support for the president's policy, the percentage of respondents who opposed it was rising.

Another issue we discussed was whether the National Guard and the Reserves should be called to active duty. Congressman Sonny Montgomery, the leading advocate on Capitol Hill for the Reserves and President Bush's closest friend in the Congress, had already publicly called for their activation. I told the president I thought activation of the Guard and Reserves was necessary in view of the scope of the buildup, and added that I thought the American people would support the move. The president was noncommittal, and I sensed he was not yet ready to take that step. Those present also recommended that the countries we were going to assist should pay for our military help.

The final point we discussed was whether Congress's approval of the deployment was required. I told President Bush that while I was fully supportive of his bold decision to deploy our forces, I thought it was imperative that he secure the approval of the people's branch of the government. I sensed Bush's reluctance to ask for it.

Inspection Trip to the Persian Gulf

Shortly after Iraq invaded Kuwait, the House Defense Appropriations Subcommittee held a hearing to receive an assessment of the overall situation from the intelligence community and the military. It was clear that this burgeoning crisis would generate great controversy in Congress and I wanted to gather all the information I could to prepare for debates, votes, and the supplemental appropriation bills that would be required to fund the deployment.

The witnesses from the intelligence community testified that the Iraqi forces were very capable and tough after their recent extensive combat experience in the war with Iran. One witness predicted many thousands of American dead and wounded in the event of a war, and none of the other witnesses disputed his estimate.

That estimate of high casualties weighed heavily on my mind, and I decided to lead a delegation of House members on an inspection trip to the region. In 100 hours we traveled over 13,000 miles in three countries. Although the flight time consumed a significant percentage of those hours, we did meet with two heads of state (Egypt and Saudi Arabia) and ministers of the exiled government of Kuwait. We also conferred with the American ambassadors to Saudi Arabia, Kuwait, and Bahrain, with General Schwarzkopf and his top officers, and with the U.S. military commanders and troops of the Army, Navy, Marine Corps, and Air Force in the field.

After refueling in Ireland, we went on to Egypt, where we conferred with President Hosni Mubarak at his summer palace in Alexandria. He had quickly responded to President Bush's request for assistance by sending thousands of Egyptian troops to join the allied buildup in Saudi Arabia. The support of Egypt was especially important because it had over 50 percent of the Arab population in the Middle East and North Africa.

President Mubarak is an outgoing, gregarious person who works a room very effectively, and as we entered the conference room he vigorously shook the hand of every member of our delegation, looked each of us in the eye, and said how happy he was to see us. We sat around a large conference table in a room that had a beautiful scene painted on the ceiling and a large ornate chandelier. President Mubarak had one assistant with him and a member of his staff to take notes.

Congressman Bill Hefner of North Carolina said, "Mr. President, our intelligence experts have estimated that America will suffer thousands of deaths and casualties if we go to war with Iraq. What is your projection?" President Mubarak gave a little smile and held his arms out wide as he said, "Gentlemen, gentlemen, gentlemen [the tone suggested "Children, children, children"] let me absolutely assure you that the Iraqi troops will collapse one day after the allies launch a ground attack. I know the capabilities of the forces in this region. Once the war begins, the Iraqis will be devastated on the battlefield." I couldn't have been more pleased to think that our experts might be wrong and a foreign head of state might be right on a major U.S. foreign policy issue.

The next day we flew on to Saudi Arabia. On that leg of the flight I recalled an earlier meeting I had had with President Mubarak, in March 1988, when U.S. naval forces were "flagging" Kuwaiti tankers. In 1984 Iraq had begun to bomb Iran's oil tankers and shore facilities in an attempt to cut off the sales of oil that were financing Iran's war effort. Since Iraq had no oil tankers, the Iranians retaliated by attacking Iraqi merchant ships. When the United States agreed to fly American flags on the Kuwaiti tankers, we were saying to the world, in effect, that we would protect those ships as though they were our own.

During my discussion with President Mubarak in 1988, he said that America's friends and enemies in the Middle East were watching closely to see whether the United States persevered in its commitment to protect the Kuwaiti tankers. "You were driven out of Vietnam after a lengthy war, and driven out of Lebanon after a terrorist attack. America is a great power but you have the reputation in this area of the world that you do not stick to your commitments."

One of our ships in the mission, the U.S.S. *Roberts,* struck a mine and came perilously close to sinking. Twenty-seven sailors were killed when the U.S.S. *Stark* was struck by an Exocet missile fired by an Iraqi jet fighter. Despite these two tragedies, the United States continued to protect Kuwaiti ships until the end of the Iran-Iraq war.

Stormin' Norman

After landing in Saudi Arabia, we drove immediately to the Saudi Defense Ministry in the capital city of Riyadh, where we met with General Norman Schwarzkopf and his key commanders. I had met Stormin' Norman about a year earlier when he testified before the House Defense Appropriations Subcommittee as the commander in chief of the Central Command. He is a barrel-chested, blunt-speaking, articulate, strong leader and was a very effective witness before the committee. He had had a very impressive career and was much decorated for his heroic actions in Vietnam. At the time of the congressional hearing, he was very near the end of his career and Saddam Hussein had not yet invaded Kuwait. Little did any of us realize then that General Schwarzkopf's rendezvous with destiny was just months away.

At the Saudi defense ministry we heard from two other generals in addition to Schwarzkopf: General Charles Horner, the head of our Air Force contingent, and General Gus Pagonis, the chief logistician of the deployment. General Schwarzkopf gave us an overview of how the personnel and equipment buildup was proceeding, the progress of our allies in the region, and the status of the Iraqi buildup in Kuwait. Although the troops currently deployed could deter an invasion of Saudi Arabia, he told us, he felt they would have to rely inordinately on airpower, so more troops and equipment were required to sustain our effort.

I said, "General, this congressional delegation supports you and the troops a hundred percent. I believe the Congress will vote to authorize the use of force. The polls show that the American people support you. My question is what equipment shortfalls are you concerned about?"

"The most critical thing I need more of is trucks. I'm also short of barbed wire, fuel bladders, and water bladders." With all the emphasis on glamorous high-tech weapon systems, it is easy to forget what a wide range of very basic equipment is needed for troops in the field.

In the aftermath of that conversation, I recalled an incident of a few years earlier. The House Armed Services Committee, chaired by Les Aspin, authorized funds above the budget request for trucks for the Army. As chairman of the House Defense Appropriations Subcommittee at the time, I supported that authorization. A factory in Les's district manufactured those trucks, and the press attacked Aspin's committee and my subcommittee for "a parochial approach to national defense matters." Here I was a few years later in Saudi Arabia discussing shortfalls with General Schwarzkopf, and the first thing he mentioned was his desperate need for more trucks. As late as the early 1990s, the Army actually had some trucks in its inventory that were procured when Harry Truman was president. Those trucks were eligible for "antique" license plates in most states. Apparently critics of the congressional budgetary increase for trucks were not aware of those Truman-vintage vehicles and the shortage of trucks when they attacked the "pork-barreling" of Congress.

The wide range of equipment needed to conduct a large-scale military campaign was dramatized a few months later when the Defense Appropriations Subcommittee received a reprogramming request from the Air Force:

it was asking us to transfer funds previously appropriated for one purpose to another of higher priority. The Air Force needed money for wooden pallets, which are used as platforms for the transportation of goods and equipment. The pallets that had gone to Saudi Arabia during the military buildup were never returned to the States for reuse because our troops used them as floors for tents, command centers, temporary warehouses, and other facilities. At one point the Air Force was down to a one-day supply of wooden pallets.

After mentioning the shortfall of trucks and other low-tech equipment, General Schwarzkopf told us of the key role played by the SL-7 cargo ships in rapidly transporting massive amounts of equipment and cargo to Saudi Arabia. In the early 1980s I offered an amendment in the House Defense Appropriations Subcommittee to add funds above the budget request for the procurement and refurbishment of eight sealift ships, which are referred to as SL-7s. These massive cargo ships, capable of traveling at great speed, were currently operating as private transport ships and were available for sale. The price was excellent, and they would increase our ability to deploy equipment. Buying these ships made eminent sense to me. The amendment was approved in committee and later that year by the Congress.

Despite the compelling arguments for buying sealift ships, the Navy was dragging its feet. Granted, these ships were not so sexy as the Navy's glamorous high-tech systems, but they fulfilled a very necessary requirement. I wouldn't have offered the amendment to fund them if that hadn't been the case.

The struggle between the committee and the Navy over spending the money for the sealift ships continued for a couple of years. Technically, the Navy had several years before it had to spend the money or lose it. Eventually Congress prevailed and the procurement and refurbishment of the ships went forward. Approximately 95 percent of the equipment deployed to the Persian Gulf region went by ship. The massive, rapid SL-7 cargo ships were the workhorses of that effort. I was pleased that the amendment I had offered years earlier had resulted in such a tremendous contribution to our effort in the Gulf War.

At the end of the meeting with General Schwarzkopf, I asked if I could see his personal quarters. I was aware of the ostentatious lifestyle of many top officers who had served in Vietnam. Schwarzkopf had one small room in the basement of the Saudi Defense Ministry, furnished with a bed, a bookcase filled with mostly military classics, and an exercise machine.

Visit to the Army's 82nd Airborne Division and the Marines

We got about five hours of sleep that night. The next day the first thing on our agenda was to inspect the Army's 82nd Airborne Division in northern Saudi Arabia, not far from the Kuwaiti border. The 82nd, which can be deployed rapidly because it has no heavy equipment, was the first American ground unit in Saudi Arabia. Both the troops and their equipment were flown to their destination. One of the 82nd's battalions was on a block leave in the States when the call went out to return to base. Troops rushed back to Fort Bragg from twenty-three states and three countries. Ninety percent were back within thirty-six hours. Although the rapid deployment of the 82nd Airborne was important as both a tactical response and a psychological move, the fact remained that these troops were lightly armed while the Iraqi troops had thousands of tanks and artillery pieces nearby in Kuwait.

Our helicopter landed at the remote desert command post of the 82nd. The commanding general of the 18th Airborne Corps, Lieutenant General Gary Luck, pulled my chain when he greeted me by saying, "Congressman, as a former Marine you should appreciate that the strategic objective of the 82nd Airborne's deployment was to make this area safe and stable for the U.S. Marines, who are now arriving in a nonthreatening environment because the elite forces of the United States Army have secured the area." After the laughter subsided we received an excellent briefing on the status of the 82nd Airborne. In an emotional moment after the briefing, we observed a brief ceremony as two young soldiers reenlisted for another four years. After the ceremony, we made the rounds and talked to dozens of enlisted personnel to get a feel for their morale and to see if they had any concerns or problems. Morale was very high; to a man they were upbeat and ready for anything that might come.

Given the absence of heavy firepower in the 82nd, it was indeed fortunate that the Iraqi troops did not invade Saudi Arabia during those early days of Operation Desert Shield. Saddam Hussein, in his own bloodthirsty and ruthless manner, had mastered the art of staying in power, but as a military strategist beyond his borders, he had a mighty poor track record.

Our next stop was to inspect the Marine contingent that had just arrived in country. As our helicopter flew to a remote site in the Saudi desert, we saw herds of wild camels running for the horizon, upset by the throb of whirling helicopter blades. When we landed, enormous clouds of sand enveloped the chopper.

The Marine base was just a bunch of tents and a few temporary structures. It seemed like a scene from a surrealistic movie. The base was surrounded by massive sand dunes. Blistering heat and constantly blowing sand made for an extremely harsh day-to-day existence. The troops had no complaints, however; they were very gung-ho. But as I viewed their living conditions, I thought it wouldn't be long before that upbeat mood would dissipate. I made a mental note that the time required to persuade Iraq to abandon its invasion of Kuwait would have to be relatively short.

The blowing sand at this remote Marine base got into everything—clothes, food, and equipment. The sands in Saudi Arabia have blown over the desert for many millennia and the individual grains are so tiny that they are more like talcum powder than sand. The intrusive sand made life very difficult and presented a tremendous challenge to efforts to maintain our equipment.

The oppressive heat made dehydration a serious health threat to our troops. The air was so dry and sweat evaporated so quickly that it was difficult to realize how much water one's body was losing. Bottled water was available everywhere, and our forces were constantly advised to drink water every fifteen minutes or so.

In his memoirs, General Schwarzkopf told an anecdote that highlighted the problem of the heat. General Gus Pagonis, the chief logistician of the deployment, was showing General Schwarzkopf a construction project at one of the bases:

> He pointed out dozens of foreign workers who were nailing together pieces of plywood. He'd hired a Saudi contractor to build gravity-fed portable showers and latrines like the ones we'd used in Vietnam. He proudly explained that the troops would have hot water whenever they wanted because the sun would heat the silver-colored tank on top. As it turned out, the system worked a little too well: the desert sun heated the water so hot that the troops could take showers only at night.[8]

The Marine commanders at the base described the rapid deployment of their troops—a remarkable logistical feat. About 15,000 of them were flown into Saudi Arabia, and within just ten days they matched up with equipment that had been disembarked in Saudi Arabia from numerous cargo ships. These "maritime prepositioning ships," which are always loaded with equipment, were based at Diego Garcia, a small island in the Indian Ocean. From there they were able to steam rapidly to the port in Saudi Arabia. Transporting the 15,000 Marines to Saudi Arabia involved a total of just 259 air sorties. If they had had to be airlifted to Saudi with their equipment from their bases in the States, the job would have taken 4,500 air sorties and many weeks.

While the rapid deployment of the Marines and their equipment to Saudi Arabia was an awesome logistical feat, there was a serious problem. The equipment aboard the prepositioned ships was quite dated. The tanks were M60A1s, which could be outgunned by the Soviet T-72 tanks used by the Iraqi military. The communications gear aboard these ships was old, and much of it was not interoperable with the current generation of communications gear. Understandably, over the years as new equipment was developed and procured, the priority was to put that equipment in the hands of our active forces and then the National Guard and Reserves. Thus updating the equipment stored on cargo ships on a distant island in the Indian Ocean had low priority in the grand scheme of things. When the time comes to use this equipment—an actual war or the deployment of troops abroad to try to prevent a conflict—it is important to provide the funds to upgrade the equipment. We addressed that issue in future legislation.

Discussion with King Fahd

After our meeting with the Marines we flew to the city of Jedda, where we were scheduled to meet that evening with King Fahd and the Saudi ambassador to the United States, Prince Bandar. No specific time had been set for the meeting; we were on standby, waiting to be called. About 11:30 that night we were summoned to the palace. In a spectacularly ornate room King Fahd thanked us for the support in Congress for the deployment of the U.S. troops, but quickly added that he hoped the American forces could withdraw as soon as they had achieved their objective. I told him that the Congress and the American people were very supportive of our troops and were confident that Saddam Hussein would not prevail in Kuwait. We discussed a wide range of issues and the meeting ended about 12:30.

John Plashal had been sitting behind the congressional delegation. He told me later that the long day and the changes of time zone during the last two days had gotten the better of him, and he had dozed off during the meeting. "The only time in my life I'll ever meet a king and I slept through it!"

On the return flight to Washington the next day I went over in my mind some of the major points we had learned thus far—the confidence expressed by President Mubarak about the outcome if a war should occur; his view that U.S. casualties would be almost nonexistent in that war; the extreme harshness of the day-to-day life of our deployed troops and the potential impact of that environment on their morale over the coming months. As I contemplated these impressions, my position began to solidify—I believed we should attack the Iraqi troops sooner rather than later.

Second Meeting with President George H. Bush

On October 30, about six weeks after the initial meeting with President Bush, he held another conference with congressional leaders. On October 28 Congress had adjourned and was not scheduled to convene again until early January. There was definitely a possibility that U.S. troops would become involved in a conflict while Congress was not in session. Brent Scowcroft wrote about that meeting:

> Foley outlined the fear in Congress that we were switching policies. "The reason for the extraordinary support you've received has been because you've used UN sanctions and an embargo. . . . The country and Congress are not prepared for offensive action." . . . Patrick Leahy also urged that we let sanctions do the job.
>
> "I agree with my colleagues about the public mood," said Les Aspin. "There's no question [the country has] moved away from a more hawkish position within the last month. The budget battle pushed Iraq off the front page."
>
> Jack Murtha disagreed. "I don't think you have any alternative to the use of force," he said. . . . "I don't think we have the luxury of time. We're already seeing exaggerated media attention on a few demonstrators. It will get more and more difficult for you to make decisions."[9]

By this time, my inspection of the deployed troops and the testimony I had heard in hearings and discussions with the intelligence community and military leaders had convinced me that barring some dramatic announcement by Saddam ordering the Iraqi troops home, war was inevitable. Our first troops to be deployed, back in August, had already been in the desert over two months. More important, as the deployment continued to grow so rapidly, it would soon be too large to permit the troops to be rotated every six months. Even though the Berlin Wall had come down about a year earlier and the Cold War was unwinding, we had major ongoing military commitments in Europe and the Pacific. If the decision was made to keep our troops in the Gulf region for an extended period of time while we waited for economic sanctions against Iraq to take effect, we would have to rotate those troops. Trying to rotate that many troops in Saudi every six months or so would have occupied the overwhelming majority of our armed forces, since the troops not deployed there would be in training for the Persian Gulf and not available for duty elsewhere.

If our troops were to sit in the desert waiting for Saddam's regime to collapse under the pressure of economic sanctions, I believed, time would clearly be on his side. The logistics of supplying his troops was simple—Kuwait was a small country on Iraq's border. The United States, meanwhile, had a supply chain one-third of the way around the world.

In briefings I received from the Defense Department, it had been pointed out that bad weather traditionally occurs in the Persian Gulf region early in the year. The effect of sandstorms on our smart weapons might be severe. Besides, the Muslim holy month of Ramadan would begin in mid-March. By that time the first American troops deployed would have spent about eight months hunkered down in the desert. Their families would (legitimately) be extremely upset, the troops' morale would be at rock bottom, our equipment would be eroded by the harsh conditions, and it would have looked to the world that as the post–Cold War world evolved, aggression paid.

The Dick and Colin Show

As the massive personnel and supply buildup of Operation Desert Shield continued, various congressional committees conducted hearings on the crisis. In addition to Secretary of State James Baker, the top Bush administration officials charged with developing our policy in the Gulf and convincing Congress and the American people of the wisdom of that policy were Secretary of Defense Dick Cheney and the chairman of the Joint Chiefs of Staff, Colin Powell. Each of them was enormously capable and knowledgeable, and as a team they were tremendously effective in congressional testimony and in appearances before the media.

I had a minor disagreement with Secretary Cheney and General Powell regarding the conduct of the hearings before the House Defense Appropriations Subcommittee. It was a disagreement I had had with nearly all Pentagon witnesses—their absolute need to come supplied with mountains of charts whenever they testified before Congress. Now I understand that different folks absorb information in different ways, and some people prefer charts and other visual aids. I personally prefer just to sit down across the table from the witnesses, look them in the eye, and question them after they have given a brief oral presentation. As chairman of the House Defense Appropriations Subcommittee, I had a standing agreement with the Pentagon that witnesses were not to use charts in presenting their testimony.

Secretary Cheney and General Powell were to give us an update on Operation Desert Shield. The hearing, open to the public, was held in the Rayburn House Office Building, which had a much larger room available than the subcommittee's hearing room in the Capitol. As Secretary Cheney and General Powell walked into the hearing room, I immediately noticed that General Powell's military aide, Lieutenant Colonel Paul Kelly, had the mother of all sets of charts with him. I'm talking *big* charts, and lots of them. They were so massive (about 6' by 8') that Colonel Kelly could barely carry them into the hearing room. I was about to inform the witnesses that charts were not welcome at this hearing, but as I scanned the room and observed a couple of hundred members of the public and a dozen members of the press, I had second thoughts about starting the hearing on a negative note.

My thoughts flashed back to the late congressman Dan Flood of Pennsylvania, a former professional boxer and actor. A very effective member, he was also flamboyant; for example, he often wore a cape over his suit. He addressed every witness at a hearing as "Skipper," no matter who it was. Once the secretary of the Department of Health, Education and Welfare (HEW; now Health and Human Services) explained that he was opposed "on principle" to spending funds for a project in Congressman's Flood district that (according to him) did not meet HEW's cost-benefit criteria. Flood raised his index finger in a circular motion and without missing a beat said in deep, dulcet, Shakespearean tones, "Skipper, at times we must rise above principle."

I decided to rise above principle and say nothing about the witnesses' charts.

Return to Saudi Arabia

I revisited the Persian Gulf region in mid-November 1990. By this time, a significant percentage of the House and Senate and a number of influential journalists were saying that continued economic sanctions against Iraq would succeed in defeating Saddam. Since I disagreed, I felt a firsthand assessment was in order. Once again we received a briefing from General Schwarzkopf, General Horner of the Air Force, and other key commanders. They gave us an upbeat assessment of how the buildup of our troops and equipment was proceeding. The in-country deployment of troops from our European and Arab allies was also proceeding apace.

The posture was changing rapidly from defensive to potentially offensive. An intense debate was going on within the administration regarding the size of the force required to achieve the United States' goals in this crisis.

By the time of my visit, our first troops to arrive in Saudi Arabia had already been there three months. After meeting with scores of enlisted troops from a number of units, I became concerned about their morale. The exhilaration and enthusiasm I had noted on my first visit had dwindled. They were still ready to carry out any mission that might be required, but their mood was somber. The constant alert status our troops had to endure, the heat and constantly blowing sand, the absence of off-base liberty time, and the long working hours were taking their toll. My personal assessment was that if these troops stayed beyond six months, morale problems would be severe and combat effectiveness would decline correspondingly.

In addition to the enormous troop buildup on the ground, the Navy had a large presence in the Persian Gulf and the Red Sea. I flew to a helicopter carrier conducting countermine operations in the Persian Gulf. The working conditions of our sailors were extremely stressful. The heat in the boiler room was so oppressive that the sailors had to work in two-and-a-half-hour shifts to avoid getting dehydrated. When I went into the boiler room to visit with the personnel on duty, the steel railings beside the steps leading down were so hot that I had to snatch my hands away.

The innumerable sailors who manned the electronic scopes in the ships' communications centers faced their own difficult working conditions. These computer screens gave out a constant stream of data from air radarscopes, maritime radarscopes, links with AWACS (Airborne Warning and Control System) aircraft, and other systems. The need for constant vigilance during these vital operations day after day, week after week, month after month, had to gradually erode the efficiency of these sailors.

I was enormously impressed by the commitment and sense of duty of all the sailors I talked to, but one I especially recall was an enlisted sailor serving aboard the aircraft carrier *Midway*. His name was Ernest Fields and he had served in the Air Force during the Korean War. He had spent a total of ten years in the Air Force and then, after being out of the service for many years, he attempted to join the Air Force Reserves. He was rejected because of his age, but he was able to get into the Naval Reserves. He had served in the Naval Reserves for many years when his unit was activated for Operation Desert Shield. At age fifty-eight Ernest Fields suddenly found himself serving his country on an aircraft carrier 10,000 miles from home. Most of the sailors had pictures of their girlfriends or wives on the bulkhead next to their bunks or inside the doors of their lockers. The door of Ernie Fields's locker bore pictures of his seven grandchildren.

An aspect of the deployment that filled me with awe was the logistical achievement of Operation Desert Shield. In a very compressed time frame, we deployed half a million U.S. troops—the equivalent of every man, woman, and child in Milwaukee—a third of the way around the world to one the largest deserts in the world and the waters offshore, and provided them with all the equipment and infrastructure necessary to wage war and all the basic necessities of life.

Major General Gus Pagonis, the chief logistician of the operation, was promoted to lieutenant general during the campaign—a well-deserved promotion. In *It Doesn't Take a Hero,* General Schwarzkopf wrote:

> Pagonis . . . was an Einstein at making things happen. . . . I would watch Pagonis pull it all together from scratch: post offices, field clinics, phone booths for calling home, recreation facilities, and mobile

hamburger stands. He had ninety-four different Reserve and National Guard units under his command. . . . Somehow he managed to integrate them all into his system. If a stevedore unit showed up when he didn't need any more stevedores, he'd say, "I hereby dub this a transportation outfit. You guys go out and drive trucks." The reservists would grumble, "I didn't come over to drive a truck." But Pagonis's attitude was, "We'll talk about that when the war's over. Right now we don't have time."[10]

We went to a remote air base in the middle of the desert where our Air Force was rapidly building up its inventory of equipment. A massive truck convoy arrived while we were there. It didn't appear to be a typical convoy, since some of the trucks looked quite different from those in the Army's inventory. The logistician at the base explained that many of the trucks were from Czechoslovakia and had been leased by the United States for the war. Many of the drivers were civilians from other countries, on temporary contracts. General Pagonis had literally gone out in the international marketplace and contracted for whatever he could find to make up for shortfalls in equipment and personnel.

At this remote air base, in a mere six weeks, our troops had constructed a base for 5,000 airmen and airwomen, not only air control facilities and weapons and maintenance facilities but a chapel, a gymnasium, a post exchange, a laundry, and a library—all temporary structures, but serviceable. Of all the branches of the armed forces, the Air Force is clearly the first among equals when it comes to providing accommodations and services. The Marine Corps is a distant last. The typical Marine base in Saudi Arabia consisted of tents, equipment, a chow hall, a few latrines, and a makeshift shower. What the Air Force considers essential to maintaining morale is considered excessive by the Marine Corps, which takes pride in its Spartan culture.

When I returned to Washington it was time to get ready for the development and passage of the fiscal year 1991 defense appropriations bill. The committee took funding initiatives to take care of some of the equipment shortfalls we had discovered in the field. Taking action to solve problems is one of the most satisfying aspects of serving on the Appropriations Committee.

The Key Role of the Guard and Reserves

An issue that quickly arose in the White House, the Defense Department, and the Congress was whether units and individual members of the Guard and Reserves should be activated by presidential order and deployed to the Persian Gulf, be sent to Western Europe, or kept in the States to "back-fill"—that is, provide key personnel as substitutes—for active-duty units deployed to the Gulf. There were two major questions: (1) How essential was the activation of these units to achieving our military objectives in the Persian Gulf? (2) What were the political implications of activating the Guard and Reserves and taking tens of thousands of citizens away from their families and jobs?

As I had told President Bush, it seemed to me that use of the Reserve Component was essential. From my perspective, the issue was not whether the Reserves should be activated but how quickly they should be called to duty and how many should be called up.

In 1973, when James Schlesinger was secretary of defense, the department adopted a policy referred to as Total Force. Lieutenant General John Conaway described it this way:

> It envisioned the integrated use of all the active forces—Army, Navy, Air Force, Marines and Coast Guard as well as their reserve components—the Army National Guard and the Air National Guard, the Army Reserve and Air Force Reserve, and the Coast Guard Reserve. . . . The reserve forces would be integrated into the war plans and force structure of the active duty forces, giving planners the ability to quickly utilize any single individual in uniform, active, Guard, or reserve.[11]

Certain military occupational specialties (MOS's) within the total military personnel structure had a very high percentage of troops within the Reserve Component—strategic airlift, military intelligence, water purification, and communications. Personnel with these skills were vitally important to the overall war effort. Thus the case for activating the Reserve Component for the Persian Gulf crisis was indeed compelling.

I strongly disagreed with the conventional wisdom that a presidential order directing such an activation would be unpopular with the individuals called up, their families, and the public. I believed the public would strongly support it. This belief was based on discussions with Guard and Reserve units in my congressional district and with constituents throughout the district. There was a strong surge of patriotism and support for the president's policy among the people I spoke with. Eventually a large number of Guard and Reserve personnel were called up and they played a key role in the dramatic victory. The Reserves also back-filled key personnel in the United States and Europe for active-duty units in the Persian Gulf.

A tragedy occurred while I was at the Pentagon meeting with General Colin Powell. Right after the meeting I was informed that thirteen members of a National Guard unit called up from my district (the 14th Quartermaster Detachment, a water-purification unit) had been killed by a SCUD missile. Others from the unit were wounded in the attack. The 14th Quartermaster Detachment suffered a greater loss of life than any other unit that served in the war.

Before the unit left for Saudi Arabia, I visited them at Fort Lee, where they were in training. I don't recall my exact comments, but I did point out that although they were not a combat unit, they should be fully aware that "there are no front lines in this war." I also mentioned the importance of training for their mission.

The very day they arrived in Saudi Arabia they were assigned to spend the night in a warehouse in Dhahran, on the eastern coast of Saudi Arabia, south of the Iraqi troops in Kuwait. After one night at that interim staging area, they were to go to the field to carry out their mission. That night a SCUD missile, which normally is not a particularly accurate weapon, made a direct hit on their quarters. It was the last SCUD missile the Iraqis fired in the war. Killed in the attack were Specialist Steven E. Atherton, Specialist John A. Boliver, Sergeant Joseph P. Bongiorni III, Sergeant John T. Boxler, Specialist Beverly S. Clark, Sergeant Alan B. Craver, Specialist Frank S. Keough, Specialist Anthony E. Madison, Specialist Christine L. Mayes, Specialist Stephen J. Siko, Specialist Thomas G. Stone, Specialist Frank J. Walls, and Specialist Richard V. Wolverton. A memorial to them reads:

> They answered the call of duty.
> They paid the ultimate price of freedom.
> They are not forgotten nor will they ever be.

I called each of the families who had lost a son or daughter in the attack. Sergeant Boxler's family lived just a block from my home in Johnstown.

Specialist Clark, a committed and devoted woman, was the first person in her family to be accepted for admission to college. She was about to begin her college education when her Reserve unit was activated. Her father was laid off from his job the day after she was killed. I talked to the Kuwaiti ambassador to the United States, Sheik Muhammed al Sabah, and explained the tragedy to him. He said he would take care of the families' economic distress until things worked out. We were able to raise $100,000 for a scholarship fund in Beverly Clark's name.

Congressional Debate on Use of Force

During my second inspection trip to the Persian Gulf, one of the major issues I discussed with General Schwarzkopf was whether the United States should declare war against Iraq. He made the point that a declaration of war by the U.S. Congress would make it appear that Iraq's only opponent was the United States, whereas much of the world community was just as much against Iraq as we were. And if Congress declared war, Saddam Hussein might make a preemptive strike on the allied forces or fire missiles at Israel. Although such a strike would obviously result in massive retaliation and a military defeat for him, it might have enabled him to save face. I was sympathetic to General Schwarzkopf's arguments, but I felt strongly that the people's branch of the U.S. government should pass legislation officially supporting the use of force.

In *On Strategy: A Critical Analysis of the Vietnam War,* Colonel Harry G. Summers wrote:

> As Alexander Hamilton explained: ". . . The whole power of raising armies [is] lodged in the Legislature, not in the Executive. . . . This Legislature [is] to be a popular body, consisting of the representatives of the people, periodically elected."
>
> Hamilton's remarks highlight a critical distinction. In other nations a declaration of war by the chief executive alone . . . may or may not represent the substance of the will of the people. By requiring that a declaration of war be made by the representatives of the people rather than by the President alone, the Founding Fathers sought to . . . insure that our armed forces would not be committed to battle without the support of the American people.[12]

Although many had doubts, I was certain that there were sufficient votes in the House to support the president if he chose to attack the Iraqi forces. An approach mentioned by General Schwarzkopf in our discussions in November was eventually tried. Rather than have Congress officially declare war, the United Nations could authorize the use of military force under certain conditions; Congress could then vote on a resolution to support the UN resolution.

The debate in Congress on the Persian Gulf crisis centered on whether we should continue economic sanctions against Iraq in an effort to force Saddam Hussein to withdraw from Kuwait, or whether Congress should grant President Bush approval for military action. The proponents of a continuation of sanctions were bolstered by the testimony of Admiral William J. Crowe (USN, ret.) who had been chairman of the Joint Chiefs of Staff from 1985 to 1989. In testimony before the Senate Armed Services Committee on November 28, 1990, he stated: "I would argue that we should give sanctions a fair chance before we discard them. I personally believe they will bring him to his knees ultimately, but I would be the first to admit that is a speculative judgment. If, in fact, the sanctions will work in twelve to eighteen months instead of six months, a tradeoff of avoiding war, with its attending sacrifices and uncertainties, would in my estimation be worth it."

Opponents of the "go slow, sanctions will work" school of thought argued that over the years the use of sanctions to achieve political goals had not been very effective, to say the least. During the eight years of the Iran-Iraq war, the Iraqis suffered enormous casualties, but at the end of it Saddam was still in power. I simply didn't believe that economic sanctions would remove him.

Finally, by the time Admiral Crowe testified, the level of our forces deployed to the region was building up to its peak of over 500,000. Keep in mind that this was at a time when the rapid downsizing of our overall force structure had begun in the wake of the end of the Cold War and we had other troop commitments around the globe, especially in Korea and Europe. If we were to remain for long in the Persian Gulf under the sanctions scenario, we would run into the rotation problem: we did not have enough force structure to rotate so many troops in and out of the region. Were all those troops going to sit in the desert for a year or a year and a half while we waited for the Iraqis to succumb to economic sanctions and withdraw from Kuwait? I felt strongly that Saddam would win the waiting game.

Saddam Hussein was aggressively pursuing the development of weapons of mass destruction, and the delivery systems for those weapons was another matter of grave concern cited by those of us who believed we should intervene. Some argued that the United States had coexisted with other Third World countries that had developed or were developing weapons of mass destruction, and questioned why Iraq should be treated differently. Congressman Stephen Solarz (D-N.Y.) effectively answered these critics when he wrote in the *New Republic*, "Why should we be any more concerned about the acquisition of nuclear weapons by Iraq than by Pakistan, India, Brazil, Argentine, or South Africa? The answer is that although the nuclear programs of these other countries are a source of legitimate concern, none of them has already used weapons of mass destruction."[13]

Saddam not only was attempting to develop nuclear weapons but had used chemical weapons against the Iranians. He also used chemical weapons against the Kurd minority in Iraq. After the war, two members of the Appropriations Committee staff, John Plashal and Del Davis, went into northern Iraq. One of the pictures they brought back was the rubble of a Kurdish village that Saddam Hussein had ordered destroyed. On the hill overlooking that rubble he had constructed a palace—one of the scores of palaces he had throughout the country.

As I took the pulse of the House, I grew increasingly confident that the votes were there by a comfortable margin for support of the UN resolution authorizing the use of force. I called Brent Scowcroft and told him that I believed the measure would pass by an 80-vote majority. On January 8, 1991, over five months after the initial deployment of U.S. troops, President Bush sent a letter to Congress requesting approval for the use of force, and the stage was set for a momentous debate in the House and Senate. The House had to deal with two separate resolutions. House Concurrent Resolution 33 supported continuing economic sanctions against Iraq as the primary policy; House Joint Resolution 77 (the so-called Michel-Solarz bill, which I co-sponsored) sought to authorize the use of U.S. forces to implement United Nations Resolution 678, which in turn authorized UN member states to "use all necessary means" to force Iraq out of Kuwait unless it ended its occupation by January 15, 1991.

Speaker Tom Foley, who was opposed to the Michel-Solarz bill, was explicit about the momentousness of the vote and made it clear that although technically the vote was on a joint resolution, it was in reality a form of declaration of war. In a rare appearance in the well of the House and speaking without notes, Foley said in part:

In twenty-six years in the House of Representatives, I have never seen this House more serious nor more determined to speak its heart and mind on a question than they are at this time on this day. . . . Those who believe that the president must now be armed with what unquestionably . . . is the virtual declaration of war should not hesitate to vote that way, should not hesitate to give him that power.

But let me suggest to you one thing. Do not do it under the notion that you merely hand him another diplomatic tool, another arrow in the quiver of economic and international leverage. The president has signaled no doubt about this. He has said again and again that if given the power, he may well use it, perhaps sooner than we realize.

The debates in the House and Senate were intense and dramatic. According to the *Congressional Quarterly,* the debate in the House was one of the longest in its history. More than 300 speeches were given during the debate in the House of Representatives. Of the 100 senators, 94 participated in the debate.

During the conduct of day-by-day business in the House and Senate, each chamber is all but empty except during votes on specific legislation and amendments. By far the greatest part of the time-consuming work done in Congress occurs in its many committees. During the debates on the Persian Gulf resolutions, emotions were running high, and so was attendance. Almost no committee hearings were held those days.

Here is what I said:

Mr. Speaker, we are here today engaged in the exercise of one of the great strengths of democracy—the elected representatives of a free people are openly debating and voting on the future course of our country at a time of national crisis. The words spoken in this debate will soon fade from memory, but the votes cast on the Persian Gulf resolutions will be forever etched in history.

Let me make clear that from the very start of this crisis, my goal has been to help find a way to a peaceful settlement. No one wants to avoid war more than those of us who have been in it. Having been wounded twice in Vietnam, I know firsthand the horrors of war, and will always be diligent in trying to prevent its recurrence.

We join here not to debate whether Saddam Hussein has committed unfathomable atrocities against the people of Kuwait—we all know he has. We join here not to debate whether Saddam Hussein must leave Kuwait—we all agree he must. We are here to debate what is the most effective method of achieving that goal, and to find the best route to a peaceful settlement of this crisis.

There are those who say economic sanctions alone will force Iraq to withdraw from Kuwait. As we are all aware, the intelligence community has concluded "that there was no evidence that sanctions would mandate a change in Saddam Hussein's behavior and that there was no evidence when or even if they would force him out of Kuwait." Also, Mr. Speaker, there are innumerable examples in history of the failure of economic sanctions to achieve the desired effect.

Mr. Speaker, only when Saddam Hussein is convinced that the nations arrayed against him may go to war will there be a possibility of peace.

In August of 1939, Winston Churchill said the following about the House of Commons.

"This House is sometimes disparaged in this country but abroad it counts. Abroad the House is counted as a most formidable expression of the British national will and as an instrument of that will in resistance to aggression."

I am confident that the House of Representatives will vote to support the president, and when it does, the world will know, and Saddam Hussein will know, that the American people are united behind their president and supportive of the American and allied troops deployed in the Persian Gulf region. America is the principal member of the coalition opposing Hussein's aggression, and we in the Congress must now confirm our support for United Nations Security Council Resolution 678.

Mr. Speaker, in a radio address to his constituents in June of 1941, Senator Claude Pepper of Florida spoke on the rising threat of Nazism. He stated that "America's strength is not great unless it is a united strength. Our power is not determining unless it is mobilized. America's will is not decisive unless it is one irresistible will."

The upcoming vote on the Persian Gulf resolutions are at a time when we need a united strength, and I am glad that the Democratic member from Florida, the distinguished chairman of the House Foreign Affairs Committee, Mr. Fascell, is supporting the Michel-Solarz Resolution.

Mr. Speaker, while mankind has made great strides in so many areas in the twentieth century, it has been a century of great tragedies:

- This has been the most violent century in the history of man;
- Tens of millions have died in armed conflicts in the twentieth century;
- The unspeakable horror of the Holocaust occurred in this century; and
- Weapons of mass destruction have proliferated in recent decades.

What lessons have we learned from the tragedies that have occurred in this century? I believe the most important lesson we should have learned is that the appeasement of expansionist, dictatorial regimes results in the eventual occurrence of armed conflict on a large scale. We are all familiar with the failure of the League of Nations to maintain global peace and its inability to check the ambition of dictators. For many years the effectiveness of the United Nations was impaired by the two superpowers' conflicting policies on the world stage. Today, as we deal with the first crisis of the post–Cold War era, we are at a crossroads of history. We stand with an opportunity to make the United Nations a truly effective instrument in the maintenance of international law and order.

There are those who say that Saddam Hussein is just another Third World dictator and that he is no threat to America's global interests. I disagree. The world knows of the human suffering and distress that he has already wrought—one million casualties in the Iraq-Iran war; his use of chemical weapons against both Iran and the Kurdish minority in his own country; and Kuwait has been invaded, occupied, pillaged, and devastated. . . . I have met with Kuwaiti citizens who have told me of the incredible suffering their citizens have been going through. Amnesty International has documented in chilling and grotesque detail the torture, mutilation, murder, and rape of innumerable Kuwaiti citizens.

But beyond the issue of the invasion and devastation of an innocent nation is the broader issue of the potential impact of Saddam Hussein on the world stage if his ambitions are not countered. Had President Bush not acted to deploy our troops shortly after the August second invasion, Saddam Hussein could have easily deployed his troops into Saudi Arabia and captured their oil fields. . . . The greatest concentration of resources in the world would have been in the hands of a ruthless dictator who not only possesses chemical weapons, but is developing even more threatening nuclear and biological weapons. Mr. Speaker, this man has demonstrated his willingness to use whatever weapons are in his arsenal in order to achieve his geopolitical ambitions.

We cannot have this debate without addressing how proud we are of our young men and women serving in Saudi Arabia. I've visited the front-line troops twice. The conditions are harsh, but their dedication is solid. . . .

In conclusion, Mr. Speaker, I would like to quote from a congressional debate of August 12, 1941, on the eve of World War II. In that debate, John McCormack, a young congressman from Massachusetts who later became Speaker of the House, said:

"We are the trustees of the present and future of our country. That is our job. It is our duty to perform it without fear of the consequences. The question that confronts us is not what we would like to do, but what we must do under the conditions that exist throughout the world today."

Mr. Speaker, I believe what we must do under the conditions that exist in the world today is vote to support United Nations Resolution 678, the president of the United States, and the servicemen and servicewomen deployed in the Persian Gulf.

The vote approving the use of force passed in the House by 250 to 183. After the vote I stayed behind, sitting in the empty chamber and reflecting on what had just occurred. I found it painful to vote to send our young men and women off to war. The fact that one of my nephews, Captain Brian Murtha, was a helicopter pilot in the Marine Corps and was deployed to Saudi Arabia caused me additional concern. But I was comfortable with my vote.

When I arrived home that evening Joyce told me that President Bush had called. When I returned his call he said, "Jack, when you told Brent [Scowcroft] the other day that the votes were there by a comfortable margin in the House to support the Persian Gulf resolutions, nobody at the meeting believed you except me."

Support for continuing the economic boycott was much stronger in the Senate than in the House. The vote was close: the resolution supporting the UN resolution passed by 52–47.

Before he was elected to the Senate, John McCain (R-Ariz.), who spent over six years as a prisoner of war in North Vietnam, briefly served in the House of Representatives. As a freshman member of the House he stated during a debate on the deployment of U.S. troops to Lebanon:

> General Maxwell Taylor, in an interview given shortly after the Indochina conflict, stated the conditions under which he thought it appropriate to introduce American combat troops overseas. First, the objectives of the involvement must be explainable to the man in the street in one or two sentences. Second, there must be clear support of the president by the Congress for the involvement. Third, there must be a reasonable expectation of success. Fourth, we must have the support of our allies for our objectives. And finally, there must be a clear U.S. national interest at stake.

With the passage in the House and Senate of the resolutions supporting the UN resolutions, all of the criteria outlined by General Taylor were in place. War was inevitable.

War

President Bush's press secretary, Marlin Fitzwater, made the first official acknowledgment of the war. He began a brief, straightforward statement with the sentence, "The liberation of Kuwait has begun." Operation Desert Shield became Operation Desert Storm. A massive campaign of air attacks by allied forces for over a month extensively rearranged the landscape of much of Kuwait and Iraq, emasculated the command and control infrastructure of the Iraqi forces, and decimated much of their equipment. America's inventory of smart bombs and missiles were used with enormous precision and devastation. The Iraqi troops in Kuwait suffered massive casualties and the industrial and military infrastructure of Iraq received enormous damage. Nevertheless, troops had to move in on the ground and occupy territory before victory could be achieved.

The ground phase of the war was a classic military campaign explained

An M-1 tank in Saudi Arabia en route to Kuwait. Although the air war lasted forty-four days and the ground war just four days, 79 percent of the Iraqi tanks destroyed in the war and 75 percent of the Iraqi artillery destroyed were "killed" by allied ground forces.

in great detail in voluminous Pentagon documents and innumerable books. There is no need to describe those details here, but I would like to mention two impressive quick fixes made to our equipment in the course of the operations. One was the adjustment made to the forward-looking infrared radar (FLIR), with which many Air Force aircraft are equipped. The FLIR enables the pilot to see objects and targets such as ships, tanks, and trucks in the dark.

Unfortunately, the FLIRs in use when the bombing campaign began were unable to differentiate between real tanks and the dummy tanks the Iraqis set up throughout the area to confuse our aircraft and draw fire. After the problem of the decoy tanks was recognized, American technicians quickly went to work and developed a program that adjusted the FLIR software. The real tanks retained much more heat than the fakes. Now the FLIRs could detect the heat radiated from the actual tanks so that our pilots could distinguish them from the fakes. Can you imagine the Iraqi commanders and troops surveying the damage after an American nighttime air attack as they tried to fathom how the American aircraft flying by at incredible speed were able to pick out the actual tanks and leave the dummy tanks untouched?

Another quick technology fix was the innovative jerry-rigging of a weapon system to penetrate the deep underground facilities used by Iraqis as command and communications bunkers. After January 16, when the allied forces began the air attacks, it became clear that although they knew the locations of those underground facilities, no weapon in their inventory, not even a 2,000-pound bomb, was capable of penetrating deep enough to destroy them. A heavier bomb with a bigger bang and greater penetrating capability was urgently required. A book published in association with *U.S. News & World Report* explained:

> Ideally a deep-penetrating bomb should be long, slender and heavy and be dropped from a high altitude. Someone thought of using old hardened steel howitzer barrels. After a search, several of the 7,500-pound barrels were found at the Watervliet Arsenal near Albany, New York.
>
> On Friday, January 25, technicians at Watervliet had begun working around the clock on the super-secret project. . . . It measured nearly nineteen feet long. . . . The big bomb had to be lowered by crane into a deep hole in the back of the high-explosive research and development facility at Elgin Air Force Base and packed with explosives by hand.[14]

Fins were added to this artillery tube to give it stability in flight. Then a laser guidance system was added so that a pilot could in effect steer the massive bomb to its target. On February 27, a mere thirty-two days after the contractor was presented with this challenge, two of these new weapons were launched from an Air Force F-111F aircraft. The weapon destroyed a deep underground bunker at the al-Taji Air Base, near Baghdad. After the bunker had withstood 2,000-pound bombs, the Iraqis felt secure there. After attack by the new weapons, one of our spy satellites that monitored communications reportedly detected a telephone conversation between top Iraqi military leaders discussing the destruction of the previously impenetrable bunker. One of the Iraqis said, "We have no place to hide now." This weapon was used effectively years later in the war in Afghanistan.

Saddam Hussein

It is distressing that Saddam Hussein remained in power in the aftermath of the Persian Gulf War. Reflecting on events at the end of the war, many people say we should have pursued his fleeing forces all the way to Baghdad and finished him. But the situation at the time was complex. President Bush had put together an international coalition that had the stated goal of driving the Iraqi forces out of Kuwait. There were many Arab states in that coalition, and none of them was prepared to expand the mission to send troops to capture Saddam Hussein. I believe the president made the right decision. As President Bush wrote in *A World Transformed*:

> Trying to eliminate Saddam, extending the ground war into an occupation of Iraq, would have violated our guideline about not changing objectives in midstream, engaging in "mission creep," and would have incurred incalculable human and political costs. . . . Apprehending him was probably impossible. We had not been able to find Noriega in Panama, which we knew intimately. We would have been forced to occupy Baghdad and, in effect, rule Iraq. The coalition would immediately have collapsed, the Arabs deserting it in anger and other allies pulling out as well.[15]

Hey, Mister! You're Mixing the Aluminum Cans with the Plastic!

One morning a few months after he retired from the military and moved to Florida, General Schwarzkopf, attired in his bathrobe, was lugging to the curb a container of recyclable materials for collection—newspapers, aluminum cans, and plastic refuse. At that moment the truck that collected the recyclables came by. The man who hopped down from the truck noticed that the aluminum cans and plastic refuse were in the same container. "Hey, mister," he called, "you're supposed to put the aluminum cans and the plastic in separate containers. Didn't you read the instructions?" A few months earlier Stormin' Norman had led American troops and their allies in one of the most brilliantly executed wars in history; now the man who collected his recyclable trash was lecturing him. Is this a great country or what?

Shortly before a congressional hearing in November 1991, General Norman Schwarzkopf told me of his recent experience when he attended the Kentucky Derby. There was a standing ovation when he walked in and took a seat. A while later, he stood up to go to the men's room and got another enormous ovation. Minutes later he returned to his seat and once again the crowd cheered!

8

HUMANITARIAN MISSION TURNS TO MANHUNT IN SOMALIA

America's intervention in Somalia was a watershed event that shaped U.S. foreign policy in the post–Cold War era. A well-meaning humanitarian mission to feed the hungry ended in bloody battles as American and United Nations troops tried to bring stability to a country that most Americans knew nothing about. U.S. forces entered Somalia as saviors, but their role changed when they were given a new mission to capture a warlord in a destitute city in one of the most impoverished countries in the world.

When the cost for this well-meaning but ill-conceived mission turned out to be American blood spilled in the streets in Somalia's capital city of Mogadishu, public support for U.S. intervention evaporated. More important, the negative public reaction affected other future global missions. A new phrase entered the vocabulary of some military circles: "Don't cross the Mogadishu line."

The Background

Somalia burst onto America's consciousness in 1992 when daily TV newscasts highlighted the suffering and hunger there. During most of 1992 many members of Congress and the media severely criticized the Bush administration for inaction and insensitivity to the suffering.

For forty years the United States had had a visible and determined foe—the Soviet Union—which presented a national security threat all of our citizens understood. After the Soviet Union collapsed, Saddam Hussein's invasion of Kuwait threatened both the stability of the new post–Cold War era and the flow of Middle Eastern oil, which was so essential to the global economy—again, a straightforward, understandable threat.

But Somalia was something new. Under the constant barrage of television reports of terrible human suffering and the natural desire of Americans to try to alleviate that suffering, a clear-eyed assessment of the risk of getting mired in a civil conflict in a distant land of no vital interest to our national security was lost in the emotion of the moment. We had no foreign policy compass for this situation.

Initial U.S. Assistance

In August 1992 the United States began to airlift massive amounts of food to Somalia. Various Somali military forces, paramilitary factions, and criminal gangs stole much of the delivered food. Over the ensuing months the situation continued to deteriorate. The 1992 American presidential election was the major news story that autumn, but the ongoing crisis in Somalia continued to be widely covered. Although President Bush lost his bid for reelection in November, he continued an activist foreign policy in his remaining months in power. In reaction to attacks on UN relief workers, he decided to increase the U.S. role from flying in food to joining a multinational force to create a secure environment for the distribution of that food.

About a day before our troops were to land in Somalia, I appeared on *Larry King Live*. The other guest, who was in favor of the deployment, was Congressman John Lewis (D-Ga.), a hero of the civil rights movement in the 1960s. He had been in Somalia the week before and had visited various villages where he observed the terrible suffering at firsthand. The guest host of the show, Bob Beckel, asked me how I could possibly be opposed to the deployment. I answered that the pictures I saw on television were very painful to watch and it caused me anguish to take this position, but I asked rhetorically, "Where do we stop? Do our troops go to Sudan, Russia, Sarajevo, or anywhere else on the globe where there is civil strife and hunger?" I was very doubtful about America's ability to resolve complex social and ethnic strife around the world. I also argued that it appeared to me that a decision to make this large-scale deployment would be a major shift in policy—that future deployments of our military might not be based on national security requirements.

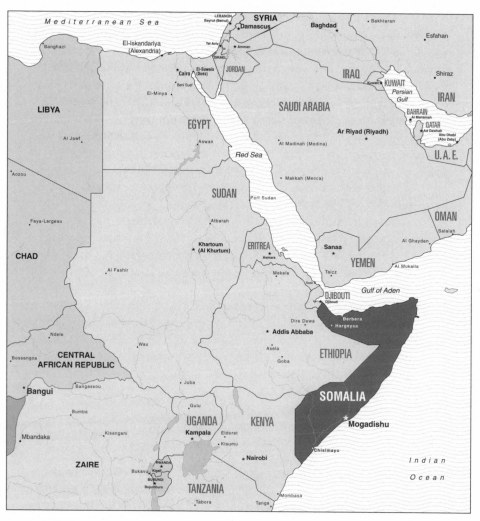

Somalia and its neighbors

American troops have been very effective in conducting humanitarian missions, especially when both active forces and the Reserves are used to assist in the recovery from natural disasters in the States. They have also carried out important humanitarian missions abroad. To me, however, Somalia was a different situation. As Congressman Lewis mentioned in our debate on the Larry King show, everywhere he looked in Somalia he saw young men with rifles and other weapons. The media had reported on the "technicals"—paramilitary groups that roamed around the cities and countryside on small trucks and jeeps with mounted automatic weapons and other military gear. Besides, the number of troops to be sent to Somalia, which turned out to be almost 26,000 by late January 1993, was an enormous deployment to a country inconsequential to our national interests.

While I was open-minded about the use of our armed forces for unconventional missions, I believe such missions should be conducted only under carefully crafted rules of engagement and only when they are essential to attain clear-cut policy goals. My concerns were that these unconventional deployments detracted from our military readiness, were expensive, had an adverse effect on our troops' morale, and invited attacks from terrorist groups seeking high-profile international exposure. A final concern was the fast tempo of troop deployments at the very time our overall force structure was being dramatically reduced. During the four years after the Berlin Wall fell, the reduction of our active military forces and Defense Department civilians totaled 578,000.

With the Cold War and the Persian Gulf War successfully concluded, attitudes toward the deployment of U.S. forces changed. In the past, people who favored the use of military forces abroad were generally middle of the road to conservative in their political outlook, whereas those of a more liberal bent tended to oppose such action. In this new geopolitical global situation, liberals tended to favor the use of the U.S. military for a wide range of missions, while those farther to the right had reservations about the wisdom of such actions or opposed them outright.

The media were strong supporters of the intervention. *Newsweek* wrote:

> Unlike the other charnel houses of the new world order, Somalia has no government to oppose intervention or allies to aid the resistance. It has no jungle, swamps or forested hills from which guerrillas can lash out at foreign intruders. It has no functioning air force and no real army, only ragtag gunmen who are far better at abusing helpless civilians than at standing up to determined invaders. Like the desert of Kuwait and Iraq, the hardscrabble Horn of Africa is a nearly ideal laboratory in which to test the theory that a high-minded application of force can right some of the world's wrongs.[1]

Putting aside for the moment the question whether or not the United States should have intervened in Somalia, one thing is clear—the intervention would never have occurred without the massive media coverage that generated widespread support for it.

The news media feel a need to project drama, violence, and action. There is a saying among some of the cynical producers of television news shows: "If it bleeds, it leads." In view of the compressed time of the evening news programs broadcast by the national networks, the wide range of stories they cover, and the competitiveness of the networks, I understand why the Somalia news coverage basically consisted of brief clips showing dramatic pictures of suffering. But it was clear from the beginning that the vast majority of the Somalia stories were superficial and provided little perspective on the historical complexity of the situation and the extent to which the famine was caused by a civil conflict rather than by drought.

Decision makers in the executive branch and members of Congress who must vote on military deployments must guard against the temptation to be overly influenced by the media. Media coverage can make involvement by the United States compelling. We have a heritage of helping others who are suffering. But deploying a massive contingent of U.S. troops without clear achievable goals and without thoughtful consideration of the risks and consequences can quickly lead to tragedy and failure. We should address each situation with our objective clearly in mind.

The actual order to deploy the troops was issued by President George H. Bush on December 4, 1992, just weeks before Bill Clinton was to assume the presidency. The Bush administration's announced objective was to create a secure environment in the hardest-hit parts of Somalia so that food could be distributed to the people most in need. Once the secure environment was established, the intention was to withdraw our troops and hand over the security mission to a United Nations peacekeeping force. It sounded like a straightforward, simple policy, and there was basically no opposition from the public. The vast majority of members of Congress were vocally supportive of the deployment.

The day after his order to deploy the troops, the president consulted Democratic and Republican leaders of the key committees with oversight of the Somalia issue. As we sat in the Oval Office in the White House, the president gave us an overview of the situation and then asked each of us for his or her views on his decision to deploy the troops. The overwhelming consensus was that the deployment was necessary and should proceed.

I had already decided a few days before that I was against the deployment, as I had publicly stated on *Larry King Live*. After all the others had spoken, President Bush turned to me and said, "Jack, I understand you have some reservations." I said, "Mr. President, all of us sympathize with the goals of the deployment, but I don't think it's in our national interest, and I believe that once we are deployed, we won't be able to get out easily." I asked the president how long our troops would be in Somalia. He replied that they would be out of Somalia by Inauguration Day, six weeks away.

The Absent Ambassador

In January 1993, about one month after our troops had arrived in Somalia, I headed a congressional delegation (CODEL) of seven members of Congress to inspect them. The other members of the delegation were Congressmen Bob Livingston (R-La.), Buddy Darden (D-Ga.), Nick Rahall (D-W.Va.), Tony Hall (D-Ohio), Curt Weldon (R-Pa.), and Jack Reed (D-R.I.). All were knowledgeable in defense and foreign affairs. Over the years I've found such on-site inspections invaluable for making an independent assessment of the executive branch's policy decisions. Meeting face to face with the individuals on location who are responsible for carrying out the decisions made in Washington gives a unique perspective.

It was a long flight and we stopped to refuel at the Mildenhall Air Base in England and in Cairo, which was the major airhead for military aircraft supplying our troops in Somalia. From Cairo we flew to Nairobi, the capital of Kenya, which borders Somalia, and spent the night there. Before leaving the States we had received a telegram from Smith Hempstone, our ambassador to Kenya, in which he agreed to meet our delegation in Nairobi to discuss America's overall policy in the region, and particularly in Somalia. In a politely worded cable he wrote, "If CODEL thinks their schedule will permit, Ambassador and Mrs. Hempstone would be pleased to host a small, informal cocktail buffet for Representatives from 7:00 P.M.–9:00 P.M. on Sunday, January 10."

We were in Nairobi the day before we went to Somalia and for part of the day on our way back to the States, but "scheduling conflicts" prevented Ambassador Hempstone from meeting with us. Three members of the delegation were on the appropriations committee and had the responsibility of providing funds for the State Department, the Defense Department, and the foreign aid program—the three agencies of the executive branch responsible for conducting the Somalia mission. Congressman Tony Hall (D-Ohio) was the leading advocate in Congress for feeding the world's hungry. For an American ambassador not to have time to meet with any congressional delegation, much less one with the responsibilities of our members, seemed strange indeed. I suspect that the State Department ordered him not to meet with us because of his and my opposition to the intervention in Somalia. Thus, even before we had set foot in Somalia, the ambassador's "scheduling conflict" had put me in an increasingly skeptical frame of mind.

Before our departure I had been privy to a copy of a cable from Ambassador Hempstone to the State Department. The cable, which had been sent before the deployment of our troops, stated in part:

> Aside from the humanitarian issue—which admittedly is compelling (but so is it in Sudan)—I fail to see where any vital U.S. interest is involved. Statecraft, it seems to me, is better made with the head than with the heart.
>
> The first question that needs to be asked is how long the American public is willing to put up with a major, expensive U.S. presence in Somalia.
>
> Somalis, as the Italians and British discovered to their discomfort, are natural born guerrillas. They will mine the roads, they will lay ambushes. They will launch hit and run attacks.
>
> This . . . operation is not a map exercise. . . . It is not a public relations exercise. Real lives (Americans and Somalis) are going to be lost. Billions of the U.S. taxpayers' dollars will be spent.

A prophetic cable!

Early on the morning of January 11 we flew on a military C-130 transport aircraft from Nairobi to Mogadishu, the capital of Somalia. Among our other stops was Baidoa, in central Somalia, where a contingent of U.S. forces was deployed. The economic situation and the living conditions we observed were among the most squalid and destitute I have ever seen. The Somali government had ceased to provide any services. There was widespread destruction from the ongoing fighting in both Mogadishu and Baidoa. There was no electricity. Many buildings and homes had no roofs. Sewage and garbage littered the streets and economic activity appeared to be minimal.

As I observed these terrible conditions, my thoughts went back to a conversation I had a few months earlier with a United Nations worker during my first trip to Bosnia. After landing at Sarajevo, we were unable to leave the airport for a time because of heavy shelling and gunfire, and I fell into conversation with a UN worker. He described for me the refugee problem in Sarajevo. When I expressed my dismay, he said, "If you think it's bad in Sarajevo, you should see what it's like in Somalia." Now, as I inspected the refugee camps in Somalia, one of the U.S. embassy staff escorting us said to me, "Congressman, if you think this is bad, you should see the refugee camps in Sudan." (A civil war in Sudan was causing an enormous refugee problem.)

The American public saw our deployment to Somalia as a straightforward humanitarian mission to distribute food to the impoverished people seen every day on TV. The disturbing reality was that we were interjecting ourselves into a civil war among clans and subclans that were using the distribution or withholding of food as a weapon against each other. They were using the food we sent them to increase their power base.

Granted, a drought had triggered a severe decline in the production of foodstuffs. But for the civil war, however, the massive influx of food from America and other countries would have rapidly solved the hunger problem in Somalia until the weather returned to normal and the land was again productive.

A Congressional Research Service book titled *Somalia: A National Profile* summed up the cultural backdrop to this unfolding drama: "Historically, Somalis have shown a fierce independence, an unwillingness to submit to authority, a strong clan consciousness, and conflict among clans and subclans despite their sharing a common language, religion, and pastoral customs. Clans are integral to Somali life."[2] Beyond the historical clan and subclan conflicts, there was outright armed looting of food warehouses in the major cities and violence in much of the country. Civil authority had broken down, and the ready availability of arms (provided by the United States and the Soviet Union during the Cold War) added even more volatility to this explosive situation.

In a paper titled "Peacekeeping, Peacemaking, and Peace Enforcement: The U.S. Role in the New International Order," Donald Snow wrote:

> Anarchy underlay the Somali crisis. The factions that collectively were capable of overthrowing Siad Barre [the former president of Somalia] in early 1991 were individually too weak and fractured to form a government to replace that which they had overturned. In-

stead, the structure of government crumbled, and "armies" of young thugs nominally loyal to one warlord or another took to the streets, terrorizing the populace and stealing or ransoming most of the food supplies intended for starving victims.[3]

While visiting one of the locations where the U.S. Marines were camped, we encountered a small group of Somalis who indicated by frantic hand-waving and gestures that they wanted to talk with us. Through an interpreter, an elderly woman in the group summarized her perception of Somalia's crisis in two brief sentences: "The drought did not destroy our country. Guns and anarchy have destroyed our country." William Shawcross wrote, "By 1992, Somalia was more a geographical expression than a country."[4]

Our delegation received briefings from Ambassador Robert Oakley, the U.S. special envoy to Somalia; Lieutenant General Robert Johnston, the Unified Task Force commander; Major General Steven L. Arnold, commander of the U.S. Army forces; and Major General Charles E. Wilhelm, commander of the Marine forces. We had many conversations with American troops and visited hospitals, orphanages, and feeding centers. While the briefers at each of these locations were candid about the challenge our forces faced, they also told us about the progress being made. Food was being delivered to the areas most in need, small markets were functioning, and our forces were engaged in a variety of civil engineering projects.

A lieutenant colonel who commanded a contingent of U.S. troops in Merca, a town south of Mogadishu, went into detail about the clans in his area of responsibility, his efforts to mediate among them, and his long-term plans for reconstructing Merca's infrastructure and political life. He was a good officer, dedicated to carrying out his duties and enthusiastically trying to find a way for the Somalis to take some responsibility for rebuilding their community.

Every time I visit our troops in the field, I am struck by their irrepressible and commendable can-do mind-set. At all levels of command they are willing to sacrifice to carry out their mission. This can-do attitude is one of our military's greatest strengths, but it can get us into trouble, too. We must take care not to go overboard in our efforts to solve other people's problems.

In addition to the almost 26,000 American troops deployed to Somalia, 13,400 troops from other UN countries were there. (The number of non-U.S. forces expanded significantly as the U.S. role declined.) These forces were under the control of the United States Unified Task Force commander.

I asked the military and civilian officials we met with about the prospects for the United Nations taking over the mission, as President Bush had promised. To my surprise, there was no UN leadership in the country to take over if the United States decided to disengage. Nor did the United Nations have any plan to establish a command and control organization, develop a concept of operations, or, from what I could observe, establish the necessary logistical support structure for a post-U.S. peacekeeping phase.

The bottom line was that there was no prospect for a smooth transition to a UN peacekeeping force in the near future. After one month into an operation in which the United States' participation was to have lasted two to three months, our forces were basically the only game in town. It was obvious to me that this was not going to be a quick, in-and-out humanitarian operation. It was also obvious that the incoming president was going to be handed a foreign policy crisis on day one of his administration.

One of the events we had scheduled was a visit to a large concentration of U.S. troops based at a soccer stadium in Mogadishu. The stadium was a convenient place for our troops to set up a temporary base. Most of our delegation and some members of the press corps were in a convoy of military vehicles on our way to the stadium when we heard small arms fire nearby. The accompanying military providing security ordered the drivers to hit the pedal to the metal. Members of the delegation riding in the backs of small trucks followed orders and hit the deck. Those inside their vehicles huddled down as close as they could to the floor as the convoy sped off. No one was wounded and the small arms fire hit no vehicles. It was an exciting moment in an eventful day and we nervously joked about it after we arrived safely at the stadium.

We spent an hour and a half at the stadium and talked with many of the troops. Their morale was good. Since Somalis were occasionally firing at the stadium from the surrounding area, our forces had a couple of snipers lying on the roof with powerful long-range .50-caliber rifles equipped with telescopic lenses. They would shoot at anyone they saw setting up a mortar or preparing to use any other weapon that would threaten our troops. The snipers fired their weapons on two occasions while we were there. When they fired, our troops in the stadium gave a brief cheer and a high five to the soldiers next to them before going back to their chores of cleaning weapons, maintaining gear, or planning the next day's operations.

The next morning we were in the Hotel Intercontinental in Nairobi. On these trips a room is always set up at the hotel to serve as a message center and gathering place. We were having coffee there before boarding a bus to the airport when the TV, tuned to CNN, reported that "a congressional delegation headed by Congressman Murtha has come under attack by small arms fire in Mogadishu, Somalia." Congressman Nick Rahall of West Virginia shot back, "Small arms fire? I distinctly remember the attack being ferocious and life-threatening!" Someone else said, "That's our story and we're sticking to it." Laughter was followed by descriptions of heroics that achieved Audie Murphy proportions. Each exaggerated tale of our intrepid actions under fire was followed by a chorus of "That's our story and we're sticking to it!"

Congressman Livingston added, "Mr. Chairman, I realize you are always attentive to the needs of those of us in the minority party who are accompanying you, but I hope you noticed that none of the Republicans received any protective flack jackets during this mission." I assured him that this was just an oversight and pointed out that the loss of every Republican on the delegation would not result in any significant change in the ratio of Democrats to Republicans in the Congress. The laughter grew even louder. It was a welcome moment of levity after a somber day.

On the flight back to Washington I reflected on what I had learned in Somalia. The actual situation in an international crisis is always far more complex than it appears to be in the media coverage. In this case, the ongoing conflicts between the clans and subclans were the major reasons the international relief effort was encountering so much trouble. Weapons were available throughout the Texas-sized country of 7 million people. The optimistic timetable for completing the U.S. portion of the mission was a fantasy.

It was hard for American troops to tell friends from foes. Despite my concern about the ability of the United Nations to conduct an effective large-scale operation, I concluded that we had no choice but to phase down our presence in Somalia and shift responsibility to an international force. Although initially there was public support for the deployment of our troops, I was certain that support for a large-scale, drawn-out U.S. military presence in Somalia was minimal.

Rather than write President Bush, who was about to leave office, I wrote my friend and former House colleague Les Aspin, soon to be secretary of defense, and UN Secretary General Boutros Boutros-Ghali about my views of the situation in Somalia. In both letters I emphasized the total lack of progress toward developing a follow-on UN peacekeeping force and called

American forces on patrol in the narrow streets of Mogadishu, Somalia.

for initiating steps immediately to address this challenge. In my letter to Aspin I also expressed my concern about the too frequent deployment of our troops and the subsequent impact on morale. I wrote:

> Les, I want to bring to your attention an additional point. One of the Marine units I visited had been deployed to the Persian Gulf during Christmas of 1991, was in Somalia for Christmas of 1992, and was scheduled for another rotational overseas deployment during Christmas of 1993. As we continue to downsize the overall force, the same units will be called on time and time again for deployment. As you are aware, my biggest concern is a fear that we may return to a hollow force if the morale of the troops should begin to decline and benefits and quality of life do not remain attractive.

All of the United States' military personnel are volunteers, and the point is often made that frequent deployments are part of the bargain struck when they enlist or reenlist. That is a legitimate point, but we must be aware of how extensively the sociological profile of today's troops has changed. A much larger percentage of today's young troops have spouses and children than those of past decades. Regular rotational deployments overseas—Europe, South Korea, aboard ship, and so on—are a fact of life. I believe, however, that when those scheduled rotations are combined with frequent unscheduled deployments—Somalia, Haiti, the Persian Gulf no-fly zone, Bosnia, Kosovo, and others—the prolonged absences from their families and the resulting strain on their personal lives can become excessive.

The United Nations Expands Its Goals

In the months after our return from Somalia, I focused on the annual defense appropriations bill. The process is time-consuming and challenging—months of hearings, marking up the bill, passing the legislation in the House, holding a conference with the Senate to resolve our differences, and then guiding the resulting legislation through the House to final passage. Throughout the process I worked closely each year with Congressman Joe McDade, the ranking minority member of the subcommittee and one of the finest and most knowledgeable members of Congress I have ever worked with.

I stayed abreast of events in Somalia through frequent briefings. I've found it very beneficial to receive briefings from the desk officer who specializes in the country of interest. The desk officers' job is to read and analyze the vast array of information available to them. The desk officers at the Central Intelligence Agency, the Defense Intelligence Agency, and the State Department are extremely knowledgeable about all aspects of current events in most countries of the world. More important, these civil servants can place these events in historical context. As I received briefings by the desk officers, participated in various other discussions, and read intelligence reports, I became increasingly alarmed by the trend of events in Somalia.

In early May, the UN passed Security Council Resolution 814, calling for rebuilding the Somali government, disarming the militias, rehabilitating the Somali economy, and developing a justice system and police force. This mission was a long way from the initial goal of feeding a hungry nation.

Each change in the policy objectives of the intervention in Somalia had its own name or acronym. Operation Provide Relief (August 1992 until early 1993) delivered massive amounts of food. The deployment of U.S.

forces became part of the next phase, Operation Restore Hope, which expanded the food-distribution role to include the provision of security. Then UNOSOM (United Nations Operation in Somalia) officially began in May, and a very ambitious agenda was implemented. This phase was called Operation Continue Hope.

As Vernon Loeb wrote in the *Washington Post,* "With almost no planning, the UN Security Council broadened the peacekeepers' mandate from securing relief operations to 'the rehabilitation of the political institutions and economy of Somalia.' . . . Madeleine Albright, then the U.S. ambassador to the United Nations, said 'the goal was nothing less than the restoration of an entire country.' "[5] From my perspective, there was an enormous gap between the policy makers' perception of what could be achieved and what was going on in the country where that policy was being executed.

United Nations Resolution 814, passed in reaction to events in Somalia, sounded impressive and noble, but its stated goals were unattainable given the resources committed to the Somali operation. At the very time the scope of America's role in Somalia was being scaled back significantly, the stated goals of the mission, as articulated by the UN and supported by our government, were being constantly expanded—a recipe for disaster.

In the six months from December 1992 to May 1993 the mission evolved from a straightforward humanitarian mission to peacekeeping to peace enforcement to nation building. The *Washington Post* correspondent Keith Richburg succinctly summarized the problem when he wrote in *Out of America:*

> The Marines earlier had steadfastly avoided being drawn into playing the role of street cops and sorting out Somalia's inter-clan feuds. But the UN came in with a different idea of its mission—they called it "nation building," which in practice meant stripping the guns away from the warring factions and trying to set up "neutral" institutions like a police force and a judicial system. Problem was that there was no such thing as a "neutral" Somali . . . and the UN, with its well-meaning but overly ambitious agenda, allowed itself to be sucked into a . . . war of attrition.[6]

During this period the Surveys and Investigations Staff of the Appropriations Committee conducted a lengthy study of the United Nations' numerous peacekeeping operations, and I asked them to brief me on the results.

An American soldier rushes for cover during the fateful battle in Mogadishu, which claimed the lives of eighteen Americans and more than five hundred Somalis in October 1993.

As they described the situation to me, the UN Security Council had relinquished its peacekeeping responsibilities to the Secretariat bureaucracy. In early 1993 the UN's military planning staff had only six people—the size of the planning staff of one U.S. Marine battalion, which has about 900 personnel. The quality of the UN staff was an issue as well. One UN officer's sole qualification for his rank and position was that he was the brother of his country's president. Yet the United Nations was responsible for fourteen military operations around the world. And the United Nations operations center in New York did not operate twenty-four hours a day or on weekends or holidays.

The United Nations' nation-building policy was a bottom-up approach beginning with economic, political, and judicial reform at the grass-roots level. As well intentioned as this approach was, the warlords viewed it as a threat because it eroded their control over the clans they headed. Aideed, the head of the largest clan, began to foment unrest among his followers, and his radio station began to inveigh against the "foreign invaders."

The civilian in charge of UNOSOM and the UN secretary general's representative in Somalia was a retired American admiral named Jonathan Howe. He had served earlier as commander of the NATO Southern Command and deputy national security adviser. Despite his impressive career, I agree with the critics who said that in this case Admiral Howe was the wrong man in the wrong job at the wrong time.

Vernon Loeb wrote in the *Washington Post Magazine* that Howe "quickly emerged as a hawkish force who saw Aideed as the root of Somalia's problem. He began lobbying U.S. officials to send in the Delta Force, America's most secretive . . . fighting unit, to apprehend the warlord."[7]

In *The Road to Hell,* Michael Maren wrote:

> Howe proved uniquely unqualified for the task. On several occasions I met with top Somali experts in his office, who were totally exasperated at their boss's refusal to deal with the complex realities of Somali politics. Howe just forged ahead doing things his way. He failed to see that offering a reward for Aideed made the warlord all the more powerful and that much more difficult to catch, and that blanketing Mogadishu with Wild West wanted posters just made UNOSOM look stupid.[8]

On June 5, one month after the UN had taken command of operations in Somalia, twenty-four Pakistani soldiers were killed in a battle with members of a clan headed by Aideed. Having fought the Viet Cong and North Vietnamese for a year, I have great respect for the skills and capabilities of an ill-equipped but focused military force. Michael Maren wrote about "the sophisticated and coordinated way the Somalis boxed in the Pakistanis, creating a killing zone. . . . The truth is that Aideed's militia had been battling in the streets of Mogadishu for four years. They knew every hiding place and every corner. A hundred times before they had set up roadblocks and cordoned off kill zones. They were conditioned to do it at the first sign of gunfire."[9] The attack on the Pakistani forces was answered within a week by U.S. helicopter gunships and ground forces. Aideed's clansmen and the U.S. and UN forces clashed repeatedly in the ensuing weeks.

The goals of the UN mission were expanded again. On June 6 the UN passed Resolution 834, resolving "to establish the effective authority of UN-OSOM II throughout Somalia" and to arrest and detain for "prosecution, trial and punishment" those responsible for the attack on the Pakistani forces. The resolution had been drafted by Madeleine Albright, the U.S. ambassador to the United Nations, and the White House staff; the Pentagon was not consulted.

Some countries that had UN contingents in Somalia reportedly disagreed with UN Resolution 834 and made separate peace agreements with Aideed's forces. In fact, some Americans believed that one of the other UN contingents was communicating U.S. troop movements to Aideed.

In an effort to achieve the goals of the new UN resolution, U.S. forces escalated their military action. Two weeks later, on June 18, American Cobra helicopter gunships attacked a villa where a large number of Aideed's key clan members were gathered. American helicopters also launched attacks on Aideed's radio station.

John R. Murphy was a Marine intelligence officer serving in Somalia at the time. In an article titled "Memories of Somalia" he reflected upon the impact of these military actions:

> The effect of this high-profile action undoubtedly led people into Aideed's camp. Somalis respect power, and what Somali could be more powerful than one targeted for death and openly fighting the greatest military force on Earth? As in so many other societies, cultural differences were not taken properly into account, with disastrous results. Radio Aideed was off the air for only a short time, as the warlord soon had a mobile radio set broadcasting his propaganda once again.[10]

In *Black Hawk Down*, Mark Bowden described a failed covert attempt to capture Aideed: "The original plan had called for a daring, well-placed Somali spy, the head of the CIA's local operation, to present Aideed an elegant hand-carved cane soon after Task Force Ranger arrived. Embedded in the head of the cane was a homing beacon. It seemed like a sure thing until . . . he shot himself in the head playing Russian roulette. It was the kind of idiotic macho thing guys did when they'd lived too long on the edge."[11]

As these events unfolded and the original objectives of the mission evolved into a series of military battles, my initial opposition to the deployment of our forces seemed increasingly wise. I decided it was time to press for the return of our troops. Not only were the stated goals of the UN resolutions unachievable with the resources provided, but the deployed UN forces were divided among themselves. The only way to ensure that the U.S. troops came home would be for me or some other member of Congress to insert a provision in a bill that "no funds in this bill, or any previous bill, may be used to fund the ongoing operations of United States forces in Somalia." That was a step I was reluctant to take. Even if the House of Representatives passed the bill, I doubted the provision would survive the Conference Committee. Furthermore, the first legislative vehicle in which the provision could be inserted was the annual defense appropriations bill, which routinely does not pass in its final form until about October each year. Also, I was hopeful that the executive branch and the Congress could develop a meeting of the minds and a common policy.

On July 14, 1993, I wrote President Clinton a letter recommending a phased withdrawal of our troops. It read in part:

> As you know, I have had reservations about the deployment of U.S. troops to Somalia from the beginning of the policy initiated by the previous administration. While the purpose of the mission is noble, we must have a realistic assessment of what goals are achievable and to what extent it is in our national interest to pursue those goals.
>
> The ongoing violence and opposition to the UN presence by many Somalis make it clear that the mission is no longer contributing to the stabilization of Somalia. I recommend that your administration develop a timetable for the phased withdrawal of U.S. forces and discuss that plan with the Congressional leadership.

I learned later that the approval of UN Resolution 834, which greatly expanded the objectives and goals of the UN mission, was followed almost immediately by a request by Admiral Howe for the deployment of U.S. Special Operations Forces. For the next two months a struggle continued between the National Security Council, which requested the deployment of those forces, and the Defense Department, which resisted it. On August 24, after a land mine destroyed a vehicle and killed four U.S. Army enlisted personnel, the president directed the secretary of defense to deploy additional troops to Somalia.

I asked Secretary of Defense Aspin for a briefing on the deployment of additional U.S. forces and he sent his military aide, who told me the United States was sending Army Rangers to beef up the reaction force. The aide did not tell me that the half of the 400 Rangers being deployed were a Delta team of elite Special Forces. Later I felt I had been misled by this omission. In congressional briefings and hearings on sensitive policy issues, you seldom get information you haven't specifically asked for.

In May, a half year after their initial deployment and four months into the Clinton administration, American forces handed over control to the United Nations. Four thousand U.S. troops remained in support roles and as a quick reaction force for use in emergency situations. By late summer 1993, however, the faltering UN operation in Somalia, the deployment of U.S. Special Operations personnel, and a speech by Secretary of Defense Aspin outlining an expanded agenda in Somalia clearly indicated that the United States was being pulled back into the conflict.

Beyond the Somalia issue, on the larger world stage the UN was beginning its deployment to Bosnia and "multilateral interventionism" was becoming popular with foreign policy officials and academicians. The post–Cold War era was beginning to look like a very troubled time. The United States, as the only global superpower, was being asked to become a global policeman to quell any conflict that caught the attention of the world media, whether or not they had anything to do with our national security.

In September 1993 I was at the White House with a small group of other members of Congress when President Clinton mentioned that he was going to make a speech on international affairs at the United Nations in a few weeks. If any of us had any ideas we would like him to consider including in his speech, he said, we should let him know. I wrote the following letter to the president.

> September 22, 1993
> The Honorable William J. Clinton
> President of the United States
> The White House
> Washington, D.C. 20500

> Dear Mr. President:
> As you prepare to address the United Nations, I want to share with you my perspective on some of the issues regarding involvement of U.S. troops in UN multilateral operations. We all recognize that

over the past decades, there have been United Nations peacekeeping operations which have been successful. . . . However, these missions have all had common characteristics:

- The conflicting parties had agreed to a cease-fire and to a UN peacekeeping mission.
- The parties were committed to attaining a meaningful peace.
- The United Nations forces did not have to militarily enforce the agreements.
- The missions predominantly consisted of small units deployed in an observer status.

Conversely, in recent years, UN missions have transitioned to a new role of peacemaking/peace-enforcing operations which have grown tremendously in number, cost, intensity, and complexity. I believe recent Security Council votes have led to the establishment of operations which the United Nations is incapable of effectively managing. The character of some peacekeeping missions has dramatically changed, and they are no longer limited to the traditional observer missions with the parties committed to peace but have developed into a combat enforcement role. We now have missions where internal conflict continues, and an intervention force must be deployed which is prepared for combat. It is these operations which have crossed a threshold which exceeds the management capability of the United Nations.

Some of the specific shortcomings of the United Nations' ability to carry out this "new threshold" of operations include:

- An inability to successfully plan and execute complex multilateral operations. For example, in early 1993, the military planning staff totaled six people, which is fewer than the United States uses to manage a 900-person battalion. Although this staff is expanding to thirty-eight, the United Nations has 90,000 personnel (including Bosnia) deployed.
- An unwillingness to use strategic and tactical intelligence information because of the issue of the sovereignty of the member states.
- Some missions proceeding with inadequate command and control and unclear rules of engagement.

- A severe mismatch between the objectives including in resolutions passed by the Security Council and the capability of the member nations to effectively carry out the directives included in the resolutions.

While I support committing additional resources to improve the UN Headquarters planning capabilities, I do not believe that a major commitment to U.S. participation in multilateral peacekeeping operations should become a focal point of our foreign policy. . . .

I am also concerned about the cost to the U.S. of various UN missions. Currently, there are 14 peacekeeping operations in progress with projected costs of $4.5 billion in 1994, of which the U.S. share is $1.4 billion. The UN is considering 20 additional "trouble spots" where peacekeeping operations may be needed in the next two years, eight of which could reach a crisis point in 1994. . . .

As you are aware, our projected defense force structure will soon reach its lowest level since before World War II. We must be cautious in accepting additional operational commitments. We cannot afford to become engaged in multinational deployments which, though noble in their objectives, are peripheral to the core national security interests of America.

> Sincerely,
> John P. Murtha, Chairman
> Defense Appropriations Subcommittee

A Fateful Battle in Mogadishu

On October 3 and 4, 1993, 18 Americans were killed and 82 wounded in a brutal battle in the streets of Mogadishu. More than 500 Somalis were killed and many wounded. Two American helicopters were shot down and the Army forces on those downed choppers were trapped for hours. The American public and the Congress were outraged at news film of the body of a dead American soldier being dragged through the streets of Mogadishu. The political impact of this battle was not unlike that of the Tet offensive in Vietnam. Morbid television coverage turned public opinion strongly against the government's policy. Just as television coverage played an important role in getting the United States involved in Somalia in the first place, it now played a key role in changing the policy to withdrawal.

Shortly after the battle, President Clinton ordered additional Army and Marine units deployed to Somalia to ensure the safe withdrawal of our forces. All U.S. combat forces would be out of the country, he said, by March 31, 1994, about five and half months away. From a foreign policy perspective, the worst had happened—the United States was being forced out without having achieved its policy objectives.

In the aftermath of this battle I went to see how the spouses and families of our troops in Somalia were coping. I traveled to Fort Drum, New York, the home of the 10th Mountain Division, the first U.S. Army unit deployed to Somalia. By that time America's commitment to the deployment in Somalia had gone on for so long that some soldiers from this division were in Somalia for their second tour. Units of the 10th Mountain Division had served as the relief force in the large battle in Mogadishu after the Ranger forces had become trapped.

The division commander, Major General Dave Meade, met me at Fort Drum and took me to the base community center to meet the families of the deployed troops. About 200 wives and children were gathered there and the mood was very somber. I gave a brief talk expressing my appreciation for all of the sacrifices they and their spouses were making, and then asked if they had any questions.

The wives told me that morale was very low; the scenes they had seen on television after the battle had devastated them. One woman said they were receiving no official information on what was really happening, and their primary source of information was the media. One mother said her four-year-old asked, "Mom, are we losing the war?" Someone asked why no one from the administration had visited Fort Drum. Another woman said she felt her husband was being used as cannon fodder in what the media called a losing effort with no public support. These women had good reason to be upset. The mission had spun out of control.

I returned to Somalia on October 9, a few days after the battle in Mogadishu. Robert Oakley met me at the airport. President Clinton had just recalled him from civilian life on October 6 to try to arrange the release of an American prisoner (Warrant Officer Durant), stop the fighting, and restart the political process. We left immediately for a meeting with Major General Tom Montgomery, who had two roles—deputy United Nations commander and the commander of U.S. forces in Somalia. We entered his headquarters in the former U.S. embassy compound, which had been badly damaged. He had in his hand an article that had just been faxed to him, holding him responsible for the disaster in Mogadishu and recommending that he be relieved of command. Our discussion turned to the command structure in place for the forces in Somalia. General Montgomery described the difficulties under which he had been operating. The command structure in place under the UN mandate allowed him to use the American quick reaction force, mostly Rangers, for force protection missions, but he did not have tactical control over the Ranger forces. The Rangers were assigned directly to the Central Command, which had Somalia within its jurisdiction, and were under the control of Major General Jim Garrison. General Montgomery added that he had a good working relationship with General Garrison and that they shared information. (Years later I discussed Somalia with Anthony Zinni when he was commander of the Central Command. He had been a brigadier general when he served in Somalia. He told me that the major problem during the Somalia deployment was that there was no single commander on the scene. In fact, there were five separate command lines.)

At the end of the meeting I asked both Ambassador Oakley and General Montgomery if there was a possibility that the United Nations could sustain the operation in Somalia after the United States had withdrawn. They said private contractors would have to provide an important component of the logistics supports, but without adequate security, no contractor would stay. They both emphasized how much easier it is to get troops into a country than it is to get them out.

We met briefly with Brigadier General Greg Gile, who was the on-site commander of the troops from the 10th Mountain Division, the unit based at Fort Drum. In addition I met with Lieutenant Colonel Bill David and members of his battalion. He had organized and led the ad hoc force of Malaysians and U.S. personnel who had fought their way through the streets of Mogadishu to rescue the embattled troops of Task Force Ranger.

I mentioned that morale was low among the dependents back at Fort Drum. General Gile pointed out how frequently the troops had been deployed. The average soldier from the 10th Mountain Division had spent about six months a year away from his or her family. Before coming to Somalia in October 1992, they had been on a training mission to Guantánamo Bay, Cuba, in December 1991 and on a humanitarian mission to Florida to assist in the recovery from the devastating Hurricane Andrew in August 1992.

General Garrison gave me an overview of the battle of a few days earlier and brought in one of the Special Forces soldiers who had been there. Captain Jim Yacone was a helicopter pilot; he and his wife had graduated from West Point the same year. His sister, Jill Yacone, was an associate staff assistant for the Defense Appropriations Subcommittee. Captain Yacone had been piloting a backup UH-60 helicopter just outside Mogadishu during the operation, ready to participate in the operation if problems developed. One of the helicopters involved in the mission was hit and downed almost immediately. A second helicopter moved into position and Captain Yacone's chopper took its place. The second helicopter was also hit; then Captain Yacone's chopper was hit, but he was able to make an emergency landing.

Other accounts have described in detail the carnage encountered in the eighteen-hour battle. One of the major reasons it went on so long was our troops' determination to bring their dead comrades back to the base camp. Two of the bodies were pinned under a downed helicopter.

Many of Aideed's clansmen had fired on our forces from second-story windows, standing back to minimize their exposure and shield the muzzle flashes from view, so that it was extremely difficult to detect their positions. Fear and confusion were sown by the constant echoes of gunfire in the narrow streets.

The Somalis organized groups of women and children and positioned them in the streets where American casualties lay to await the U.S. convoys that would come to rescue them. When the trucks arrived, the women and children dropped to the ground and behind them Aideed's forces fired on our soldiers. It was a cowardly but effective tactic.

The fog of war was dramatized in this battle between the elite forces of the United States and elements of a clan in a country that had no defense budget. One of the convoys sent to rescue the survivors of the downed helicopters was being constantly ambushed as it slowly proceeded toward its destination. A Black Hawk command-and-control (C2) helicopter was flying overhead to help direct the convoy to the downed chopper. In *Black Hawk Down*, Mark Bowden wrote:

> Flying about a thousand feet over the C2 helicopter was the navy Orion spy plane, which had surveillance cameras that gave them a clear picture of the convoy's predicament. But the Orion pilots were handicapped. They were not allowed to communicate directly with the convoy. Their directions were relayed to the commander at the

JOC (Joint Operations Command) who would then radio . . . the command bird. Only then was the plane's advice relayed down to the convoy. This built in a maddening delay. The Orion pilots would see a direct line to the crash site. They'd say, "Turn left." But by the time that instruction reached McKnight in the lead Humvee, he had passed the turn. Heeding the belated direction, they'd then turn down the wrong street.[12]

At the end of the meeting with General Garrison and Captain Yacone, General Garrison was informed that the Somalis had just agreed to free the captured pilot, Chief Warrant Officer Durant, along with a Nigerian colonel held by Aideed. Ambassador Oakley had secured their release. It was a welcomed bit of good news in a somber day.

The equipment available to our troops in Mogadishu became a focal point of debates in the House and Senate. In late September, a few weeks before the battle, Secretary of Defense Aspin had denied a request to send a reinforced armor company to Somalia. Now controversy raged around Aspin's decision. A "Dear Colleague" letter was circulated in the House, demanding Aspin's resignation.

As a footnote to history, at the end of my meeting with General Garrison, he handed me a four-page letter written in longhand on legal-sized paper and asked me to give it to the president when I returned to Washington. General Garrison wrote that before the bloody battle of October 3 and 4 he

- Had conducted six previous similar operations with no casualties.
- Received and assessed all available intelligence.
- Was comfortable that sufficient forces were available to conduct the operation.
- Provided for a ready reaction force that he considered adequate to reinforce the elements performing the operation should it become necessary.

He concluded that those above him in the chain of command and the Defense Department were not responsible for the events of October 3 and 4. In his professional opinion, he wrote, the armor that had been requested (four M-1 tanks and fourteen Bradley fighting vehicles) would not have significantly changed the outcome. He assumed full responsibility for the operation—a gallant position.

I met with Lieutenant General Cevik Bir, the Turkish commander of the

UNOSOM force. He told me candidly of his frustration in attempting to carry out the UN's policy. He had military units from about thirty countries under his command. Each of the commanders of those units had his own views on military tactics, and of course there were language barriers. Before undertaking any major military initiative directed by the UN, the military contingents from many of the participating countries would check through their own national chain of command for final approval.

The loss of lives in the battle and the dramatic images of the body of a dead American soldier being dragged through the streets of Mogadishu ended whatever support the American public had for the continued presence of our troops. Overwhelming political pressure was building in Washington to "bring the troops home." On the return flight to Washington, I received a phone call telling me that the Senate leadership was strongly considering introducing legislation that required the withdrawal of our forces from Somalia by January 15, 1994.

Although I had been opposed to the deployment of our troops to Somalia from the beginning, I was worried about the geopolitical and policy implications of a precipitous withdrawal. It is always much easier to inject our troops into an international crisis than it is to attain our policy objectives after they are deployed and withdraw them in a reasonable time frame.

From the plane I phoned Senate Majority Leader George Mitchell and Senator Robert C. Byrd, the chairman of the Senate Appropriations Committee, to express my concerns. From my perspective, a quick withdrawal right after the attack in which eighteen American lives were lost had major drawbacks. If a perception developed that the United States would cut and run after it incurred any casualties during a deployment, our adversaries would have tremendous leverage over our foreign policy. Another concern was the practical one of the time and planning it takes to remove our troops and equipment. Many of the thousands of foreign troops in Somalia relied on the United States for transportation back to their homelands. Also, although Congress has the constitutional right to cut off funding for a specific deployment of our troops, I believed it was vastly preferable to have the executive and legislative branches agree on foreign policy. I felt that my conversations with the Senate leaders had an impact. Senators Mitchell and Byrd agreed with my assessment, and the date in the proposed legislation for withdrawal was altered. Eventually the date set by President Clinton for the withdrawal of U.S. troops was the one at which the deployment to Somalia ended.

The last American combat units left Somalia on March 31, 1994, 481 days after the order to deploy to that distant land. Marine security forces protecting our State Department contingent and individual U.S. military personnel on various staffs continued their presence until the final withdrawal in March 1995.

Our troops had fought with tremendous courage and valor as they protected and rescued their downed comrades in Mogadishu. I would point out, however, that beyond the issue of the type of equipment that might have made a difference in the outcome is the larger question of why the raid was launched at all. As Edward N. Luttwak wrote in *Foreign Affairs:* "The Somali intervention came to a sudden end after the bloody failure of a daring helicopter raid in true commando style—a normal occupational hazard of high-risk, high-payoff commando operations. But given the context at hand—a highly discretionary intervention in a country of the most marginal significance for American interests—any high-risk methods at all were completely inappropriate in principle."[13]

9

WAR IN THE BALKANS

The breakup of Yugoslavia in 1991 triggered an international tragedy in the Balkans. Old religious and ethnic rivalries and hatreds rose to the surface. Accurate statistics concerning the scope of the tragedy have been difficult to develop, but published estimates have been in the range of 200,000 dead and up to 3 million refugees displaced from their homes at one time or another during the long intermittent conflicts. Estimated costs to the West are roughly $50 billion. There is little doubt that some level of NATO and U.S. forces will be in the region for a long time.

After a decade of war and atrocities throughout the Balkans, it appears that relative peace has finally descended on the region. The dramatic overthrow of Serbia's president Slobodan Milošević by a people's revolt considerably brightened the prospects for peace. Although the ultimate outcome of these events has been beneficial to U.S. interests in the region, I take issue with the conventional wisdom on two important aspects of our policies in regard to this region over the years. First, I disagree with the argument that U.S. ground troops should have been sent to Bosnia much earlier. Second, I don't believe that a policy relying almost totally on airpower offers a blueprint for the United States to follow in future crises.

I was involved in these events in the Balkans periodically, albeit in relatively minor ways. I served as the chairman of a congressional delegation monitoring an election in Bosnia; conducted inspection trips to Bosnia, Croatia, Macedonia, and Kosovo; participated in numerous congressional hearings on the intermittent crises that erupted in the region; and provided the president and executive branch officials with my perspective and advice.

The Balkan states and their neighbors

The Background

In *Kosovo Crossing*, David Fromkin eloquently put into perspective the historical context of the events in the Balkans:

> The situation and physical features of the Balkans have played a large role in shaping their political culture. The peninsula adjoins the Middle Eastern Fertile Crescent and, with it, forms the crossroads of Africa, the Middle East, Asia, and Europe. From the days of the first

humans . . . the peoples of the earth often have been in motion. Countless tribes and nations have passed through the Balkans on their way from one continent or river or sea to another, and left some legacies behind. Unlike Iberia and Italy, each sealed off on the north by forbidding mountain chains, the Balkans are easy of access. . . . Potential invaders find the way open.

Internally, however, the mountainous terrain keeps its diverse peoples isolated and apart: it works against unity. Cut off from one another in a mosaic of different communities, the inhabitants of the Balkans have retained their own religions, their own languages, their own style of dress, their own architecture, their own alphabets and their own calendars.[1]

The ethnic and religious diversity of the now independent countries that until the early 1990s were part of Yugoslavia is described in a Library of Congress book profiling the area:

Modern Yugoslavia had its genesis in a nineteenth-century idea that the South Slavs . . . should be united in a single independent state. . . . The Yugoslavia created after World War I was a virtual realization of this idea.

The South Slavs lived for centuries on two sides of a disputed border between the Eastern and Western Roman Empire, between the Eastern Orthodox and the Roman Catholic Churches, between the Islamic crescent and the Christian cross. . . . Besides the South Slavs, the Yugoslav state contained a mélange of minority peoples, many of them non-Slavic, who professed different religions, spoke different languages, and had different and often conflicting historical assumptions and desires. With over twenty-five distinct nationalities, Yugoslavia had one of the most complex ethnic profiles in Europe.[2]

One of the newly independent countries, which had been part of the former Yugoslavia from 1919, was Macedonia. In an insightful book, *Balkan Ghosts,* Robert Kaplan captured the essence of the roots of much of the conflicts:

Macedonia, the inspiration for the French word for "mixed salad" *(macédoine),* defines the principal illness of the Balkans: conflicting dreams of lost imperial glory. Each nation demands that its borders revert to where they were at the exact time when its own empire had reached its zenith of ancient medieval expansion. Because Philip of Macedon and his son, Alexander the Great, had established a great kingdom in Macedonia in the fourth century B.C., the Greeks believed Macedonia to be theirs. Because the Bulgarians at the end of the tenth century under King Samuel and again in the thirteenth century under King Ivan Assen II had extended the frontiers of Bulgaria all the way west to the Adriatic Sea, the Bulgarians believed Macedonia to be theirs. Because King Stefan Dushan had overrun Macedonia in the fourteenth century . . . , the Serbs believed Macedonia to be theirs. In the Balkans, history is not viewed as tracing a chronological progression. . . . Instead, history jumps around and moves in circles; and where history is perceived in such a way, myths take root.[3]

Despite these historic rivalries, the region had been peaceful in a multicultural, multireligious environment for long periods of time. In 1984 the Winter Olympics were held in Sarajevo, where Serbs, Croats, Christians and Muslims had intermarried extensively. The city had been relatively prosperous and peaceful for decades, yet beneath the surface centuries-old enmity simmered.

Under the dictator Josip Broz Tito, who ruled from the end of World War II until his death in 1980, there was peace in Yugoslavia. Although Tito's regime was communist, he declared the country to be "neutral." Soviet troops did not occupy Yugoslavia, as they had the countries of Eastern Europe, but there was always a concern that the Soviets might cross the border. Tito's state police and the people's fear of the Soviets resulted in a tranquil populace. When fear of the Red Army collapsed with the Soviet Union, long-simmering rivalries among ethnic and religious subcultures reemerged.

Potential U.S. Intervention

Yugoslavia began to unravel on June 25, 1991, when Slovenia and Croatia declared their independence. Yugoslav tanks attacked Slovenia two days later, and fighting broke out between Serbs and Croats in Croatia.

As violence flared intermittently, Washington saw the problem as one to be handled by our European allies. President George H. Bush's secretary of state, James Baker, stated, "We have no dog in that fight." I agreed with him. Near the end of the Bush administration, Lawrence Eagleburger, a career State Department official, replaced Baker as secretary of state. At that time blood was being shed in Kosovo, an autonomous province of Serbia, as the Serbian minority attacked the Kosovar majority of Albanian descent. Secretary Eagleburger wrote a letter to Milošević, warning him that the United States would not tolerate Serbian dominance of the autonomous province of Kosovo, whose population was overwhelmingly of Albanian descent. "In the event of a conflict in Kosovo caused by Serbian action," Eagleburger wrote, "the United States will be prepared to employ military force against Serbians in Kosovo and Serbia proper." A similar warning was sent to President Milošević early in the Clinton administration.

By themselves, these two letters are mere footnotes to history. Upon reflection, however, they symbolize the classic dilemma faced by the United States when violence and instability flare elsewhere in the post–Cold War era. On the one hand, if America keeps relatively silent and takes no steps to counter the violence, the inaction implies cynicism, lack of compassion, and disinterest in the outcome. On the other hand, when we react to a crisis by formally stating that we are "prepared to employ military force," we begin to slide down the slippery slope toward military engagement. Military action may not be important to the United States' security interests and it may not have the support of the American public or the Congress.

Inspection Trip

As the pace of violence and atrocities increased in the early 1990s, the media coverage of the ongoing conflicts in Croatia and Bosnia expanded. The United Nations deployed forces to the region, but there were no U.S. ground troops in the contingent. I alerted John Plashal to keep me updated on the intelligence community's perspective on events in that troubled corner of the world. I also received periodic briefings from experts in the Defense Department and the intelligence community. As chairman of the Defense Appropriations Subcommittee, I kept myself updated on all potential hotspots where U.S. troops might be sent. The fact that citizens of Croatian and Serbian descent are among my constituents was an additional reason for my concern.

Pressure began to mount in Congress, the media, and the public for the commitment of U.S. troops as the violence continued and the flow of refugees increased. Atrocities were being committed against ethnic and religious groups. Pictures of prisoners whose only crime was their religion or their ethnic background began to appear. Images of refugees fleeing from the violence appeared frequently in the press and on television. Like the Serbs, proponents of U.S. intervention had lost their fear of retaliation by Russia.

The conventional wisdom was that the United States should have sent in ground troops much earlier than it did, that lives could have been saved if we had intervened sooner. That may be true; and perhaps more lives could have been saved if U.S. troops had become involved in the fifty-four other conflicts going on around the world. But at what cost in American lives and well-being?

By mid-1992, although our massive force in the Persian Gulf was being rapidly reduced, a very large contingent of troops remained in the region to enforce the no-fly zones over northern and southern Iraq. In late 1992 and early 1993, 26,000 American troops were deployed to Somalia. Eighteen months later, 25,000 U.S. troops intervened in Haiti. It didn't seem prudent to make another major commitment of our forces, especially when it was not clear that vital national security interests were involved. Besides, as the former Soviet troops withdrew from Eastern Europe in the wake of the USSR's collapse, the threat to Western Europe dissipated; it appeared that the European democracies should handle this crisis, which was, after all, in their backyard.

As political pressures for U.S. intervention continued to grow, I decided to make an on-site inspection in early August 1992. An analyst from the CIA accompanied me. He was the desk officer for the area. He briefed me for hours on the historical background of that troubled corner of the world. He explained that the Battle of the Blackbird Fields, in which the Serbs fought against the Ottoman Turks in 1389, was a central factor in Serbian history and culture. He talked about the ethnic diversity, religious strife, cultural strains, and balance of military power among the competing forces in the region. He had color-coded maps showing the varied ethnic and religious mix of Yugoslavia's population. Talk about needing a scorecard to keep track of the players!

My introduction to the intensity of the ethnic hatreds came shortly after we arrived in Zagreb, the capital of Croatia. Serbian forces had been attacking parts of Croatia and had driven many people from their homes. We went to a refugee camp where a large gymnasium was filled with cots for the displaced. A wrinkled, stooped man who appeared to be about ninety got up slowly from his cot and walked over to me. Through an interpreter, I asked him if he had enough food. He ignored my question. His thoughts were elsewhere. He looked me in the eye and said emotionally, "I can remember World War I and I fought in World War II and I think every day about what the Serbs did to us. When I get out of this camp, I'm going to kill every Serb I see."

From Zagreb we flew to Sarajevo, where Bosnians of Serbian descent were shelling the city. The United Nations was providing humanitarian assistance to the embattled citizenry. We flew into Sarajevo on a C-130 military transport aircraft. The C-130 is a mid-sized aircraft with canvas web seats that parallel the sides of the plane. The workhorse of America's tactical airlift fleet, it was designed to fly troops and cargo into small airfields. There are only two small circular windows in the cargo portion of the C-130, where I sat during the flight. It's impossible to see much from them, so as we neared our destination I went to the cockpit and sat in the jump seat behind the two pilots. From there I could get a wide view of the topography of the region. As I observed Sarajevo in the distance, I thought of the flight into Beirut in 1983. Sarajevo, too, is partially surrounded by hills and mountains—a precarious position when your adversaries have the high ground. As we approached for the landing, the pilot emitted metallic chaff to draw any ground-to-air missiles away from the aircraft.

As soon as we landed we heard gunfire. The ongoing fighting in the area was so intense that we could not drive into Sarajevo. While we waited, two children were killed when their bus was fired on near the airport. We met with the military logistics personnel and the UN refugee officials, who were doing a courageous job under extremely stressful conditions.

As violence continued and the political pressure for the deployment of U.S. forces increased, I wrote President Clinton on February 4, 1993. The letter read in part:

> I believe American troops should not become engaged on the ground in that troubled area of the world. Numerous factors indicate it would be extremely difficult for Western forces to conduct an effective military campaign. These factors include the mountainous terrain of much of the region, a large indigenous armaments industry,

and a vast reserve of experienced military personnel who are trained in guerrilla warfare. . . .

I also have serious reservations about the utility of airpower in this complex situation. I am not convinced that the enhanced weapons which worked so effectively in the desert terrain during the Gulf War would be as successful in this situation. The target selection for tactical air strikes would be very complicated and the utilization of airpower may lead to hardened political positions. Also, if the air strikes did not achieve their objectives, we would face the dilemma of what additional military options are available, including the use of ground forces. Furthermore, there is a danger that the use of airpower may result in some units of the deployed UN contingent being held as hostages.

United Nations Policy

Meanwhile, the UN Security Council was passing resolutions that I believed it would not or could not enforce. UN Resolution 836, for example, called for contingents of a UN Protection Force (UNPROFOR) deployed in Bosnia to provide safe havens for Bosnian Muslims. This was an honorable goal, but the UN force was too limited and lacking in firepower to achieve it.

At the time this resolution was passed, the Dutch contingent of the UN forces was trying to establish safe havens in one area of Bosnia. The mandates of 1993 had significantly changed UNPROFOR's role. The UN's commander in Bosnia at the time, General Francis Briquemont, complained about the "fantastic gap between the resolutions of the Security Council, the will to execute these resolutions, and the means available to commanders in the field." Briquemont, wrote William Shawcross, "said he had stopped reading Security Council resolutions."[4]

"Resolution 836, which set up the safe areas, was ambiguous if not deceptive," Shawcross wrote. "The areas would never be safe. Resolution 836 had been designed not to defend the safe areas but to 'deter attacks' against them. And the Security Council never provided the UNPROFOR with the number of troops needed to achieve this lesser mission."[5] To me the UN's approach in Bosnia resembled its approach in Somalia—it set forth a goal but failed to provide the resources needed to achieve it.

The situation continued to deteriorate and the West's military role increased. In response to limited air attacks, the Serbs took UN soldiers hostage, as I had predicted in my letter to President Clinton. "Four unarmed military observers were handcuffed to a fence outside the Pale ammunition dump. . . . Nothing showed the impotence of the United Nations so vividly as the plight of its soldiers chained to potential targets."[6]

In reaction to this crisis the Security Council adopted Resolution 1004. Once again William Shawcross provides insight: "It demanded that the Bosnian Serbs cease their offensive and leave Srebrenica immediately. It demanded that all the parties respect the status of Srebrenica as a safe area. It demanded that they respect the safety and freedom of UNPROFOR personnel. It demanded that the Bosnian Serbs release immediately all UN personnel they had detained. It demanded immediate access to Srebrenica for the Red Cross and other humanitarian agencies. . . . The demands and threats of the Security Council meant nothing."[7] Soon thereafter forces under the control of General Ratko Mladić massacred thousands.

In late 1993 I met with Manfred Wörner, the secretary general of NATO, who presented his case for aggressive U.S. military involvement in Bosnia. He said sending American ground forces to Bosnia was very important. He did say, however, that U.S. troops should be committed only if they had a precisely defined role. "It's important to come in strong. Show your teeth. Show force if need be. If people speak the language of tanks, then you answer with tanks." UN peacekeepers often paint their jeeps and armored vehicles white and wear blue helmets. To me, this practice did not project the kind of force that instilled respect or fear in anyone. Wörner made a strong case for an expanded U.S. military role in Bosnia, but I was still not convinced that we should send in ground troops.

Air Strikes

One of the major events in this intermittent war occurred at the beginning of August 1995. A large number of Serbs lived in an area of Croatia called Krajina, where Serbian military forces had also been recently deployed. Croatia had undertaken a multiyear buildup of its military's capabilities, and in a lightning ground attack that took only a few days the Croatian military drove the Serbian forces from Krajina. A large number of Croatian refugees of Serbian descent also fled to Serbia. Our intelligence community had predicted that the Croatian offensive would fail; they were wrong.

In *To End a War,* Richard Holbrooke wrote:

> The Croatian offensive proved to be a wedge issue that divided not
> only Americans but the top echelons of the American government
> itself. Most officials saw these military thrusts as simply another
> chapter in the dreary story of fighting and bloodshed in the region.
> They felt the duty of our diplomacy was to put a stop to the fighting,
> regardless of what was happening on the ground. For me, however,
> the success of the Croatian . . . offensive was a classic illustration of
> the fact that the shape of the diplomatic landscape will usually reflect
> the balance of forces on the ground. In concrete terms, this meant
> that as diplomats we could not expect the Serbs to be conciliatory at
> the negotiating table as long as they had experienced nothing but
> success on the battlefield.[8]

In late August–September 1995, in reaction to atrocities committed by
Bosnian Serbs in the city of Srebrenica, NATO began air attacks against Bosnian Serb military targets. Shortly after, airlifts of humanitarian aid resumed
and plans for a peace conference were being made. The improvement in
prospects for a peace conference after the air attacks probably convinced
many observers that airpower was the key to achieving the West's goals in
Bosnia. "In fact," writes Shawcross,

> the bombing was only partially successful. It was hampered by bad
> weather. NATO ran out of suitable targets and had to bomb some of
> them several times in order to keep up any air campaign at all. Bomb-
> ing alone did not break the will of the Bosnian Serbs. The bombing
> was accompanied by other pressures which were equally vital, in par-
> ticular the aggressive use of artillery of the Rapid Reaction Force.
> Also absolutely vital was the Croat offensive through Krajina and
> into Bosnia, which cost the Bosnian Serbs large swaths of land which
> they had hoped to retain. The Bosnian Serbs were also given political
> inducements. The Holbrooke plan included a Bosnian Serb entity in
> Bosnia, which meant that they were no longer compelled to surren-
> der their independence to the government in Sarajevo.[9]

A few air attacks, then, were not alone the answer to Serb aggression.

Surreal Dinner at the Holiday Inn

I talked with the president on numerous occasions about events in the former Yugoslavia. Shortly before the Dayton Accords were finalized, I played golf with him at the Army-Navy Country Club and told him of my concern about sending troops to Bosnia. He said it was the right thing to do if we could reach an agreement. Peace talks were being held at the Wright-Patterson Air Force Base, outside Dayton, Ohio, under the able and forceful leadership of Ambassador Richard Holbrooke. A cease-fire was finally agreed to but the negotiators had to work out additional details for a final settlement, including the presence of troops from the United States and other NATO countries to keep the warring factions apart.

I felt it was important to make a firsthand assessment of the volatile situation in which our troops would be involved. There would be many debates and votes in the Congress regarding this controversial deployment, and the Appropriations Committee would have to pass legislation to provide funds for the operation. I wanted to have current firsthand information for those upcoming debates and votes, so I went on an inspection trip on October 9–10, 1995.

Jim Dyer, the staff director of the House Appropriations Committee, accompanied me. Jim is one of the most influential staffers on Capitol Hill and has encyclopedic knowledge of foreign affairs. Greg Dahlberg of the staff was also in the delegation, as was John Plashal. Our plan was to fly from Andrews Air Force Base in Maryland, refuel en route, and then land at the Aviano Air Base in Italy. From there we would catch a C-130 transport aircraft to Sarajevo.

We were denied permission to fly over France and had to fly around it and approach Aviano by way of Switzerland. The French government never explained why. Because of this petty snub, we almost missed the plane scheduled to fly us to Sarajevo. We finally landed at Aviano at 8:45 A.M., jumped into a minibus that was waiting on the tarmac, and sped down an access road to a C-130 aircraft that had its engines running. The crew gave us Kevlar helmets and flak jackets, recommending that we sit on the jackets and wear the helmets when we approached Sarajevo.

The C-130 was a U.S. aircraft flying under UN auspices. It carried medicine, food, and other essential supplies to the people of Sarajevo. These flights were called "hot loads" because the engines were kept running after the plane landed while ground crews quickly unloaded the cargo. Only a few minutes later the plane was in the air again. This quick turnaround minimized the chance that the aircraft would be hit by mortar fire on the ground. As we began our descent into Sarajevo, this pilot, too, dispatched metallic chaff to counter any anti-air fire.

We spent the afternoon at meetings with the top military and civilian officials of UNPROFOR. The commanding officer was Lieutenant General Rupert Smith, a British officer who had commanded the famous Desert Rats armored division in the Persian Gulf War. I told him that many of my colleagues in the Congress repeatedly asked, "Why can't the Europeans handle this crisis by themselves?" General Smith was unequivocal in his belief that without U.S. ground forces, the mission to restore peace in Bosnia would fail. Another participant in the meeting said, "If the United States deploys to Bosnia and then decides to pull out, the other NATO forces would quickly follow and disengage from Bosnia." General Smith and his staff told us they believed the cease-fire, scheduled to start the next day, would hold.

During the meeting an officer came in and whispered something to General Smith. "Gentlemen," the general announced, "there has been a little problem. Since you landed at the airport there's been firing at incoming and outgoing aircraft. All flights in and out of Sarajevo have been canceled until tomorrow."

We had left our luggage in Italy, since we had expected to return there that day. Our options now were to sleep on the floor at the UNPROFOR headquarters or stay at the only functioning hotel in town, a Holiday Inn. We chose "The Nation's Innkeeper." The hotel had been shot up pretty badly by Serb forces and was heavily pockmarked. As one of the tallest buildings in the city—about ten stories high and a startling chartreuse—it was an easy target. Its few habitable rooms had plastic covers over the shot-out windows. We were the only guests. Each room cost about $180 a night. The price seemed steep in view of the fact that one side of the hotel, as the desk clerk warned us, was known as Sniper's Alley: anything that moved there drew rifle fire.

Since we had no luggage, our military escort, Lieutenant Colonel Dan Cunningham, went out—not by way of Sniper's Alley—to see if he could find us any toiletries. When he returned he said the shops he had found (not many) had sandbags piled high around their entryways as protection against incoming mortar rounds. Dan went to a few of these establishments before he finally found one that had a few cans of tuna fish and some disposable razors. No shaving cream, though.

Earlier he had traded a recent copy of the *Washington Post* for a half tube of toothpaste with someone from our diplomatic mission. He had the toothpaste with him. As our little group gathered in the corridor outside our rooms, he kiddingly stood at attention and slowly squeezed out a little bit of toothpaste on the index fingers of the assembled delegation, and we proceeded to brush our teeth. That took care of our personal hygiene and it was time to go to dinner.

Given the constant gunfire we could hear in the background, it seemed like a pretty smart idea to stay in the hotel. We ate that night in the basement of the hotel, in a large room that had been a discothèque before the war. We were the only patrons. Waiters in tuxedos took our orders in the dimly lit room. A pianist played classical music on a grand piano. The Mozart (a classical music aficionado in the delegation assured us it was Mozart) was accompanied by occasional sounds of gunfire and shelling. (A report the next day estimated that up to 4,000 rounds had been fired that night. Evidently the factions involved in this tragic war were getting in their licks before the cease-fire took place the next day.) Toward the end of the meal, a few French officers dressed in fatigues and snappy red berets sat down at a corner table and held an intense discussion. Classical music, waiters in tuxedos, constant gunfire in the background, French soldiers dining in their fatigues—only in Sarajevo could such a surreal setting for an evening meal seem normal.

The Cease-Fire Holds

After the dinner, which was very good, I turned in for what turned out to be a cold and restless night. The noise from the frequent firing of weapons was not conducive to a good night's sleep. When I awoke early in the morning, there was no sound of gunfire. It appeared the cease-fire was being honored. In the few hours before our return flight we decided to take a quick tour to assess the situation. One of our stops was at the national library of Bosnia, a magnificent old building of classical architecture, severely damaged by mortar fire. It had contained thousands of priceless books, many of them centuries old. The fact that the national library and a marketplace filled with shoppers had been targets underscored the depth of cynicism and hatred in this tragic conflict.

Just down the street from the library, in a picturesque section of Sarajevo where an ancient little arched bridge crossed a river meandering through the city, we stopped at an old building. A plaque on the wall marked the spot where Archduke Ferdinand, heir to the throne of the Austro-Hungarian Empire, was assassinated in 1914, precipitating World War I.

Bosnia was the southernmost territory in the Austro-Hungarian Empire, and although the Bosnians harbored considerable resentment against the empire, Archduke Ferdinand went there as inspector general of the army. An UNPROFOR officer refreshed our knowledge of history when he told us that an anarchist group called the Black Hand plotted the killing. Seven men with a variety of weapons were stationed along the archduke's route. One of the assassins threw a bomb at the archduke's car. It bounced off and exploded, wounding members of the delegation in the next vehicle, but the archduke was not injured. Despite the attack, the delegation continued on its designated route.

The archduke then decided to visit the wounded. En route to the hospital, the driver of the archduke's car took a wrong turn. Realizing his mistake, he stopped and backed up. Incredibly, one of the seven Black Hand assassins was at that very location with his pistol hidden beneath his coat. He was despondent about his failure to assassinate the archduke earlier in the day, as planned. He looked up, saw the archduke's car, and calmly walked over and shot and killed the archduke and his wife. Soon after, Austria-Hungary invaded Bosnia and the slaughter of World War I was under way.

As we walked the streets of Sarajevo, we were struck by the silence after the constant firing the night before. Viewing the destroyed library and standing on the spot where World War I was set in train made it hard to be optimistic about peace in Sarajevo. But it was a beautiful day, and as we walked I noticed small vegetable gardens on available patches of land. A couple of vendors were selling flowers. We stopped at a small shop filled with crafts. I noticed an attractive ornamental copper plate that a local craftsman had skillfully hammered into a rural scene. I asked him the price and he replied, "Because you are an American it is free. Please take it as a gift from the people of Sarajevo, who are hopeful that peace has finally arrived." I insisted on paying him.

Hope springs eternal. The gunfire of the night before seemed to be a distant memory. A few vegetable gardens, enterprising vendors selling flowers, and a grateful shopkeeper selling his wares persuaded me that peace had finally come to this war-torn city.

"Make My Day"

Although a cease-fire was in place at the time we left Sarajevo, not all the details of how the Dayton Accords were to be implemented had been worked out. I was encouraged by my visit to Sarajevo, but I was determined to do what I could to ensure that when U.S. troops were sent to Bosnia, they would operate in the safest possible environment. I kept thinking of the weak rules of engagement operable for our troops in Lebanon over a decade earlier—"No round in the chamber," "Use only a minimum degree of force to accomplish the mission." I also thought of Somalia, where mission creep and an unwise execution of policy put our troops in unnecessary danger.

On October 13, 1995, I wrote President Clinton a letter that read in part:

> Dear Mr. President:
>
> I recently returned from an inspection trip to Sarajevo . . . where I met with UNPROFOR and NATO commanders about the status of affairs in Bosnia. . . . While the people of the region still harbor a healthy skepticism about the ultimate success or failure of upcoming negotiations, it is universally agreed that American leadership is responsible for the progress made so far. . . .
>
> My concern is that we not lose sight of the very real possibility that upcoming negotiations on the details of the peace accord will be protracted and difficult. . . . We should not let the current optimism and high expectations in the press cause us to commit to a vague and ambiguous peace accord that leaves it to U.S. troops on the ground to settle the fine details.
>
> Any peace accord that contemplates a commitment of U.S. ground forces must be ironclad and specific. It should spell out clearly the peace enforcement mission, roles, and responsibilities of the NATO ground troops with achievable goals. . . . There must be no room for "mission creep" as we had in Somalia. It also should clearly specify what conditions must exist on the ground prior to deployment and make clear that no long-term or permanent deployment of U.S. troops is involved. All sides must agree that NATO will be authorized to use force as its commanders see fit to carry out the mission. Most important, the senior military commanders responsible for imple-

American peacekeepers on patrol in Bosnia in 1996. The doctrine of "disproportionate response"—replying with overwhelming force to any challenge—was the guiding tactical policy.

menting this plan in the field should continue to participate in developing the specifics of the agreement to give it the best chance of success.

The details of the peace agreement were finally ironed out. While I had been opposed to the deployment of U.S. troops to Bosnia, once the peace treaty was signed, I supported it. Under the agreement, our troops would not be interjecting themselves into the middle of a civil war, but rather would be keeping apart factions that were exhausted after many years of conflict and had agreed to a peace settlement. This was a much more achievable mission than earlier proposals to interject U.S. ground troops into an ongoing civil war.

I was pleased when I learned that our troops would be operating within a carefully defined doctrinal framework, which I believe made an important contribution to keeping the peace. I am referring to the doctrine of "disproportionate response," a sort of Clint Eastwood "make my day" policy. It was simple. The Bosnians were told that if they fired on or attacked NATO forces with any kind of weapon, including small arms, the response by our forces would be disproportionate to the level of the attack on our troops—it would be massive and decisive, and it would definitely ruin their day. Although widespread problems remain, relative peace has prevailed in Bosnia since the deployment of U.S. and NATO forces and the execution of a no-nonsense policy.

Return to Bosnia

As violence subsided in Bosnia, elections were scheduled. Because of the sensitivity and importance of the vote, it was necessary to send in international monitors to ensure fairness. Ambassador Richard Holbrooke was the head of the vote-monitoring delegation; I led the congressional component. The turnout of voters was large and the delegates were all impressed by the fairness of the election.

As we always did, we divided into small groups to cover as many voting locations as possible. Our interpreter was a young woman of about twenty who was majoring in English at Sarajevo University. John Plashal asked her about her goals and where she would like to go if she visited the United States. She immediately responded, "I would like to go to Chicago and see Michael Jordan in a Bulls game." Later, when our group stopped at a red light, we heard music coming from a radio in a nearby restaurant. It sounded Middle Eastern to me. John asked her if that was the kind of music she enjoyed. She said the music she really liked was the kind she heard on MTV. The pervasiveness of American culture around the world is an amazing thing.

With President Clinton in Bosnia

In November 1998 I was invited to accompany President Clinton to Bosnia during the Thanksgiving holiday. Included in the delegation were Senators Ted Stevens, Chuck Robb, and Pat Leahy and Congressmen Dave Obey and Bob Livingston. On the flight over, three of us were sitting together, each reading a book on the current *New York Times* best-seller list. President Clinton came back from the front of the plane and joined us. He noticed our books and began to discuss each of them with us, sometimes in great detail. I found it amazing that the president of the United States had time to read so much.

We found the troops in good spirits and very appreciative of the president's visit. Turkey dinner with all the trimmings was served. Everyone was in a festive mood. A show put on by USO entertainers was a big hit. Relative calm had prevailed in Bosnia since the implementation of the Dayton Accords and refugees were streaming back to their homes.

Little did we realize on this festive Thanksgiving that the commitment of U.S. and NATO forces would soon dramatically escalate. Just 120 days after our visit, U.S. and Western forces began air strikes against Serbia and Serb forces in the province of Kosovo.

Air War Against Serbia

Kosovo is an autonomous province within Serbia, about the size of Connecticut, with a population of approximately 2 million. By the 1990s, citizens of Serbian descent made up about 10 percent of Kosovo's population. The vast majority of the people were ethnic Albanians. The stress and rivalries were exacerbated by the religious differences between the Orthodox Serbs and the Muslim Kosovars of Albanian descent. Kosovo has many ancient shrines that are of cultural significance to the Serbs.

Events leading up to the war against Serbia have been described in *Kosovo and U.S. Policy,* by Julie Kim and Steven Woerhel of the Congressional Research Service: "In February, 1989, the Serbian Parliament passed amendments to the Serbian Constitution sharply limiting Kosovo's autonomy. . . . In 1990, Serbia approved further constitutional amendments that eliminated Kosovo's autonomy and abolished Kosovo's parliament and government. Over 100,000 ethnic Albanians in government, the police, enterprises, media, educational institutions and hospitals were fired and replaced by Serbs." In reaction to this oppression, the Albanian Kosovars started an armed insurrection. "Starting in 1996, a shadowy group called the Kosovo Liberation Army (KLA) . . . claimed responsibility for killing several Serb policemen and other officials, as well as alleged ethnic Albanian collaborators."[10] Although both the Bush and Clinton administrations had warned Milošević many years before that America would not stand by if

Serbia became militarily involved in Kosovo, Serbian forces became increasingly aggressive.

Negotiations to end the conflict between the Serb forces in Kosovo and the Kosovo KLA were held in Rambouillet, France. "The Rambouillet accords would provide for a three-year interim agreement on democratic self-government for the people of Kosovo. The accords would establish political institutions and offices in Kosovo, free elections, and human rights provisions. A NATO force would ensure compliance with the accords and provide a secure environment. The United States pledged to contribute up to 4,000 troops."[11]

The Kosovars signed the agreement at Rambouillet but the Serbs refused to agree to foreign troops in Kosovo. Weeks later President Clinton told me his advisers had led him to believe that the Serbians would sign. A last-ditch effort by Richard Holbrooke to persuade Milošević to sign the Rambouillet accord failed. Serb forces had begun a large buildup of troops on the border and on March 20 they moved into Kosovo. Four days later, on March 24, 1999, NATO (largely U.S.) forces began air attacks against targets in Serbia and Serbian ground forces in Kosovo.

Ultimately, Serbian forces withdrew from Kosovo and Slobodan Milošević was overthrown when, in the aftermath of the war, he attempted to steal an election. Regarding these historic events, Javier Solana, then secretary general of NATO, wrote: "For the first time, a defensive alliance launched a military campaign to avoid a humanitarian tragedy outside its own borders. For the first time, an alliance of sovereign nations fought not to conquer or preserve territory but to protect the values on which the alliance was founded. And despite many challenges, NATO prevailed."[12] NATO suffered no casualties and the people of Kosovo returned to their homes.

Many observers point to this air war as a classic victory for airpower and a blueprint for U.S. involvement in future crises. My assessment is quite different. Initially, key policy makers believed that a few air attacks would change Milošević's policies. Eventually, however, over 23,000 bombs and missiles were fired by U.S. and NATO forces over almost three months. Milošević finally backed down when he believed NATO forces were about to launch a ground attack. He was overthrown when hundreds of thousands of Serbian citizens stormed key government and industrial facilities in rage at his attempt to steal the election.

The military and economic imbalances between the two adversaries were as lopsided as one can imagine. The total population of the countries in the

NATO alliance was 775 million. The population of Serbia (about the size of Ohio) was 11 million. The combined gross national product (GNP) of the member nations of NATO was 57 percent of the world's GNP. The gross domestic product (GDP) of Serbia was so minuscule that it did not even register as a percentage of the world's GDP. According to the CIA's annual *World Fact Book*, the GDP of Serbia in 1998 was $24.3 billion. (That would make the total economic output of Serbia worth about half the value of Bill Gates's stock in Microsoft at the time.) Years of economic mismanagement, hyperinflation in the early 1990s, economic boycotts by most of the industrialized world, and intermittent wars with Serbia's neighbors had left its economy in shambles.

The imbalances were just as extreme militarily. The Serbs had had no weaponry comparable to NATO's. NATO, especially the United States, had all the latest high-tech and most effective weapons in the world. The CIA did not officially list Serbia's defense budget in 1998, but the agency's *World Fact Book* listed Serbia's defense budget in that year as 6 percent of the country's GDP, or roughly $1.5 billion—about equal to the cost of one B-2 Stealth bomber.

Yet the overwhelming imbalances of population, economies, defense budgets, and military capabilities were not indicative of how events would turn out (at least over the short term) when U.S./NATO air forces began their attack. Once again the United States underestimated the tenacity of its adversary. Although the U.S./NATO bombing campaign began at a low level, it built up steadily, and by the time it ended, almost three months later, over 38,000 sorties had been flown (one flight by one plane is one sortie). To put that number in perspective, the United States flew a total of 70,000 sorties during the Persian Gulf War.

Over 23,000 bombs and missiles were launched in the Serbia/Kosovo air campaign, a massive and expensive effort. At the peak of the bombing attacks, 1,200 NATO aircraft were used. Of that total, 980, or about 88 percent, were U.S. aircraft. The attacks became so intense that Air Force officials told Congress that no more aircraft were needed because of "air space constraints." In other words, there was no room for any more.

Doctrine—Gradual Escalation or Decisive Force

The lessons of the air campaign conducted against Serbia and its forces in Kosovo are extremely important. The first lesson regards the gradualness of the U.S./NATO response to Milošević's aggression once the decision was made to intervene with airpower. That approach repudiated the opinion that evolved after the Vietnam War: if you are going to intervene, do so decisively. Second, I believe the air attacks against fixed targets in Serbia and those against the Serb armed forces in Kosovo were in effect two very different campaigns.

As it became increasingly clear that NATO would act, the use of ground troops was ruled out. Statements by the administration precluding the use of ground forces were frequently cited as a major tactical error. That was probably true, but it should be remembered there was strong opposition in the Congress and almost no support from the American people for the use of U.S. ground troops. Also, Kosovo's terrain and its very limited road infrastructure made the interjection of ground troops with heavy equipment such as M-1 tanks very challenging. At any rate, the decision was made to limit the intervention to airpower

Immediately after the air attacks began, a reporter called me and asked if I agreed with sources who had told him that "things should be over in about two or three days when Milošević backs down because of the air attacks." I replied, "You've got to be kidding me. Your sources said two to three days? How about two or three months!" He said he was "basing his projections on very high sources within the administration." There is little doubt in my mind that his sources were in the State Department. Soon thereafter, Secretary of State Albright replied to a press inquiry that our goals could be achieved in a relatively short time frame.

Air Force General John P. Jumper testified before Congress that "NATO's initial guidance was based upon the hope its objectives could be achieved by bombing a limited set of targets over a few days." A Congressional Research Service stated that "the air campaign's actual objective from the start was political, not military—i.e., to bring President Milošević back to the bargaining table. This in turn contributed to a constrained, incremental approach to targeting."[13]

Michael Ignatieff wrote: "Immediately, however, it became clear that 'strategic bombing lite' would not work. In fact [General K. Wesley] Clark had wanted a different approach from the outset. He and his air commanders, led by General Michael Short, a blunt, outspoken veteran of 276 combat missions in Vietnam, wanted to 'go downtown' on the first night, hitting the power, telephone, command-and-control sites and Milošević's bunkers."[14] They were overruled.

Granted, other factors significantly affected the implementation of the policy. Members of the NATO alliance had to be included in the planning and target selection. Their inclusion was absolutely necessary, but it added layers to the decision-making process. In the aftermath of the war, I requested (along with Bob Stump, chairman of the House Armed Service Committee) that the General Accounting Office conduct a study to determine to what extent military doctrine had been followed in the execution of the air war. One of the study's conclusions was that the need for a consensus among the NATO alliance members led to many departures from doctrine. "The vague objectives adopted by NATO were difficult for the military to attain."

Each foreign policy crisis has, of course, unique and complicated circumstances. In the aftermath of the Vietnam War, however, two basic doctrines evolved in regard to the intervention of U.S. troops. The Weinberger Doctrine, articulated by Reagan's secretary of defense, Caspar Weinberger, was: Become engaged militarily only for core national security reasons. The Powell Doctrine was: If you get involved in a situation that may not be a core national security issue, have clear objectives and use overwhelming force to achieve your goals. (A third school of thought favored frequent deployment of U.S. troops for humanitarian purposes.) Ivo Daalder and Michael O'Hanlon wrote in *Foreign Policy:*

> What Powell rejected was the idea of using force without clearly defined and achievable objectives or ample means for accomplishing them. "Decisive means and results are always to be preferred, even if they are not always possible. So you bet I get nervous when so-called experts suggest that all we need is a little surgical bombing or a limited attack. When the desired result isn't obtained, a new set of experts comes forward with talk of a little escalation. History has not been kind to this approach."[15]

In Kosovo—at least in the initial phase—neither the Weinberger nor the Powell doctrine was applied. It was not clear to me that the vital national security interests of the United States were involved. Granted, the fact that this violence was occurring in Europe added an important dimension. There was obviously an enormous humanitarian problem. But such crises arise daily in many corners of the globe and our armed forces cannot be sent to all of them. When Madeleine Albright claimed, "The future of NATO is at stake," her statement alone seemed to make the outcome of events vitally important to our security interests. But rather than apply the Powell Doctrine and use overwhelming force, a sort of reverse Theodore Roosevelt foreign policy was used: Speak loudly and carry a small stick.

After the limited air attacks failed to change Serbia's policy in Kosovo—indeed, the air attacks spurred the Serbs to increase their military intervention there—the intensity of the bombing rose steadily. There was no turning back. The staff of the Military Readiness Subcommittee of the House Armed Services Committee put the eventual level of these air attacks in perspective in a report that read in part: "The Air Force is 40% smaller than it was in 1990 and . . . over 40% of its assets were necessary to meet the mission requirements of Operation Allied Force. This was a higher percentage of aircraft than was committed by the Air Force during Operation Desert Storm."[16] General John P. Jumper, commander of the U.S. Air Force in Europe, made the same point in congressional testimony, and he added that "the American aircraft used in the conflict were also higher in percentage terms than U.S. aircraft used during the Vietnam conflict."[17] Congressman Jerry Lewis and I noted in a *Washington Post* column that the United States committed nearly 100 percent of operational intelligence, surveillance, and reconnaissance aircraft such as U-2s and AWACS, and committed so many of our electronic jamming aircraft that Korea was left uncovered.

All of the countries on Serbia's borders and in the region, with the exception of Russia, cooperated in the campaign against Serbia. The agreements, which varied from country to country, included housing for refugees, the right for NATO aircraft to fly over the country, and, in some cases, troop basing arrangements. However, even this enormously escalated effort and the opposition of almost all the nations in the region were not enough to change Milošević's policy.

In late May, President Clinton called me and expressed his concern about the air war, but he added forcefully, "Jack, we are going to prevail." I told him that in light of the implications of a failure of our policy, I was willing to support the use of ground troops and told him I would write him a letter to that effect.

As the air campaign continued to fail to reach its objectives, the policy changed from the original "no ground troops" to an admission that they were probably necessary. An article on this issue in the *Washington Post* read in part:

> At noon on June 2, [Sandy] Berger, the president's national security adviser, met with several foreign policy experts who had publicly

advocated that NATO consider sending in ground troops. . . . According to a participant, the group was surprised to hear Berger hint strongly that the administration was prepared to back a ground invasion, if that was what it would take to win the war.

Berger made four points, according to notes from the meeting. The first was: "We're going to win." The fourth was: "All options are on the table." Asked directly whether Clinton would support ground troops, he replied: "Go back to point one."

That afternoon, Clinton's national security staff stopped short of recommending an invasion but urged swift planning. "We had to prevail, even if it meant preparing for a ground option. We all recognized this," Berger recalled in an interview last week.[18]

As usual, weather played a part in the decision-making process. Almost a million Kosovars were huddled in refugee camps in Macedonia and Albania. If they could not return to their homes before winter set in, a tragedy would be made even worse. Further, if the air war did not achieve its objectives relatively soon and intervention by NATO ground troops became necessary, they would have to deploy well before winter began.

A Congressional Research Service report read in part: "On May 21, the United States urged a rapid build-up to a force of 45,000–50,000 in Macedonia, with a U.S. contingent of 7,000. U.S. officials said that a decision must be made by mid-June to establish such a force if refugees are to be returned to their homes before winter. The force would enter Kosovo, even without a final peace agreement."[19] As NATO's buildup of ground troops continued, reports were published that through diplomatic channels the Serbian government had been informed that a NATO intervention of ground forces into Kosovo was imminent. A few months after the air war ended, General Wesley K. Clark, the supreme allied commander in Europe, told a think tank that he thought Milošević's intelligence had plenty of indicators that would have made him conclude that the West would conduct a ground campaign.

Milošević finally withdrew his troops from Kosovo when he realized the odds against him were overwhelming. Much of Serbia's infrastructure—bridges, oil refineries, and industrial facilities—lay in ruins. The country was faced with an economic boycott, continued massive air attacks, and an imminent ground invasion by NATO troops into Kosovo. Daalder and O'Hanlon wrote:

Many who favor the use of force to support diplomacy reject General Powell's supposed dictum for using overwhelming force, believing that there must be a place for its more limited deployment. However, even in Kosovo, NATO did not prevail until it tripled its air armada, bombed for many more weeks than originally planned and talked convincingly about deploying ground forces. In other words, it succeeded as its military strategy became increasingly muscular and decisive—or to put it differently, increasingly Powell-like.[20]

Two Separate Air Wars

The capability of America's airpower is awesome. The mix of strike aircraft, strategic bombers, electronic jamming aircraft, air-to-air attack aircraft, smart bombs, smart missiles, and tactical and strategic intelligence technology to select targets overwhelmingly exceeds the capability of any other air force in the world. In the air war against Serbia, the United States' air capability was enhanced by the participation of our NATO allies.

Although the air war against Serbia was one integrated campaign, in reality there were two separate types of air campaign—one attacking fixed targets in Serbia and Kosovo and another attacking Serbian ground troops in Kosovo. The air strikes against fixed targets played to our technological strengths. Those missions were attacking stationary, exposed targets—bridges, military installations, ammunition dumps, oil refineries, petroleum storage facilities, industrial facilities. In an air campaign of this nature we used many of America's high-tech assets: intelligence satellites helped select targets and pinpoint their location, jamming aircraft suppressed enemy radar, the Global Positioning System (GPS) satellites gave our pilots their precise location, and smart weapons hit targets with awesome precision. Cruise missiles launched from our ships hit their targets with great accuracy. Michael Ignatieff described the attack of an F-15E Strike Eagle aircraft

> high over the mountains above Peć, Kosovo's second largest city. Its target was a military communications tower located among a dozen houses laid out on an upland meadow above the city. About five miles from the tower, the "wizzo"—the weapons system officer—released a laser-guided munition with a camera lens on the tip which homed in on the target. The strike . . . severed the tower's metal

A munitions technician performs a final check on a missile before the aircraft takes off for a bombing run against Serbia. More than 23,000 bombs and missiles were fired by U.S. and allied forces.

frame from its concrete base. Now the mangled frame lies on its side across a water-filled bomb crater, located just twenty-five feet from the homes.[21]

During the attacks on fixed targets, our pilots skillfully used a top-secret weapon never before used in combat. An American aircraft ejected filaments that attached themselves to electric transmission lines, causing the grid systems to short out. The resulting blackouts caused economic dislocations, a sort of psychological warfare that sent the message to Serbia that although we hadn't destroyed their electricity supply, we could turn their lights out any time we wanted. Even these bombings, however, did not deter Milošević. Finally, on May 24, heavier bombs destroyed the electrical grid. "Hitting these yards," Ignatieff wrote, "turned out to be the single most effective military strike of the campaign. Everything from the computers which run a country's banking system to the systems which operate air-defense radar stations depends on the grid. Hitting it also sent a powerful message to the civilian population."[22] After the grid was destroyed, both the political elite and the people knew that NATO had secured control of the regime's central nervous system.

Two months after the air attacks began, a newspaper article described the fifty-eighth day of the air campaign. One of the targets destroyed that day was a large petroleum storage facility. In view of the intensity of the air attacks—over 1,200 planes were involved at their peak—and our tremendous capabilities to destroy fixed targets, the question arises as to why NATO hadn't taken out all the major petroleum storage facilities well before the attacks were about to enter their third month. It seemed logical to me that strikes against those petroleum storage facilities early in the campaign would have severely set back the Serbian military effort, saved lives, and contributed to an early conclusion of the war.

Reading about that particular attack, I recalled a book about World War II I had read decades earlier. In *Inside the Third Reich*, Albert Speer, Hitler's chief architect/industrialist, wrote that "the war could have been decided in 1943 if instead of vast but pointless area bombing the [Allied] planes had concentrated on the center of the Third Reich's armaments production. . . . In those days we anxiously asked ourselves how soon the enemy would realize that he could paralyze the production of thousands of armaments plants merely by destroying five or six relatively small targets."[23]

A NATO official made a similar point when he described the air attacks against fixed targets in Serbia: "We have hit one type of target air defense—petroleum or industry—on one day and then shifted to a whole different group the next. As a result we never finished the job in one category before moving on to the next."[24]

NATO forces may very well have had reasons for not destroying those petroleum storage facilities earlier than the fifty-eighth day of the air campaign. Nevertheless, I raise this issue for consideration by military planners.

Although the air attacks were conducted with overwhelming precision and professionalism, a tragedy and diplomatic fiasco occurred when smart weapons from a U.S. aircraft accidentally struck the Chinese embassy in Belgrade. Three people were killed and twenty wounded. The irony of this tragedy was the juxtaposition of high-tech weaponry and human error. The aircraft that launched the smart weapon, a B-2 Stealth bomber, had flown from Whitman Air Base in Missouri, fired the weapons, and then returned home nonstop. The flight lasted about seventeen hours, requiring multiple airborne refuelings.

The development and production of the B-2 strategic bomber was an incredible technical achievement. The weapons these planes launched were 2,000-pound bombs that sought out their targets with great precision. The Air Force testified that B-2s flew a total of forty-nine sorties and that "the B-2 with Joint Direct Attack Munitions (JDAM) was our only manned aircraft that could strike targets with precision in any weather. . . . Furthermore, the B-2 and JDAM demonstrated their impressive flexibility when we devised a procedure to retarget them in flight. This innovation proved crucial when addressing target changes during . . . en route time."[25]

In the Chinese embassy mishap, however, an intelligence technician used an "unclassified military map to try to pinpoint the building's location, based on a limited knowledge of addresses on a parallel street."[26] The intended target was the Yugoslav Federal Directorate of Supply and Procurement. The map identified that building as China's embassy. The Chinese had bought the building from the Serbian government and occupied it as their embassy for several years. Our intelligence community failed to note the change. This was a classic instance of Murphy's Law in operation. The most expensive and sophisticated military aircraft in history flew all the way from the United States, launched one of our most sophisticated weapons, and struck the wrong building because of a simple human error. The CIA technician involved was eventually fired and others received administrative punishment.

The B-2 was originally designed to have a crew of three, but it was decided to make it just two. This change freed space behind the two pilots. Before the seventeen-hour round-trip flight to Kosovo from Missouri, the pilots had been up for many hours to check out their aircraft and prepare for their mission. I was told that the two pilots of at least one of the flights went to their local Wal-Mart and purchased a $19 lawn chair—one that opened out into a chaise longue. They put it behind their seats and stretched out from time to time during their lengthy mission.

Aside from the B-2 that mistakenly hit the Chinese embassy, the missions against stationary targets were another stunning example of U.S. military capabilities. Lest we become overconfident, however, it must be kept in mind that although the Yugoslav military had purchased some relatively high-quality radars, much of the Serbs' air defense system consisted of equipment manufactured by the Soviets in the 1970s.

Air Attacks against Serb Forces in Kosovo

The Serbian targets in Kosovo—small troop concentrations, clusters of mobile tanks and trucks, towed artillery pieces, armored personnel carriers— were widely dispersed, hard to find, and extremely difficult to hit from high altitudes. Frequent bad weather also greatly impeded the pilots' efforts.

U.S. News & World Report quoted one NATO official as saying: "The campaign against mobile targets was a near failure."[27] A chart showed the discrepancy between the Serb military equipment that NATO declared destroyed and the number found by NATO ground troops after they entered Kosovo.

Serb military equipment	Number NATO claimed destroyed	Number found in Kosovo
Tanks, self-propelled artillery	110	26
Armored personnel carriers	210	12
Mortars, towed artillery	449	8

The Serbs did use decoy tanks to draw the fire of allied aircraft. Perhaps that accounts for the discrepancies. "You don't fight atrocities from an altitude of 15,000 feet," Ignatieff points out. "The extraordinary fact about the air war was that it was more effective against civilian infrastructure than against forces in the field. . . . The hard fact is that the mightiest air forces in the world were unable to destroy Milošević's army in the field."[28]

The Pentagon's *Kosovo/Operation Allied Force after-Action Report* read in part:

> Battle damage assessment and the evaluation of the effectiveness of allied attacks against the various targets in Serbia proper and Kosovo remained at the forefront of NATO and U.S. efforts and concerns. . . . Allied strikes against fixed targets including bridges, airfields, tunnels, bunkers, petroleum facilities, and other above ground facilities were highly successful and inflicted very limited collateral damage. However, Serbia's mobile Army and Interior forces presented a targeting and damage assessment challenge.[29]

My translation: In some situations, America's airpower and cruise missile capability can take out fixed targets almost at will, but successfully attacking mobile ground forces by aircraft in the terrain of Kosovo is a whole other ball game.

The commander of NATO's air war, Lieutenant General Michael Short, said on May 21, 1999: "If the alliance continues the bombing campaign for two more months, we will either kill their army or have it on the run." The air campaign had been going on for almost two months and approximately 25,000 sorties had been flown by that time. Nevertheless, it was being said that at least two more months and tens of thousands of additional sorties would be needed to attain the objectives.

Soon after, Pentagon spokesman Kenneth Bacon said, "No one can guarantee at this stage that the air campaign will produce all of the objectives by fall." Think about that for a moment. The air war had started in March 1999. The main proponent of the air attack, the State Department, thought limited attacks over a few days would force Milošević to sign a peace agreement. Ultimately, we used a higher percentage of our air assets than we had used during the Persian Gulf War or Vietnam. Now, two months into this massive air campaign, it was not certain that NATO's objectives could be achieved by airpower alone even after eight months of intense bombing. Keep in mind that these massive air attacks were against a fourth-rate military power with a minuscule GNP. Unlike the open terrain of Desert Storm, the mountainous and tree-covered terrain of Kosovo did not lend itself to an effective air campaign.

These observations do not detract from the enormous skill with which our pilots conducted their assigned missions. As General Wesley Clark noted in *Waging Modern War*: "The truth was that this was a theater with significant distances, no matter how small it might look on a map. Each mission for one of the single-seat F-16's, for example, was the equivalent of taking off in Washington and flying almost to Chicago before facing Serb defenses, then flying through hostile airspace, and returning to Washington. Usually two air-to-air refuelings were required, and flying times of five, six, seven, or more hours were routine."[30]

I went to Kosovo shortly after the war, accompanied by Greg Dahlberg of the committee staff and Charles Horner of the Pentagon. Greg later became undersecretary of the army and then acting secretary of the army. Subsequently he returned to the committee staff. It is a tribute to the professionalism of the staff that individuals of Greg's ability and stature serve as committee staffers. We went to the French and U.S. sectors. Both the French and the American commanders described a bleak situation in which relations between ethnic Albanians and ethnic Serbs were extremely tense.

The Kosovar refugees returning to their cities and villages from refugee camps in neighboring Albania and Macedonia found widespread destruction of homes and facilities, and no functioning government, police, or judicial system. We visited the Trepca mining facility in a section of Kosovo called Mitrovica. It was a Soviet-style complex of the 1950s that had produced batteries, fertilizer, and zinc before the war. At its peak it was the largest employer in Kosovo, employing 20,000 workers. It looked as though it had been abandoned for years. Most of the windows were broken, refuse was piled everywhere, and tanks and railroad cars filled with phosphoric and sulfuric acid were parked dangerously close to buildings.

One of the officials told us that whereas the participants in the ethnic conflict in Bosnia were tired of fighting by the end of the war, many of those who fought in Kosovo were looking forward to evening the score. Bosnia had a functioning government, but there was none in Kosovo. Clearly the cost of rebuilding Kosovo and maintaining Western troops there to keep the peace was going to be enormous.

It looks as though NATO forces will remain in Kosovo for many years. On a day-to-day basis they are involved in tedious police work. The tensions between ethnic groups and widespread economic deprivations remain throughout Kosovo. Miranda Vickers of the International Crisis Group wrote, "The international community, which aimed to make Kosovo a multiethnic protectorate, vastly underestimated the level of hatred between Serbs and Albanians. The West has now abandoned the phrase 'multiethnic society' and instead refers to 'peaceful coexistence,' but even that is wishful thinking at this late stage. A tolerant multiethnic society can only be achieved following a substantial period of political stability and economic development."[31]

Slobodan Milošević's record as president of Serbia and Yugoslavia—four wars fought and lost, ethnic cleansing, international economic sanctions, diplomatic isolation, and an economy in ruins—finally brought him down shortly after an election held on September 24, 2000. His major opponent, Vojislav Kostunica, won a decisive victory, but Milošević declared that his opponent had won less than 50 percent of the vote and a runoff was in order. In reaction to this brazen attempt to counter the will of the people, hundreds of thousands of demonstrators stormed the parliament building, the state television station, coal mines, and other key sites. The people's tolerance of his repressive dictatorship had finally run out. When the military and the police refused to follow orders to fire tear gas and take other steps to crush the rebellion, Milošević's resolve quickly crumbled.

An article in the *Washington Post* revealed how out of touch with reality he had become. "Milošević began his campaign this summer genuinely believing he could win the election. When he lost it, he believed he could steal it. And when he couldn't steal it, he believed—finally and desperately—that the police and the army would crush the people to keep him in power. He was wrong on all counts." One of his opponents said, "Milošević did not foresee those faces in Belgrade. They were not middle-class faces. Those were faces with real anger in their eyes, the faces of workers and peasants who had come to the capital to finish the job."[32]

Although Milošević was still in power at the end of the allied air campaign, clearly those massive air attacks had been the key factor in his downfall. Ultimately, however, he was overthrown by ground troops. Those ground troops did not have tanks, artillery, or mortars. They did, however, have enormous numbers and a will to succeed. The ground troops who overthrew him were the hundreds of thousands of Serbian citizens he had driven beyond endurance.

10

SEPTEMBER 11, 2001

Just as earlier generations of Americans remember where they were on December 7, 1941, when Pearl Harbor was attacked, all of us will remember for the rest of our lives where we were when we found out about the tragic terrorist attacks of September 11, 2001. When the planes struck the twin towers of the World Trade Center, I was in the Capitol, where the House Defense Appropriations Subcommittee was meeting to decide on the funding levels for the many programs requested by the Defense Department for fiscal 2002. My wife, Joyce, was also in the Capitol, where she was about to begin a meeting with other members of the executive board of the First Ladies' Library.

Soon after the attacks on the World Trade Center, the Capitol was ordered evacuated because of a belief that it might very well be a target. People were milling around outside when security personnel said, "Folks, this is the real thing. We don't want you anywhere near the Capitol." I ran into Joyce and we started to walk up the street to get some coffee until we could reenter the Capitol. As we walked up Pennsylvania Avenue, we heard a loud boom. Apparently, it was the sonic boom from a jet fighter deployed to the area. Suddenly in the distance we could see smoke billowing up from the Pentagon. I learned later in the morning that a plane that probably had been heading for the Capitol or the White House had crashed in Pennsylvania, in the congressional district I represent. We all owe a deep debt of gratitude to those heroic passengers who foiled the terrorists' plan on that aircraft. Had the plane struck the Capitol, few lives on the ground might have been lost because we had all been evacuated, but the destruction of that magnificent

Although fewer lives were lost and less property was destroyed at the Pentagon than at the World Trade Center, the fact that terrorists were able to attack the nerve center of our national security operations strained belief.

building surmounted by the massive Princess of Freedom statue would have been a terrible psychological blow to America.

Terrorism and the Changing Nature of America's Enemies

My concern about terrorism and the lack of an adequate counterterrorism effort began in the early 1990s. It was triggered by the poison gas attack in the Tokyo subway by an extremist cult, the attack against the World Trade Center in 1993, and, ironically, the stunning success of the United States and our allies in the Persian Gulf War. The attacks in Tokyo and New York killed few people, but they could easily have been a major catastrophe. What particularly struck me at the time was how vulnerable a modern society can be to unconventional attacks. In 1995, in the aftermath of those attacks, I offered an amendment (which was accepted) to include an additional $50 million in the defense appropriations bill to fund a program to give the National Guard and the Reserves the capability to counter bioterrorism. The increased funds met with a lukewarm response by the National Guard, since such a program was beyond the scope of their mission at that time. Today National Guard units in twenty-seven states have such a capability. I have offered similar amendments over the years to increase funding for the antiterrorism effort.

After the fall of the Berlin Wall in 1989 and the decisive victory in the Persian Gulf War, it appeared much less likely that America's core national security interests would be challenged in conventional war. That belief does not detract from our need to enhance our capability to meet any challenge. Indeed, remaining rigorously prepared to conduct conventional warfare is the best insurance policy against such a threat. In light of our awesome capability to effectively counter any such challenge, however, it seemed to me likely that our enemies would turn to asymmetrical warfare—that is, unconventional low-tech attacks at our most vulnerable points.

In early 2001 the U.S. Commission on National Security/21st Century, whose co-chairmen were former senators Gary Hart and Warren Rudman, published a study that read in part:

> One of the Commission's most important conclusions . . . was that attacks against American citizens on American soil, possibly causing heavy casualties, are likely over the next quarter century. This is because both the technical means for such attacks and the array of actors who might use such means are proliferating despite the best efforts of American diplomacy.
>
> These attacks may involve weapons of mass destruction and mass disruption. . . . America's present global predominance . . . makes the American homeland more appealing as a target, while America's openness and freedoms make it more vulnerable.[1]

America's major wars of the twentieth century were conventional responses to aggression. With terrorism, aggression has taken on a whole new dimension. In the days after September 11, David Kennedy wrote, "nothing was more eerie and unsettling than the silence of our attackers and their studied refusal to specify their demands." Their aim was not simply to destroy the buildings they targeted but to demoralize us, "not to seize territory but to sow chaos, not to conquer so much as cripple and corrupt. They are targeting not only our lives and property but also our most fundamental values, including our commitments to personal liberty and to the institutions of an open society."[2]

It is remarkable how low-tech the weaponry and tactics of our enemies have been in many conflicts over the past decades. For example:

- As I can personally attest, during much of the Vietnam War, a major fear was stepping on a punji spike or being shot in a hit-and-run ambush.
- In Lebanon in 1983 we withdrew after 241 Marines were killed in a terrorist attack carried out by a fanatic driving a dump truck filled with dynamite.
- We left Somalia after a militia group shot down a U.S. helicopter with a rocket-propelled grenade. When our troops went to carry out a rescue mission, they were fired on with elementary weapons in the congested streets of Mogadishu, one of the most impoverished cities in the world.
- In the Balkans, the atrocities that caused us and our NATO allies to intervene were often committed by people with ethnic and religious scores to settle, using rifles and pistols.

Shortly after September 11, Secretary of State Colin Powell made the point that while the planning for the attacks was complex and involved, carrying them out was remarkably simple. Indeed, while the twin towers succumbed to the fire caused by the impact of jet aircraft with full loads of fuel, the weapons with which the terrorists commandeered the aircraft were box cutters and a fake bomb.

Shortly after Bush, then governor of Texas, was elected president but before he was inaugurated, he invited a number of members of Congress to Austin to discuss national security issues. We sat around a table and expressed our views in turn. I said, "I recognize the highest priority defense issue in your party's platform is the rapid development and deployment of a limited national missile defense to counter the potential of a missile attack from a nation such as North Korea or Iraq. Personally, I think a much more probable danger is a terrorist attack." I added that nuclear proliferation was my other major concern.

According to the Office of Management and Budget (OMB), the pre–September 11 defense budget submitted to Congress included a 59 percent increase in research and development for missile defense while the proposed funds for antiterrorist programs for all national security accounts would increase by only 3 percent. My disagreement with the emphasis on the missile defense program may be simplistic, but it was logical to me. On the one hand, it would take an enormous and extremely expensive effort for a rogue state to develop even a few operational international missiles with warheads capable of carrying weapons of mass destruction—programs that we could detect as they attempted to bring them to fruition. Also, the ultimate deterrent for the use of such a weapon against us is the knowledge that our satellites would immediately know where it had been fired from, and that rogue nation would quickly become a FORON (former rogue nation). (If the Pentagon can have thousands of acronyms, I thought I was entitled to devise at least one.)

On the other hand, low-technology weapons of mass destruction are relatively inexpensive to develop and much more difficult to trace. Consider shipping containers loaded with explosives or even more dangerous substances set off at key transportation or industrial nodes. The Coast Guard and Customs Service manage to inspect only 2 percent of the million-odd containers that are unloaded in U.S. ports every month. "It would be a simple matter," Thomas G. Donlan points out, "—simpler at least than hijacking four airliners simultaneously—to equip a container with a satellite navigation system and a communications device to let a controller know the container's precise location. The communications device—a cell phone, for example—could also trigger something dangerous in the container's cargo." Donlan quotes Coast Guard Commander Stephen Flynn as saying that "shipping companies controlled by Osama bin Laden have owned 20 freighters that the Coast Guard knows about."[3]

A so-called dirty nuclear device is a conventional explosive surrounded by fissile material. Granted, development of such a device is a significant technical challenge, but it is infinitely easier than developing an intercontinental missile with a warhead capable of carrying a weapon of mass destruction. I make these points not to detract from the desirability of a national missile defense program but to put in perspective the kind of attack

On September 12, 2001, I toured the crash site of United Flight 93 in Shanksville, Pennsylvania, about twelve miles by air from my hometown of Johnstown. The phrase "Let's Roll" became a clarion call of America's will to defeat terrorism. (AP Photo/Gene J. Puskar)

we are most likely to face and to emphasize the need for homeland security programs that will effectively counter these much more probable scenarios. The fiscal 2002 budget submitted to Congress, however, reflected the opposite priority.

In recognition of this reality, the House Defense Appropriations Subcommittee, under the leadership of Chairman Jerry Lewis, trimmed numerous accounts in the defense budget request (including $400 million from the $3.1 billion requested increase for missile defense research) and created a new $1.67 billion account to boost key counterterrorism programs. The newly created Counterterrorism and Operational Response Fund accelerates promising work to improve our defenses against chemical and biological agents at home and abroad, and will accelerate development of our defenses against other unconventional threats, such as an attack on our key computer systems. The funds will also be used to accelerate promising research on new anthrax and smallpox treatments and vaccines, speed up the procurement and deployment of the latest technology to detect biological warfare agents, expand the stockpiles of critical antibiotics and vaccines, conduct training exercises across the United States for first responders to attacks by weapons of mass destruction, train more military teams to respond to chemical and biological pathogens, and improve our capability to track down terrorists' money-laundering and other financial activities.

The Congress also agreed with my proposal to increase the budget by $75 million to implement a new nuclear protection program to detect nuclear devices hidden in trucks, ships, or other vehicles. This program, which follows the recommendations of the prestigious Defense Science Board, is to be conducted jointly by the Defense Department's Defense Threat Reduction Agency and the Energy Department's National Security Administration, so that they can pool their nuclear detection equipment, array it in a networking system, and demonstrate its effectiveness for protecting both military and civilian ports, airfields, and other key installations. The experts believe effective detection technology already exists; the main hurdles are the networking and integration of those systems. With proper organization and a relatively modest commitment of resources, I believe we can significantly improve our defense against unconventional nuclear attack. In all, for fiscal year 2002, the Congress increased the funding for national security programs aimed specifically at the terrorist threat from the proposed 3 percent to over 29 percent. The administration submitted a much more robust budget for the antiterrorism effort in fiscal year 2003.

Despite our success in routing the Taliban and Osama bin Laden from Afghanistan, we are in the early stages of a long battle against terrorism. Unless some rogue nation threatens us, I believe that over the long run the war against terrorism will be analogous to the war against drugs—a series of small-scale interdictions and actions taken by military, intelligence, and law enforcement personnel around the world.

It is absolutely essential to maintain a global coalition in this long battle. As President Bush said in his address to a joint session of Congress shortly after the attack, "there are thousands of terrorists operating in over sixty countries." Clearly we will need the cooperation of the intelligence, military, and law enforcement communities of many other countries if we are ultimately to achieve victory against the terrorists.

Having a robust and effective American diplomatic presence in countries around the world is also essential in the fight against terrorism. From my perspective, many members of Congress and business leaders have had a schizophrenic approach to America's role abroad since the end of the Cold

War. On the one hand, they are totally supportive of free international trade and the rapid expansion of American companies throughout the world. On the other, they have been reluctant to support the steps necessary to enable the U.S. government to have a robust presence abroad in pursuit of that and other objectives. Indeed, the State Department's budget proposals and any kind of foreign aid have been the favorite punching bags of many members of Congress over the years. Yet we expect our State Department to be the first line of communication to help resolve international crises. I have found inadequate communications equipment and staffing at many U.S. embassies.

Earlier I made the point that my on-site inspections convinced me that the United Nations' military capabilities are inadequate for anything but basic peacekeeping functions. I have also been critical of the Security Council's penchant for passing sweeping resolutions that set goals the UN has neither the will nor the capability to achieve. Nevertheless, in the fight against international terrorism, I believe it is essential for a cooperative effort to be worked out within the framework of UN resolutions. It is imperative that the war on terrorism not evolve into or be perceived as a U.S.-only operation. The passage of well-conceived United Nations resolutions is important for those coalition partners that have large Muslim populations. Some nations participating in this effort may have to keep political distance between themselves and the United States, and UN resolutions and initiatives can help in that respect.

11

Reflecting on the Past/Looking to the Future

I have been very fortunate in being able to combine my military experience with my service in Congress to help develop a more effective fighting force for our country. Over the years in which I have observed U.S. forces deployed in combat and in peacekeeping missions, I have learned many lessons. So have our government and our military. However, although there have been some stunning successes, often administrations have tended to underestimate or misinterpret these lessons when they formulated and executed policy.

The Importance of Intelligence

When I was an intelligence officer in Vietnam, Marine Gunnery Sergeant Wolf gave me a plaque bearing the words "Victory is knowing your enemy." I cannot stress enough the importance of those words.

The United States' intelligence arsenal is vast. Its satellites provide photographic, signal, voice, weather, and location information to our forces; intelligence aircraft provide photo surveillance, electronic surveillance, and signals intelligence; specialists in almost any country you can name analyze the data; HUMINT and other programs supplement these efforts. In addition, tactical military intelligence systems provide massive amounts of information on the locations of enemy troop concentrations and their communications. The United States' civilian and military intelligence infrastructure dwarfs that of any other country in the world.

In all the crises I have witnessed, the common thread has been the importance of intelligence. The intelligence challenges have ranged from the macro to the micro. In Vietnam, would China intervene if the bombing of North Vietnam was escalated? Where were the Viet Cong's tunnels? In Lebanon, which of the intelligence reports of a threatened terrorist attack against our troops was credible? In Panama, where had General Noriega gone in the aftermath of our intervention? In the Persian Gulf, how effective would the Iraqi forces be? In Somalia, where was Aideed? In Afghanistan, where was Osama bin Laden? What is the status of Iraq's effort to build weapons of mass destruction?

Robert M. Gates, then director of the CIA, stated in December 1992:

> In reality it is the daily collection and analysis of millions of bits of information that consume nearly all of our resources and fuel the decision-making process. Who is killing whom in Bosnia? How long are the runways in Somalia? Where are the 30,000 nuclear warheads in Russia and who controls them? How far along is Libya's chemical weapons plant? To whom is North Korea selling its missiles? . . . What are the frequencies of Iranian radars? These and thousands of other questions pour in to us twenty-four hours a day from policy makers, the military, and the Congress—all three with insatiable appetites for information.[1]

I have been greatly concerned about the deployment of American forces to countries that are so peripheral to our national interests that we have very little intelligence about them. Vernon Loeb wrote in the *Washington Post* about the CIA contingent in Somalia. Garret Jones, "a former Miami police detective, . . . had just finished a year's study at the Army War College in Carlisle, Pa., where he'd written a paper on UN peacekeeping missions' need for a dedicated structure for analyzing intelligence. Three other temporary station chiefs had already rotated in and out of Somalia, and Jones was the only candidate left back at Langley who wanted to go and knew anything about Africa." Jones's aide in Mogadishu, John Spinelli, had arrived just a week before Jones, having been torn from a plum assignment in the CIA's Rome station. He knew nothing about Africa, but he spoke Italian, and the Italians in the UN peacekeeping force weren't getting along with their American counterparts. When Spinelli took Jones to the CIA station, the new chief's jaw dropped: It consisted of two windblown rooms in the vandalized former residence of the U.S. ambassador. Only one room had a door. Spinelli told him they had no business being in the middle of this war zone, trying to meet secretly with agents in a city where they couldn't drive down the street without getting shot at.[2]

Over the decades the capabilities and effectiveness of our national intelligence programs have fluctuated. Accurate and timely intelligence is the ultimate force multiplier—that is, the key to using our military effectively. A robust and effective intelligence capability is absolutely central to our national security posture.

In 1993 I offered an amendment to the defense appropriations bill that set up and funded a National Drug Intelligence Center (NDIC). Over the years I had noticed the lack of cooperation and policy coordination among the proliferation of agencies involved in the effort to counter illegal drug trafficking. It is a simple fact of life that bureaucracies are so turf-conscious that they frequently fail to share information with each other even if they have the same goals. NDIC brought together officials from all of the agencies involved and has streamlined the antidrug intelligence effort.

As we have seen in the investigations and revelations of the events leading up to September 11, the failure to connect the dots was at least partly attributable to the lack of coordination among the many agencies and departments involved in the intelligence component of the antiterrorism effort.

Criteria for Deployment of U.S. Forces

The vast majority of Americans agree that the United States should maintain a strong international military presence and be willing to use its military power when appropriate. As Joseph S. Nye Jr. wrote: "Polls show that the American people are neither isolationist nor eager to serve as the world's police."[3] It is distressing to contemplate the number of conflicts and atrocities around the world. As the undisputed world leader, the United States will increasingly be called upon to intervene militarily in a wide variety of situations. So we must be extremely cautious about when, where, and for what purpose we deploy our troops.

In the last two decades the most successful U.S. military interventions have been those in which a clear national security issue was involved and decisive force was used to attain our objectives. The classic example is the Persian Gulf War. A nation important to the United States and NATO had been invaded and stability in a key region of the world with vital economic resources was threatened. The United States and its allies reacted decisively. Congress authorized military action and the American people overwhelmingly supported it. So did the Kuwaitis. In the intervention in Panama, the key factors were the long historical ties between our two countries, the strategic importance of the Panama Canal, the stealing of the election by Noriega and his cronies, and the mistreatment of American citizens by Noriega's troops. Again the United States acted decisively. Ninety percent of the Panamanian people supported U.S. intervention. In Afghanistan our national security was clearly jeopardized by the Taliban's provision of a safe haven for bin Laden's al-Qaeda terrorist organization. A massive bombing campaign combined with effective ground attacks by our Afghan allies and American Special Forces rapidly defeated the major Taliban contingents. Once again, the vast majority of Afghans supported our efforts; they had had enough of the oppressive policies of the medieval-like Taliban regime.

Conversely, when U.S. military interventions have failed, the vital national security interests of the United States were not involved and we did not act decisively. In Lebanon our troops were in an untenable geographic position and our force was not large enough to carry out the mission effectively. In Somalia a well-meaning humanitarian intervention ended in failure because we interjected ourselves into a civil war. I am not arguing that we should have acted decisively with a larger military force in either case. As I have explained, I opposed the intervention in Somalia from the day the decision to intervene was made.

When the decision was made to deploy the United Nations troops in a peacemaking role in Bosnia, the initial insertion of those forces was tepid and they did not end the violence. After the Dayton Accords were signed, however, a large force was deployed, including a significant American contingent. Those troops made it clear that if they were fired upon, they would react massively and decisively; they would adhere to the doctrine of disproportionate response. Here again the Powell doctrine worked. Relative peace ensued.

In the air war in Serbia and Kosovo, the initial limited air attacks escalated steadily to massive and prolonged bombing. Once again a weak military response had to be intensified. In the end the NATO forces had to issue a credible threat of massive invasion by ground forces and the people had to revolt en masse before success was achieved.

Our military forces have frequently been deployed for short periods to deliver food and other supplies after a natural disaster. Such humanitarian missions are laudable, but they have to be chosen very carefully. Michael O'Hanlon of the Brookings Institution has written:

> For a humanitarian intervention to be wise and ethical, it must be attempted only if the odds are excellent that it will make a bad situation better and not worse. Intervening to stop Russia from killing tens of thousands of innocent Chechens, for instance, would have risked a major-power war between nuclear-weapon states with the potential to kill far more people than the intervention could have saved. Invading North Korea to bring food to its starving people would probably precipitate all-out war on the peninsula, quite possibly killing as many civilians in Seoul (to say nothing of soldiers on both sides of the war) as the food aid would save in North Korea. Entering into the Angolan civil war would force us to choose sides between our former anti-Communist associate Jonas Savimbi, a maniacal killer who has violated two major peace accords, and the corrupt dos Santos government.[4]

David Fromkin provides a perspective on the intervention in Somalia that applies far beyond that particular crisis:

> One lesson of Somalia was that there is no such thing as a purely humanitarian intervention. A military intervention in a foreign country, unless undertaken at the request of its government, is political. It occurs because the United States, believing that the other country isn't being ruled properly, acts to overthrow the local leadership; but of course that obliges America to take over the government itself. . . .
>
> Somalia should have taught Americans that invading, occupying and administering a foreign country may not be as easy as it looks at first. Above all, the lesson of Somalia was that, even in the absence of enemy great powers . . . , America is not completely free to make the world do as Americans wish.[5]

In June 2000 the *New York Times Magazine* quoted Richard Holbrooke, then U.S. ambassador to the United Nations, as saying that he disagreed with Henry Kissinger's view that "you don't get in these things unless your chance of success is 85 to 90 percent." He could understand that view during the Cold War, Holbrooke said, when "any setback to the United States was a gain for the Soviet Union, but in the post–Cold War world, where the United States is the single leader and great things are expected of us, we should try even if our chances of success are less than 50 percent."[6]

I have known Richard Holbrooke for many years. He is a dynamic and courageous man. However, I disagree with him on this issue. First of all, we must remember that although we are the world's largest military power, the size of our military has shrunk dramatically since the end of the Cold War. While peacekeeping missions may not involve a large number of troops by wartime standards, those numbers are far from negligible. The United States had 6,000 troops in Bosnia and 4,000 in Kosovo. Those 10,000 military personnel were overwhelmingly from one branch—the Army. Troops sent on peacekeeping missions serve in six-month rotations, so we are talking about 20,000 personnel a year from one of the services. Add those involved in training and supporting those troops and you are talking about a fairly significant number. A related problem is that the nature of the peacekeeping mission inevitably causes a short-term decline in the fighting capability of the deployed units. In February 2001 the Third Infantry Division, which had units deployed on a peacekeeping mission in the Balkans, was downgraded "to the Army's second-lowest rating for wartime readiness, effectively removing it from its traditional role: standing by to defend the nation."[7] Granted, that downgrade was temporary, only until the division could resume its training for its traditional role, but any decline in war-readiness is troubling, and it becomes more so when the same U.S. military units are deployed for peacekeeping and humanitarian missions time after time.

If serious consideration is being given to sending American troops to a country whose importance to our national security is not clear, it is especially important for policy makers to ascertain the relative strength of our interests and those of our adversaries. Nina Serafino of the Congressional Research Service wrote: "Some situations may not be winnable with limited force because the opponent has a much greater interest in the outcome than the intervening parties, and thus is willing to sustain greater costs and to cede only in the face of a crushing defeat. Once committed to an intervention in such circumstances, the intervening party is faced with a Hobson's choice: to bear much higher costs than originally anticipated, or to withdraw."[8]

As our policy evolved in Somalia, for example, Aideed and his clan had a much greater interest in the outcome of events than we did. The average

American was concerned about the suffering and hunger in Somalia but couldn't have cared less about who the clan leaders were.

I think the greatest danger of military deployments to countries of minimal interest to the United States' security is the loss of credibility if we suffer setbacks and have to withdraw. We risk being seen as an unreliable ally by nations that are important to our national security. And the case for military intervention for humanitarian missions loses its strength in comparison with the enormous effort we must commit to fighting terrorism.

These are the major criteria I would apply to the deployment of U.S. troops:

- The mission should be related to our national security.
- The mission should be clear and achievable.
- We must know ahead of time the implications of failure and being forced to leave without achieving our objectives (the key question is not how we get out but why we are getting in).
- The force deployed must be large enough to achieve the objectives with minimal casualties.
- The force must be sustainable.
- Decision makers should be cautious about being overly affected by reports in the media.
- Rules of engagement should be forceful and clear.
- Congress and our allies should be consulted early and frequently.

The Quality of America's Armed Forces

It is absolutely essential to retain high-quality personnel in our armed forces. Over the years the quality of personnel has fluctuated. After the great performance of U.S. troops in the 1990s, we tend to forget that in the late 1970s and early 1980s the quality of many of our personnel was a problem, morale was low, and there was a significant drug problem. When I made an inspection trip to the Marine Corps boot camp at Parris Island, South Carolina, in 1979, a drill instructor said, "Congressman, I hate to tell you this, but if there was a war, I don't believe these guys would fight." I passed his comment along to the Marine commandant.

Shortly after that I conducted a surprise inspection at the Marine Corps headquarters in Virginia. I found the morale abysmal. Marines were selling blankets and other government gear to get money for drugs. Soon the Marine Corps downsized by a total of 10,000 troops, removing the least qualified. After a zero-tolerance drug policy was instituted, the quality of our forces improved significantly. I believe our highest priority should be the recruitment and retention of high-quality personnel in all the services.

The Quantity of America's Armed Forces

Many people simply do not realize how many personnel are needed to conduct military operations. It would seem that the proliferation of high-tech weapons would reduce the number of personnel required, but that is not the case.

During the early days of the Persian Gulf War, we all marveled at the pictures on our TV screens of the smart bombs dropped down the airshaft of the Iraqi Air Defense Headquarters and on other Iraqi military facilities. Those missions seemed to involve only a handful of pilots and aircraft. What we did not see was the massive support required for success:

- The crews of the aircraft jamming and suppressing the Iraqi radars and communications to ensure that the attack aircraft involved in the actual bombing could successfully carry out their missions.
- The crews flying the intelligence aircraft to support the attack mission.
- The ground crews and mechanics keeping all of these aircraft combat ready.
- The logisticians, perimeter defense personnel, motor pool mechanics, ammunition technicians, cooks, chaplains, and administrative personnel at the air bases in Saudi Arabia.
- The soldiers and technicians manning the Patriot anti-air missile systems defending those bases.

In addition to the personnel directly involved in those operations, a vast array of other personnel labored in support roles around the world:

- The technicians who operated the control centers responsible for the reconnaissance satellite systems involved in target selection and gathering of other intelligence data for the deployed troops.

- The technicians who operated the control centers responsible for the satellite signals intelligence systems.
- The linguists and analysts who interpreted the information received from those satellite systems.
- The personnel that operated the Defense Department's international communications network, transmitting vast amounts of data to operators in the field.
- The personnel that ran the vast international supply network supporting Operation Desert Storm.

An analogous situation is the aircraft carrier task force group whose awesome capabilities played such a central role in the war in Afghanistan. The actual size of an aircraft carrier task force varies with the purpose and scope of its mission. Typically there are about 8,000 sailors in a task force—5,000 on the carrier and 3,000 on the escort ships. These "floating airfields" enable the United States to deploy a great military asset to distant corners of the globe.

An aircraft carrier typically has about 85 planes: 50 combat aircraft and the additional aircraft to serve such functions as jamming the enemy's radar emissions, performing reconnaissance, bringing provisions to the task force, and rescuing downed pilots. Many highly skilled personnel are required to keep these aircraft operational. The ship's communications centers and their navigation and radar systems must be staffed twenty-four hours a day. All of the thousands of sailors in a carrier task force, from jet pilots to cooks, fulfill roles required for the successful missions of the 60 combat aircraft on the carrier.

A global network of ground stations is processing information from satellites and other sources to provide information to the carrier task force. A typical U.S. manufacturing company operates 40 hours a week—8 hours a day, 5 days a week. Many of our national defense programs providing non-stop information to our military around the world must operate 24 hours a day, 7 days a week—168 hours a week. When vacation time and holidays are factored in, the national security operations for receiving, processing, and disseminating this information need almost five shifts to carry out their duties.

Also, a large percentage of the thousands of sailors in a task force have spouses and children at bases back in the States, requiring personnel to provide medical care, housing, and other services. Those bases have other personnel to maintain their infrastructure. The ports and harbors where the carrier task force is based must be dredged. When the carrier task force returns to its home port, the planes must be repaired and upgraded and the ships must undergo maintenance and occasional complete overhauls. Thus, although the actual number of naval *attack* aircraft in one carrier task force is about 50, tens of thousands of support personnel are needed to enable the pilots to carry out their missions successfully. We must not lose sight of the sheer size and complexity of the effort involved in having these capabilities always available to carry out America's national security objectives.

Airpower

Since its first use in warfare, airpower has had a significant impact on the outcome of numerous battles and wars. Air attacks played the central role in achieving NATO's goals in Serbia. Airpower, ranging from B-52 bomber attacks against large troop concentrations and supply nodes to F-4 fighter aircraft, attack helicopters, and C-130 gunships for close air support, was essential to our effort in Vietnam. The air attacks against Libya ordered by President Reagan ended state-sponsored terrorism by that country. In the Persian Gulf War, weeks of the most intensive bombing since World War II inflicted extensive damage to Saddam Hussein's defense infrastructure and significantly weakened the Iraqi forces in Kuwait before the allied ground invasion. And in Afghanistan, the use of smart bombs and laser guidance by ground forces to pinpoint targets and the introduction of UAV's (unmanned aerial vehicles) armed with Hellfire missiles helped bring an extraordinary victory over the Taliban and al-Qaeda forces. Indeed, writes Karl Mueller, there have been "revolutionary advances in munitions guidance, aircraft sensors, flight simulators, and battle management, together with more evolutionary developments in airframe, engine, and other technologies."[9] Despite these stunning advances and successes, I believe America must not become overconfident of the ability of airpower to resolve complex foreign policy crises.

U.S. forces and our South Vietnam allies did not prevail in Vietnam, despite our overwhelming advantage in the air. The Soviets found in Afghanistan that their air superiority—indeed, their opponents had no air assets—could not prevent their defeat by sophisticated anti-air weaponry and a focused guerrilla force. In the Persian Gulf War, despite the enormous allied bombing effort, Kuwait was retaken by land forces in tanks and armored vehicles in a classic ground invasion. Of the total kills of Iraqi tanks during the Persian Gulf War, 21 percent were destroyed by air forces over forty-four days and 79 percent by ground forces over four days. The statistics for destroyed Iraqi artillery are similar—75 percent destroyed by ground forces and 24 percent by air attacks. In 1998, Tomahawk cruise missiles launched against the terrorist camps of Osama bin Laden in Afghanistan and the suspected terrorist facility in Sudan did not achieve the intended objectives. In Serbia, despite the fact that 40 percent of America's air assets were used, along with a significant air contribution by our allies, and 23,000 bombs and missiles were launched, Milošević backed down only after he was convinced that a massive intervention by NATO ground forces into Kosovo was imminent. For discussion purposes, let us assume, as many people have done, that it was the air war alone that caused Milošević to back down. As John Keegan wrote in the *Wall Street Journal,* "It was the destruction of the Serb civilian infrastructure rather than the direct attack on the Third Army that eventually persuaded Slobodan Milošević to withdraw his troops."[10]

Relying exclusively on airpower to stop atrocities in less developed countries is unlikely to be effective. Ivo Daalder and Michael O'Hanlon wrote:

> In many of the worst civil and ethnic wars around the world there are few strategic and armored targets ripe for air attack. Coercive bombing is also unlikely to be of much use, since atrocities are often committed by militias or rebel forces that do not have clear dependencies or vulnerabilities that can be targeted by airpower. . . . A B-2 bomber simply is not a very effective instrument to stop genocide committed largely with machetes or machine guns. That task calls for ground troops—and usually more rather than less. And once troops are deployed, the aim must be to achieve the objective decisively in order to minimize risks to U.S. and allied forces. To do so requires decisive force, rather than gradual escalation. . . .
>
> Far from heralding a new age of humanitarian intervention, the war in Kosovo highlights the difficulty of pursuing such a course.

The single most important lesson of the conflict is that there is no cheap, easy way to prevent genocide or mass killing. Airpower alone will not generally determine what transpires on the ground. Only when paired with ground forces—and only if used decisively—can airpower be expected to work. That, of course, raises the cost of using force, making it more important that operations enjoy international legitimacy and that allies and others bear their full share of the burden.[11]

Another cautionary note about overreliance on airpower: the United States must be careful when it decides the threshold for intervening militarily. We should not lower the threshold by thinking, "Since we're most likely to suffer only minimal casualties by using airpower, we should act." We must always strive to minimize our casualties, but making a policy decision to intervene with airpower alone could lead to the deployment of ground troops if our objectives are not attained through airpower alone. If the country is of such marginal national security interest to the United States that we would not consider deploying ground troops there otherwise, we should think long and carefully before we send in those aircraft.

Despite these reservations, I strongly support upgrading America's weaponry and combat support systems. In addition to the high-profile weapons procurement programs, the technological capabilities of tactical intelligence, communications, and other functions for application in the use of future weapon systems are being increased dramatically.

United Nations Military Deployments

In recent years the United States' military involvements have been in concert with the United Nations. With so many crises arising in countries outside of our traditional vital national security interests, it is logical that the United Nations has been the leader in developing the international community's response. My on-site inspections and observations, however, have given me serious reservations about the capability of the United Nations to carry out large-scale military missions effectively, as I told President Clinton in 1993. When a peacekeeping mission develops into a combat operation, it has crossed the line into territory for which the UN is unequipped. I recall Speaker Tom Foley saying, "Never shake your fist at someone first and then point your finger at them later." This is what the United Nations has done too often. Time after time the ambitious goals embodied in UN resolutions have outstripped the political will and capability of the United Nations to act decisively. (It must be admitted that these impractical resolutions have often been supported and even inspired by the United States.) In Somalia, as I noted earlier, the United States was scaling back its role significantly just as the UN, with the support of our government, was expanding its goals—a recipe for disaster.

A few years after the UN left Somalia, a UN contingent of fifty-one Dutch soldiers was captured by Serb forces in Bosnia. In response to their capture, the Security Council adopted Resolution 1004, which, as William Shawcross explains, demanded that the Bosnian Serbs "leave Srebrenica immediately. It demanded that all the parties respect the status of Srebrenica as a safe area. It demanded that the Bosnian Serbs release immediately all UN personnel they had detained. It demanded immediate access to Srebrenica for the Red Cross and other humanitarian agencies. As the resolution was passed, General Mladić was still holding the Dutch peacekeepers captive. . . . The demands and the threats of the Security Council meant nothing."[12]

Five years after that fiasco, in May 2000, Richard Holbrooke reflected on a new hostage-taking in the West African country of Sierra Leone: "I must say . . . that the sight of UN peacekeepers being taken hostage by murderous thugs in Sierra Leone five years to the week after UN peacekeepers were similarly taken hostage by murderous thugs in Bosnia is not only outrageous but sobering."[13]

Passing tough-sounding resolutions that cannot or will not be carried out has a twofold effect. The hopes of the suffering parties are raised falsely; then, when the resolutions and tough rhetoric are not acted upon or ineffectively enforced, further UN pronouncements are not taken seriously.

The United Nations' inability to conduct military operations effectively and the United States' understandable reluctance to send ground forces on humanitarian missions to countries of minimal interest to its security presents a serious problem. A strong case can be made for the international community to intervene to stop violence and atrocities, but this is a moral issue, not a strategic one. I believe that U.S. military involvement in such situations (if it is required) should be limited to operations such as airlift, logistics, communications, tactical intelligence, and training. To the extent practicable, the ground forces for these UN operations should come from nations in the region and from developed countries whose foreign policy embraces the military intervention. Efforts must continue to be made to upgrade the UN's ability to conduct these missions.

Conclusion

Martin Wolf, paraphrasing the opening of Charles Dickens's *Tale of Two Cities*, gave his perspective on the twentieth century: "It was the worst of centuries. It was the best of centuries. It was the age of progress; it was the age of madness. Never before has humanity made such leaps in knowledge and wealth. Never before has it suffered such cruelties and frailties."[14] Those few sentences capture the irony of the last century. It saw unspeakable violence by human beings against human beings—over 100 million deaths in warfare between nations, in civil conflicts, in atrocities committed by tyrants against their own people, and by ethnic and religious groups against each other. But that same century brought enormous increases in longevity, health, wealth, communications, and quality of life.

To ensure that the scourge of terrorism is defeated and the horrors of the twentieth century are not repeated, it is vital that the United States conducts a vigorous and engaged foreign policy, complemented by a superior military capability. Richard Hart Sinnreich wrote: "Historically, the most profound strategic transformations, from the French Revolution to the collapse of the Soviet Union, have burst upon the world unheralded. Not one of America's major military conflicts in this century was anticipated. As late as 1991, only two years after the Iron Curtain evaporated, America found itself at war in the Persian Gulf with an adversary that only months earlier had been considered a regional ally."[15]

I believe the most important lesson of the twentieth century for America is that we can expect our national security to be challenged when our military is weak or when we are perceived as being irresolute. The meager capability of our armed forces before World War I and World War II and the precipitous downsizing of our defense budget after each war should be lesson enough. When America entered World War II in 1941 our army was seventeenth in the world in size. Within five years after the end of World War II, we were engaged in another major conflict in Korea. Once again we were unprepared. (As I noted earlier, when I joined the Marine Corps as a teenager during the Korean War, I had to wear my civilian clothes during my first two weeks in boot camp because no uniforms were available.) In the aftermath of the Vietnam War the quality of our military personnel declined significantly.

Although America will be the world's only superpower for years and decades to come, future generations should remember the words of Loren Thompson, who wrote: "History is strewn with the remains of great civilizations that lost the capacity to protect themselves from external challenges. The hard part for America, as for Rome, seems to be maintaining a sense of purpose when threats recede. Given enough time, Americans are masters of military mobilization and execution. Where they have proved wanting is in preserving their might during periods of peace."[16]

EPILOGUE

From Vietnam to 9/11 was initially published well before the war in Iraq. When I was informed that the book would be published in paperback form, I felt it appropriate to include an epilogue on the Iraq war and its aftermath.

Since the attack on 9/11, I have traveled to Iraq and nearby countries on five occasions to conduct inspections and assessments. I have a number of concerns regarding the central policy issues involved in this momentous foreign policy crisis: intelligence failures, our preemptive strike policy, the excessive tempo of operations for our troops, the inadequate equipment provided for them, our allocation of resources in the global war against terrorism, and the potential obstacles to the Bush administration's goal of spreading democracy throughout the Middle East. My observations are based on extensive conversations with military leaders and the troops in Iraq, intelligence briefings, congressional hearings, and discussions with experts and scholars on the Middle East.

Background

After the end of the Cold War, national defense policy was set, to some extent, on an ad hoc basis as we responded to crises in Somalia and the Balkans and tried to make breakthroughs in the Israeli-Palestinian conflict. Neither political party paid significant attention to the other threats that some of us saw as more probable and more dangerous—terrorism and the proliferation of weapons of mass destruction—or to the need for enhanced homeland security. As I noted in Chapter 10, when I traveled to Texas prior to President Bush's inauguration, I urged him to make nuclear nonproliferation and counterterrorism the centerpieces of his administration's defense strategy. Despite this advice—and the warnings contained in the prophetic study on the terrorist threat written by former senators Gary Hart and Warren Rudman, the increases above the budget approved by Congress to counter terrorism, and the proposal by some in Congress to form a Department of Homeland Security—terrorism was basically not on the radar screen of most Americans or of the new administration.

When President Bush took office, his administration's national security policy emphasized ballistic missile defense, saw China as our chief future adversary, and rejected America's traditional approach of "constructive engagement" when it left Israel and the Palestinians to fend for themselves. Any policy option that sounded even remotely like "nation building" or "peacekeeping" was discredited. This perspective on America's national security interests, of course, underwent a 180-degree change on September 11, 2001, when the country experienced what some had been predicting: terrorist attacks on our soil. The perpetrators struck at the very heart of our society and showed their determination to use every means at their disposal to disrupt our way of life and counter our geopolitical interests. The dramatic events of that day cleared away all the haze in the debate about defense policy. The American people rightly understood that terrorism, and the potential use of unconventional weapons against us, was the number one threat.

In the wake of 9/11, the United States conducted a decisive war to overthrow the Taliban regime in Afghanistan, where a safe haven for Osama bin Laden and training camps for his al-Qaeda operatives had been established. The administration made an irrefutable case for toppling the Taliban regime: we had been attacked, Afghanistan was the home base of our enemy, and there was broad international support for our going to war.

In 2002, however, the administration began a steady "drumbeat" of publicity regarding the threat posed by Iraq. This drumbeat included weekly appearances on television and radio talk shows by administration spokespersons, testimony by numerous administration witnesses before congressional committees, and press interviews by key administration personnel. On October 5, 2002, in his weekly radio address, for example, President Bush remarked, "The danger to America from the Iraqi regime is grave and growing." Two days later he stated, "Some ask how urgent this danger is to America and the world. The danger is already significant, and it only grows worse with time. If we know Saddam Hussein has dangerous weapons today—and we do—does it make any sense for the world to confront him as he grows even stronger and develops even more dangerous weapons?"[1] Regarding Iraq's weapons of mass destruction, National Security Advisor Condoleezza Rice argued, "We don't want the smoking gun to be a mushroom cloud over America."[2]

A massive U.S. troop buildup in the Middle East was initiated to confront the Iraqi regime. Pressure against Saddam Hussein began escalating steadily, threatening Iraq with severe consequences if it did not disarm as called for in a UN Security Council resolution. With information provided to the Congress by administration witnesses as well as other factors, such as Saddam Hussein's past history of attacking neighboring countries and his programs to develop and produce chemical and biological weapons (which he had used against Iran and his own people), the House and Senate passed a resolution authorizing the use of force to remove Hussein from power. I voted for the resolution. On March 7, 2003, the United States, Britain, and Spain proposed ordering Hussein to give up banned weapons by March 17 or face war. Ten days later, the same three countries declared that the time for diplomacy was over. They withdrew the resolution after it became apparent that the UN Security Council would not adopt it. On March 17, President Bush issued a forty-eight-hour ultimatum: Hussein and his two sons had to leave Iraq. The invasion began on March 20.

A rapid and effective military campaign was launched. Just six weeks later, on May 1, the President declared the end of major military combat operations. A cruel tyrant no longer oppressed the citizens of Iraq. But in the wake of a quick military victory, a number of unsettling issues arose concerning the aftermath of the war in Iraq.

Intelligence

Anyone who has read the Preface to this book will understand how crucial I believe the role of intelligence to be in the conduct of foreign affairs and in the policy making that leads to any decision to deploy America's armed forces. The points I made there are very relevant to the events surrounding the Iraq war and should be in the forefront of the minds of American leaders. As I put it, "the way we go about collecting, analyzing, and using intelligence information is one of the most important determinants of our success or failure in world events. Unfortunately, it is a lesson we have had to re-learn too often, at a heavy price in American blood and treasure."

Much has been written about the various intelligence failures surrounding the Iraq war. First of all, let me underscore the obvious successes. The national and tactical intelligence systems for the actual invasion—e.g., knowing the positions of enemy tanks, the locations of Iraq's key command and control centers, and the most effective way of attacking them during the invasion—performed extremely well, just as they had years earlier, during the Persian Gulf War.

Despite these achievements, there were many mistakes. Congressional hearings have investigated these failures in great detail, questioning the lack of timely data providing the targets for the initial air strikes that were supposed to take out Saddam Hussein and his sons, the nonexistent uranium contracts (when Iraq was supposedly buying uranium in Africa), and the absence of Iraq's weapons of mass destruction. Indeed, the administration's own chief weapons inspector, David Kay, stated that "we were all wrong" about the weapons of mass destruction.[3] And as of this writing, there is no proven connection between Saddam Hussein and al-Qaeda during his presidency. Regarding these and other intelligence failures surrounding the Iraq war and its aftermath, it is not yet clear whether the intelligence reports themselves were largely faulty or whether senior officials may have "cherry-picked" nuggets from a variety of intelligence reports in order to reach their preconceived conclusions. What is certain is that intelligence must always be used as a tool of statecraft, not as a political tool.

I cannot emphasize enough that "intelligence" means much more than the accumulation and interpretation of classified reports developed from input derived from top secret reconnaissance satellites, communication intercepts, tactical intelligence reconnaissance systems, and HUMINT—i.e., spying by human agents. In a broader sense, intelligence must obviously include a deep understanding of the complexities, the social dynamics, and the ethnic diversity of the countries with which we interact or in which we intervene, as well as the potential of those factors to affect America's policy objectives and military missions favorably or adversely. In a television interview with Jim Lehrer, Kay underscored this point, saying,

"The strange thing, Jim, is this isn't the first time we failed to understand what is going on in a society. You can go back to the Second

World War. We missed what was going on in Germany under strategic bombing. Much more recently . . . when the Soviet Union fell, this giant, this superpower, . . . we suddenly discovered we had a basket case on our hands. They couldn't feed their own people. It was falling apart. In Vietnam . . . we misread Vietnamese society as well.

"We are not very good as a nation in our intelligence capability at reading the most fundamental secrets of a society, what are its capabilities, what are its intentions? You can't photograph those."[4]

A classic case of our government's underestimating the realities of a country where we intervened militarily (albeit mainly through proxies) was the CIA's program to train and equip guerrillas to invade Cuba in 1961, a few years after Fidel Castro had taken over Cuba and imposed a communist dictatorship. The CIA assured the Kennedy administration that once the guerrillas landed on Cuban soil, a massive uprising by the Cuban people to overthrow Castro would occur. Instead, the invasion was a fiasco, and there was no uprising.

Elsewhere in this book, I have touched on several instances in which America intervened militarily when we had a very rudimentary knowledge of the social complexities and diversity of the culture and little knowledge of how those factors would affect the goals of our military mission. In some cases, that lack of knowledge and understanding played an important role in events that led up to a failed policy. Lebanon and Somalia are just two examples of our misreading what our troops would face when they were deployed. And in the Balkans, we confronted a very steep learning curve regarding our involvement in that enormously complicated region of the world.

In Iraq, the Bush administration assumed that our troops would be greeted with open arms. And one week after the war had begun, Undersecretary of Defense Paul Wolfowitz addressed the postwar costs of rebuilding Iraq in an appearance before the House Appropriations Committee. He asserted, "There is a lot of money to pay for this. . . . It doesn't have to be taxpayers' money. We are dealing with a country that can really finance its own reconstruction, and relatively soon."[5] Thus on three key issues—the postwar environment our troops would face, the cost of the postwar occupation, and the presence of weapons of mass destruction—the information provided to Congress and to the American people turned out to be wrong.

I noted earlier that intelligence failures fall into two categories. In the first, the intelligence agencies get it wrong and provide bad information to decision makers. In the second, intelligence personnel and policy planners make accurate assessments and recommendations, but the architects of the policy do not listen to them. The case of postwar Iraq belongs to the latter category. It has been widely documented that the State Department and the Army, in particular, performed extensive and detailed planning for the postwar events in Iraq. Those studies foresaw the very challenging environment facing our troops.

Indeed, before the war had even begun, a study group at the Army War College in Carlisle, Pennsylvania, concluded in part that "long term gratitude is unlikely and suspicions of U.S. motives will increase as the occupation continues. A force initially viewed as liberators can rapidly be relegated to the status of invaders should an unwelcome occupation continue for a prolonged time. Occupation problems may be especially acute if the United States must implement the bulk of the occupation itself rather than turn these duties over to a postwar international force."[6] Similarly, David Reiff wrote, "What went wrong is that the voices of Iraq experts of the State Department almost in its entirety and indeed, of important segments of the uniformed military, were ignored. As much as the invasion of Iraq and the rout of Saddam Hussein and his army was a triumph of planning and implementation, the mess that is postwar Iraq is a failure of planning and implementation."[7] And in an article in *Atlantic Monthly*, James Fallows commented on the extensive planning that took place and the issues dealt with by the civilian government officials and military officials who warned about the challenges of the postwar environment when they researched the probable environment we would face in postwar Iraq. Fallows observed, "Almost everything, good and bad, that has happened in Iraq since the fall of Saddam Hussein's regime was the subject of extensive pre-war discussions and analysis. This is particularly true of what have proved to be the harshest realities for the United States since the fall of Baghdad: that occupying the country is much more difficult than conquering it; that a breakdown of public order can jeopardize every other goal; that the ambition of patiently nurturing a new democracy is at odds with the desire to turn control over to the Iraqis quickly and get U.S. troops out; that the Sunni center of the country is the main security problem; that with each passing day Americans risk being seen less as liberators and more as occupiers, and targets."[8]

Despite these voluminous studies and warnings by our own experts in the government and military about the challenge of the postwar environment, the chief architects of the policy to invade Iraq preferred to believe the soothing assurances of Iraqi expatriates who had been living abroad for decades but convinced some in the administration that the postwar period would be a walk in the park. Beyond the issue of that mistake, though, are the implications for future foreign policy decisions potentially based on the doctrine of the "preemptive strike."

Preemptive Strike

The framework rationalizing the strategy for invading Iraq appears in a twenty-one-page document entitled *The National Security Strategy of the United States of America,* which presents a justification for unilateral intervention by the United States. There is a logic and simplicity at the heart of the document that could be described as "Get the bad guys before they get you." In the case of Afghanistan, America's decision to invade was faultless. Osama bin Laden was funding terrorist training camps in Afghanistan, and not only had his followers attacked America but he also had vowed continued attacks on America itself and American interests around the world.

But in the case of Iraq, we now know that it posed no imminent danger, no threat to our nation's core interests. Moreover, our having a preemptive strike policy at the center of our doctrine for intervening militarily in other countries marks a transition to a foreign policy at odds with our entire history. Invading without a clear indication that our core national interests are threatened violates one of America's fundamental principles for going to war. In any future crisis, an administration making a case for a preemptive strike must present totally reliable—dare I say almost perfect—intelligence. Considering the faulty intelligence we had regarding Iraq, it is clear that the world (and indeed the American public) will be very skeptical of future interventions whose rationales rely heavily on evidence from America's intelligence community.

In his interview with Jim Lehrer, David Kay also noted that "our credibility . . . as a nation is what allows us to cooperate with others and influence others towards our own ends. If they doubt the honesty and the objectivity of what we're saying, we're going to be in a world of hurt."[9] Forty-three years ago, the Soviet Union placed nuclear missiles on Cuban territory. President Kennedy sent former secretary of state Dean Acheson to brief key foreign leaders on the threat this posed to America and to ask for their support of an American policy to ensure the missiles' removal. Acheson briefed French president Charles de Gaulle and asked for his support in this grave crisis. At the end of his briefing, Acheson advised de Gaulle that he had photographic evidence of the Soviet weapons. De Gaulle responded, "I do not need to see the photographs. The word of the President of the United States is good enough for me." Sadly, such confidence in our leadership is now a thing of the past. The word of the United States is no longer held in such high regard, and we have lost international credibility.

Excessive Tempo of Operations

While it will take a long time to sort out the causes of our intelligence failures and to develop policies and programs to rectify them, another effect of the events in Iraq is very quantifiable and is already reaching crisis proportions: our troops are spread too thin because of America's current extensive global commitments. The Iraq war and its aftermath have caused an enormous strain on our armed forces personnel. This issue is of vital importance, because if our forces continue to be overextended, we will quickly see an erosion of morale, retention, and recruitment. This would seriously hollow out the quality of our future armed forces. We must focus on whether the United States has a force structure sufficient to carry out the Bush administration's strategy of placing such heavy emphasis on the manpower-intensive polices of peacekeeping and nation building.

The history of nation building during the past decade—Somalia, Haiti, Bosnia, and Kosovo—does not suggest that it can be accomplished swiftly or inexpensively. As Carl Bildt wrote, "In 2003 we learned again that it is far easier to win a war than to build a peace. To destroy regimes is relatively easy; many even do it to themselves. But to build new and stable ones is extraordinarily demanding. There are no quick fixes, early exits or purely military solutions."[10] There have been successful nation-building efforts in the last sixty years in the aftermath of past wars, such as those in Germany, Japan, and South Korea. To a very large extent, however, these countries had a homogeneous populace, which contributed to the stability of the postwar environment. By comparison, Iraq's populace is heterogeneous, comprising mainly Kurds, Sunnis, and Shiites. There are also many tribal loyalties within these major groups. Iraq's multiethnic nature and ancient religious and ethnic strife ensure that realizing America's objectives will take a very long time. (The ancient rivalries among the warlords and clans in Afghanistan are also foreboding in terms of the future of nation building there.) History suggests that in the aftermath of U.S. military intervention, the length of U.S. military presence and financial assistance will most likely be measured in decades, not months or years.

Two months prior to the war, Paul Wolfowitz stated, "First—and this is really the overarching principle—the United States seeks to liberate Iraq, not occupy Iraq. . . . If the president should decide to use force, let me assure you again that the United States would be committed to liberating the people of Iraq, not becoming an occupation force."[11] Months after the war, though, when reality set in, L. Paul Bremer—the head of U.S. operations in Iraq—said, "As long as we're here, we are the occupying power. It's a very ugly word, but it's true."[12]

I believe an imbalance between our military's infrastructure (especially personnel levels) and the Bush administration's foreign policy has already occurred. The commitment of U.S. troops deployed abroad puts a strain on personnel levels well beyond the actual number deployed. In addition to the enormous number of troops needed to provide logistical support for our deployed troops, many national intelligence programs must direct personnel and resources to assist in the support and operations of the deployed force. Finally, because the deployed troops must be rotated, other troops must simultaneously train stateside, preparing to replace the deployed troops. The reality is that large segments of America's force structure—especially the Army and the Reserve—are considerably strained just in conducting the current deployments for any prolonged period.

Army

As of this writing, the total deployment of active and Army Reserve/ National Guard forces in Iraq and the nearby region stands at about 150,000. There is, of course, a massive logistics, intelligence, and communications infrastructure in the region to support the force in Iraq, including 27,000 troops in Kuwait. The unwillingness of so many other countries to send sizeable forces for the postwar peacekeeping operation puts additional strain on our forces.

At the time of peak deployment to Iraq and the region, 73 percent of the Army's active combat forces were deployed either in the Middle East,

Korea, or Afghanistan. Other peacekeeping missions are also ongoing, especially in the Balkans. Additionally, a large commitment of American armed forces remains in Europe. In the words of General Eric Shinseki, the former army chief of staff, the administration has a twelve-division foreign policy but only a ten-division force structure.

National Guard and Reserve

As noted in Chapter 6 above, the National Guard and the Reserve have played a central role in America's national security policy for many years, especially since 1973. In that year, the Department of Defense implemented the Total Force policy, which involved integrating the Guard and Reserve into the war plans of the active forces: "As a ready source of manpower, Guard and Reserve men and women are a bargain. They number more than 1.2 million and allow the nation to nearly double its armed forces if necessary while accounting for just 8.3% of the defense budget."[13]

From the end of World War II until 1989—almost half a century—there were only four activations of the Guard and Reserve. In the last fourteen years, however, they have been mobilized six times. The following statistics put this into perspective.

- Since the Cold War began to unwind in 1989, the Selected Reserve (those reservists and Guard personnel who train regularly and are mobilized for situations such as the Iraq war) has been reduced from about 1,200,000 to fewer than 900,000—a 25 percent reduction.
- In the Persian Gulf War, about one out of five American troops came from the Reserve and the National Guard.
- In the Iraq war, reservists and Guard personnel deployed to the region made up the highest percentage of deployed troops in any U.S. military campaign in modern history.
- U.S. troops serving in Iraq for yearlong tours of duty were replaced by new troops by May 2004. Now, 40 percent of the Army troops deployed to Iraq are from the National Guard and Reserve.
- Since 9/11, more than 400,000 reservists have been mobilized.
- One out of every two Marines in the Marine Corps Reserve has been called to active duty since 9/11.

Many personnel who previously served on active duty volunteer for the Reserve and National Guard after their tour of duty in the active service is complete. As reservists, their commitment would normally involve training one weekend each month as well as two weeks during the year. Many of the military occupational specialties in which large numbers of Reserve units concentrate—military police, civil affairs, transportation, and logistics—are the very specialties needed on a large scale for the administration's vast peacekeeping and nation-building missions.

The Reserve component has played a key role in recent military operations. Reservists served, and continue to serve, with great distinction in Iraq. We must be very concerned, however, about the effect frequent extended call-ups to active duty will have on morale, recruitment, and retention. As noted above, a significant portion of the men and women who serve in the Reserve enter after finishing their active-duty tour. Some soldiers who are now considering joining the Reserve after completing their active service will have second thoughts, given the increased likelihood that reservists will be mobilized. Simply put, it will be harder for potential reservists to make a commitment to the Reserve and National Guard if many of them believe that they will be activated for extended periods of time. Frequent calls to extended active duty would so interfere with reservists' long-range personal goals that retention and recruitment could plummet.

With reservists making up an enormous percentage of troops involved in the current conflicts, we must also be concerned about the support systems in place for their families. As a recent article about Guard and Reserve personnel noted, "They work and fight in a military that is taking casualties in places such as Afghanistan, dealing with all the wartime trappings of separation and sorrow. But their spouses and children, who were never part of a self-supporting military culture the way most active-service families are, remain in a civilian world where neighbors and friends have long since put away the flags they flew after 9/11 and are going about their daily lives."[14]

Indeed, the current widespread use of "stop-loss" orders demonstrates the extent to which large segments of our military already have serious personnel problems. When issued, the stop-loss order can extend the time individuals must remain in the service even though their scheduled time for retirement has arrived or the time they had signed up to serve is complete. As Lee Hockstader put it, "Through a series of stop-loss orders, the Army alone has blocked the possible retirements and departures of more than 40,000 soldiers, about 16,000 of them National Guard and reserve members who were eligible to leave the service this year."[15] Granted, the use of stop-loss orders is an important management tool enabling the services to retain unit cohesion and to keep individuals in vital specialties. Having said that, I have no doubt that the frequent mobilizations, combined with long-term deployments and stop-loss orders, will result in negative recruitment and retention for Reserve personnel. Indeed, this is already happening. In early fiscal year 2004, the Army National Guard announced that it had missed its recruitment goals in fiscal year 2003 by 8,000 personnel, or 15 percent.

A decline in the quality and size of the Guard and Reserve would have an especially adverse effect on our nation's long-range national security interests. If the massive deployment to Iraq (with the 40 percent Army Reserve component presence) were to continue for a long period of time, and another crisis suddenly erupted, U.S. threats to intervene might ring hollow, especially if that new crisis involved the need for a postwar occupation along with peacekeeping and nation building by American forces. We simply do not have the force structure to conduct such a policy.

Another important policy issue that must be addressed is the fact that many of the Guard and Reserve units sent to Iraq lack the proper training for the missions to which they have been assigned. The experience of a constituent's son offers an example. After serving in Iraq for more than a year and being extended once, he was all packed and ready to return home when he was suddenly extended for a second time. He was then assigned to "ride shotgun" for contractor supply convoys because the civilian truckers refused to drive without armed military escorts. This reservist had no training for this mission. He didn't even have basic gear with which to communicate with other security personnel in his own convoys. (By the way, in addition to his service in Iraq, he had been activated a few years earlier and served in Bosnia for ten months.)

Although this soldier personally did not serve at the prison at Abu Ghraib, he told his father about others in his unit who had. It is clear from that account—and others I have heard—that the tragedy at the prison can be partly attributed to chronic shortages in personnel as well as a lack of training and supervision. Most of the unit's personnel had no formal training in running a prison, and the entire American prison contingent was at half strength, compared to Army standards. This—coupled with the mixed messages coming from the command structure about how much pressure to bring upon these prisoners and what was allowed and not allowed—was a recipe for disaster.

I met with five Egyptian generals who told me that while what was done to the prisoners would be humiliating in any culture, the particular acts perpetrated at Abu Ghraib were especially demeaning to those in Arab and Muslim cultures. One of the generals told me that some were so demeaning that many view the humiliation to be worse than the physical torture. These acts have had far-reaching ramifications across the Muslim world. They have set back America's reputation and moral standing at the very time when the central focus of the administration's foreign policy is to spread democracy.

Equipment Shortfalls

I traveled to Iraq in August 2003 to meet on-site with our military and civilian leaders and assess our operations. Although major combat had ended several weeks before, U.S. and allied forces experienced attacks almost daily. My conversations and briefings addressed a wide range of topics. What I uncovered is included in the following letter, which I sent to Secretary of Defense Donald Rumsfeld after I returned.

August 24, 2003

The Honorable Donald Rumsfeld
Secretary of Defense
The Pentagon
Washington, D.C.

Dear Secretary Rumsfeld:

As you are aware, I recently returned from travel to the Iraq theater of operations during which I met with Ambassador Bremer and our senior military leaders in the region. In a matter of days, the President will receive a letter from me outlining my broad findings, conclusions and recommendations. In the meantime, however, I want to raise with you several specific items that I believe require your immediate attention. In my discussions with our senior military, I received information about parts and equipment shortages that are adversely affecting our troops' ability to conduct their mission and provide adequate protection for themselves and others. These are:

Personnel Protection:

1. Body armor: It was reported that some 40,000 troops in theater lack protective Kevlar plates for body armor vests. Many of the troops I've visited in military hospitals who were wounded in Iraq claim that these Kevlar plates saved their lives.

2. Portable RF jammers: Remotely controlled radio devices are detonating many of the land mines and bombs being used against our troops. There are several portable radio frequency jammers that have been deployed that serve as an effective counter-measure against this threat. Yet, the Army division patrolling the so-called "Sunni Triangle" has a total of only nine portable jammers, and the 2nd brigade of the division only had one. The division leaders with whom I met reported that these jammers are urgently required for convoy and patrol protection.

3. Kevlar blankets: Division Commanders reported a shortage of Kevlar blankets for the HMMWVs.

Parts Shortages:

1. Bradley Fighting Vehicles: Of the 140 Bradleys deployed within the 1st Armored Division in theater, I was told that some 46 of these personnel carriers had been "dead-lined" due to lack of vehicle tracks.

2. HMMWVs: It was reported that roughly 80 of the 1st Armored Division's HMMWV wheeled vehicles had been taken out of service due to a lack of spare parts. In addition, the Division reported that it is still waiting for 125 "up-armored" HMMWVs.

3. Parts distribution: Perhaps the most troubling information I received regarding spare parts was that in-country distribution problems resulted in a zero balance in 46 percent of the spare parts inventory for the HMMWVs and Bradley fighting vehicles.

Mr. Secretary, I know you are as concerned as I am about these shortfalls and the need for a quick resolution.

Sincerely,

John P. Murtha

There have been subsequent improvements. By early 2004, everyone in theater had been provided protective armor, and the supply of Kevlar blankets was sufficient. The supply of the radio frequency jammers has increased, too, but a shortfall still exists. This basic equipment essential to the safety of our armed forces should have been available from day one. To some extent, equipment shortfalls were unavoidable. Having said that, it must ultimately be determined to what extent the architects of the war, confident that we would be widely accepted by the populace after the war and that our troops would encounter a relatively benign environment, did not give high priority to making protective equipment available.

For a few years, Congress added funds above the Bush administration's budget request for the procurement of armored Humvees. Armoring the Humvees "helps protect occupants from armor-piercing bullets, mines up to 12 pounds and 155-millimeter artillery blasts overhead."[16] The administration opposed the increase, but fortunately, because of this congressional intervention, the program went forward—and at least there were some armored Humvees in the Army's inventory. While production of the armored Humvees was ramped up after the end of major combat operations in Iraq, there is still a serious shortage of them.

The intensity of our operations and the harsh weather conditions in Iraq have placed an additional strain on much of our equipment. In an interview, General Paul Kern of the Army Materiel Command noted that one of the most critical shortages "was track and suspension systems for the Bradley fighting vehicles, which normally run only 800 miles in an average year but are running 1,200 miles per month escorting convoys in Iraq. . . . They are changing track every 60 days when normally they would do that only once a year."[17] The equipment of our forces in Iraq is being operated at an average of one year's worth of "optempo"—i.e., the tempo of operations—every month. Bringing this equipment back to full operational capability will carry an enormous cost. As Joseph L. Galloway noted in an article in the *Miami Herald,* "The Army's chief logistics and materiel commanders said that although they try to prepare for the worst, few saw any need for

130,000 troops in Iraq this long after the war, and no one anticipated that mines and rocket-propelled grenade attacks would require Bradley Fighting Vehicles to escort every convoy running from Kuwait into Iraq."[18]

Allocation of Resources in the War on Terror

In setting a national security strategy, communicating that strategy to the public, and analyzing alternative proposals to national security policies, leaders must, first and foremost, view matters through the lens of the threat. What is the primary threat to America's national security? How do we best protect ourselves from that threat? What resources should we allocate to which programs in order to counter the threat in the most cost-effective manner? If we step back from the rhetoric of the war on terrorism and dispassionately analyze the question of the most cost-effective way to counter the terrorist threat, we realize, first, the immense cost of the war in Iraq and the postwar occupation and nation building. These expenditures dwarf those of the budgets of all of the other programs in place to fight terrorism. Our nation's safety depends on the Department of Homeland Security, which combines the operations of twenty-two federal agencies. It has a budget of approximately $40 billion for the next fiscal year. Juxtaposed with its budget is the funding (thus far) of about $150 billion for the invasion, occupation, and economic reconstruction of Iraq. A supplemental appropriation for $25 billion has been submitted to the Congress, and I believe that another $50 billion will be required in fiscal year 2005. It won't be long until the actual and projected cost of the Iraq war, its aftermath, and the economic reconstruction will reach a quarter of a trillion dollars—an amount six times the total annual budget of the Department of Homeland Security.

The National Security Strategy of the United States of America, the document mentioned earlier, reads in part: "Enemies in the past needed great armies and great industrial capabilities to endanger America. Now shadowy networks of individuals can bring chaos and suffering to our shores for less than it costs to purchase a single tank. Terrorists are able to penetrate open societies and to turn the power of modern technologies against us."[19] Budgeting resources and allocating personnel to counter these low-cost terrorist threats effectively while simultaneously spending vast sums on the war in Iraq and its aftermath presents an enormous fiscal challenge—to say nothing of the strain on the personnel, budgets, and equipment of our armed forces.

While there is a deep division among the American people about the war in Iraq, I believe there would be overwhelming public support for the Bush administration's Iraq policy if our citizens believed that the war was driving a stake into the heart of al-Qaeda and eliminating potential future terrorist attacks on America and American global interests. But at a joint news conference in 2003, President Bush and British prime minister Tony Blair were asked if there were a link between Saddam Hussein and al-Qaeda. President Bush stated, "I can't make that claim," and the prime minister concurred.[20]

On Sunday, December 13, 2003, we woke up to the great news that Saddam Hussein had been captured the day before. One of the world's most vile dictators, a man who had so frequently strutted in a macho fashion before his people and the world, meekly surrendered as he crawled out from a hole dug in the dirt in a hut near Tikrit, Iraq, his ancestral home. Radio and television stations announced the news that morning, but the story had broken too late for the Sunday morning newspapers to cover. Interestingly, the lead story on that same Sunday morning in many papers was "International Funding for al-Qaeda Goes On Unabated." A few weeks after Saddam's capture, various flights had to be canceled due to intelligence reports of specific threats that planes would be hijacked and flown into targets. And during the holidays, concerns about a possible attack brought federal agents to major cities with special equipment to detect radiation that terrorists' "dirty bombs" would emit. A recent report by the International Institute of Strategic Studies concluded that since the invasion of Iraq, the pace of recruits joining al-Qaeda has increased and that al-Qaeda membership now is 18,000.[21]

I raise these points not to detract from the great accomplishment of the rapid military victory in Iraq and the eventual capture of Saddam Hussein. A ruthless dictator has been removed from power; initial steps are being taken toward democracy in Iraq. Those who perceive the military victory in Iraq as a great setback for international terrorism, however, should put things in perspective.

I disagreed with the President when he stated, "The war on terror, you can't distinguish between al-Qaeda and Saddam when you talk about the war on terror. And so it's a comparison that I can't make because I can't distinguish between the two, because they're both equally as bad, and equally as evil, and equally as destructive."[22] On the contrary, I believe that combining the war in Iraq with the war against al-Qaeda detracts from the reality of the international challenge America faces. As an article in the British periodical *The Economist* (which supported the invasion of Iraq) read, "Yes, Saddam terrorized his people and his neighbors. But to lump all America's enemies together as 'terrorists' is to play with words and, worse, to risk making a muddle of policy. Osama bin Laden is a religious fanatic with an apocalyptic vision of permanent Islamic war against the infidel. . . . Saddam had to be stopped, but his defeat has not necessarily hastened the defeat of al-Qaeda, and might even make victory harder if it continues to stoke up Muslim rage against the West."[23] And as the President said before a joint session of Congress, "there are thousands of terrorists operating in over sixty countries." That fact dramatizes the extent to which we will have to count heavily on the cooperation and action of the intelligence, military, and law enforcement agencies of countries around the world to achieve ultimate victory against the terrorists. We must remember that the fight against al-Qaeda and the international terrorist movement involves many functions in which the intimate cooperation of other countries' police, intelligence, and military is absolutely essential—functions such as taking out the key figures of al-Qaeda and their successors one by one, infiltrating terrorist cells and organizations, tracking the whereabouts of suspected terrorists, tracing the funding for terrorist groups, and developing cooperative programs to ensure that the vast amount of cargo shipped internationally is safe when it enters our ports and airports. The fight against terrorism must not evolve into or be perceived as basically a U.S. operation. In the words of Michael Ignatieff, "The Achilles' heel of American power has been its inability to understand its dependence on other nations, and without friends and allies, a war against terror will fail."[24]

The Challenge of Exporting Democracy to the Middle East

The central rationale for the Bush administration's policy toward Iraq has evolved from "an imminent danger posed by weapons of mass destruction" to "getting rid of a despicable dictator" to a "long twilight struggle to bring democracy to the Middle East." Attempting to spread democracy in the Middle East is a noble goal. Recent decades have seen progress toward America's objective of increasing the number of democratic governments around the globe. This accomplishment stands as one of the great achievements of our foreign policy, and I believe that a continuation of the trend toward worldwide democracy is inevitable over the long term.

Most countries in the Middle East have held out against this historical trend, however. In the case of Iraq, as of this writing, important initial steps have been taken toward the goal of establishing democracy. An interim constitution has been agreed upon. Elections are scheduled to be held in early 2005. We all hope that this scenario plays out successfully. I have reservations, though, as to whether the interim constitution will prove workable. Will a constitution forced on an interim Iraqi government (one whose members are paid by the United States) give that governing body the legitimacy, respect, and confidence it will require to govern effectively and to withstand future political pressures and hardships?

I would also offer a word of caution regarding the goal of spreading democracy in the Middle East. This is a difficult, arduous, long-term challenge, and we must question to what extent such a trend can be imposed by U.S. intervention and involvement and to what extent the countervailing "law of unintended consequences" might affect such a policy.

We are all familiar with the old saying "Be careful: You might get what you wish for." In his recent book, *The Future of Freedom,* Fareed Zakaria, the chief foreign correspondent of *Newsweek,* quoted a senior Saudi official who said:

> The Arab rulers of the Middle East are autocratic, corrupt and heavy-handed. But they are still more liberal, tolerant and pluralistic than what would likely replace them. Elections in many Arab countries would produce politicians who espouse views that are closer to Osama bin Laden's than those of Jordan's liberal monarch, King Abdullah. Last year the Emir of Kuwait, with American encouragement, proposed giving women the vote. But the democratically elected Kuwaiti parliament—filled with Islamic fundamentalists—roundly rejected the initiative. Saudi Crown Prince Abdullah tried something less dramatic when he proposed that women in Saudi Arabia be allowed to drive. (They are currently forbidden to do so, which means that Saudi Arabia has had to import half a million chauffeurs from places like India and the Philippines.) But the religious conservatives mobilized popular opposition and forced him to back down.[25]

A similar argument was raised by *The Economist,* which editorialized,

> Now that he has stated his belief in democracy, however, Mr. Bush cannot simply confer his blessings on the Arabs with a wave of the wand. . . . To be sure, those who advocate this course of action have an interesting case to make. Since the September 11th attacks, they argue, it should be clear that the absence of democracy is one of the things that turn Arabs toward Islamic extremism and against an America widely seen as the propper-up of repressive regimes. This argument is probably right. So is its corollary that the creation of a liberal, democratic order in the Arab world is in America's own long-term interest. But there is a fine distinction—and a world of differ-ence—between a policy of advocating democracy and a policy of imposing it. Apart from being questionable in principle . . . any crude attempt to impose democracy on the Arabs is liable to backfire in practice.
>
> One way such a policy could backfire is by knocking over bad regimes only to see even worse ones take their place. The existence of a general Arab appetite for democracy does not mean that the alternative to a repressive, authoritarian regime is bound in every case to be a liberal democracy.[26]

The complexities of attempting to bring democracy to Iraq were dramati-cally displayed in January 2004, when massive numbers of demonstrators in Iraq held marches in support of having elections. L. Paul Bremer came to the United Nations and pleaded with UN Secretary-General Kofi Annan to send a UN delegation to Iraq to convince the Shiite Iraqis *not to hold elec-tions in the time frame they wanted.* The administration had developed a complex five-milestone plan to gradually transition to an electoral democ-racy. The first milestone was to agree on a law defining how to choose constitutional delegates. Then regional caucuses would select a transitional assembly, and that assembly would select a provisional government to re-turn sovereignty to the Iraqi people. Elections were to be held in 2005. The case in favor of this approach, as opposed to going straight to a popular election, is a strong one: the lack of a current census or registration of voters made it clear that an early vote was not practical.

The Shiite majority, however, disagreed with Bremer's approach and de-manded a popular vote quickly. Massive demonstrations calling for popular elections were held at the behest of the Grand Ayatollah Ali al-Sistani. Susan Sachs wrote that "the most important political figure in Iraq today is Grand Ayatollah Ali al-Sistani, an elderly Shiite Muslim cleric. He has not set foot outside his home for six years, yet the white-bearded ayatollah has effectively commandeered the Bush administration's planning for postwar democracy."[27] After consulting with an assessment team from the United Nations, the Shiites agreed to conduct elections later than they had originally demanded. While the initial steps toward democracy are evolving in Iraq, it is far from clear how long it will be until a viable Iraqi democracy can function. Switching for the moment to the process in Afghanistan, as of late February 2004, 2 percent of Afghan women had registered to vote, and 8 percent of eligible Afghan voters had been enrolled. Nevertheless, a national election was scheduled for June.

As Quentin Peel observed, we must not confuse "purely electoral democracy—the right to vote and the establishment of parliamentary institutions—with full fledged liberal democracy."[28] Without the robust institutions of a free press, a secure environment, an effective police force, a fair judicial system, and an impartial system of laws and regulations, a nation cannot truly function as a vibrant democracy. Achieving these goals in Iraq (to say nothing of Afghanistan) will take a prolonged period of time, effort, and enormous sums of money.

In a column entitled "Dysfunctional Democracy," the author and journalist Georgie Anne Geyer succinctly expressed this concern: "We're way too tied up with the magic word 'democracy.' It's almost like the ancient alchemists who thought they could make gold from common metals: The modern one-note Americans, rife in this administration, who insist only the mechanism of democracy is important are the modern political alchemists. Yet, while forms of democracy are surely desirable everywhere—I prefer the less purist phrase 'representative government'—the mechanism of electing leaders doesn't mean much without the cultural, legal, social, economic and psychosocial stuff of democracy."[29] Don't get me wrong. I believe that our foreign policy should support trends toward more open Arab societies— culturally, economically, and politically open. The failure of many of the governments in the region to meet the hopes of their citizens is causing significant societal strains there. Let me quickly add, however, that a policy emphasizing the rapid expansion of democracy in the Arab world must be tempered by prudence and historical perspective. It must be guided by a set of achievable goals. It must have a realistic timetable and an appreciation of the limitations to enforcing change. It must have the support of the American public and the Congress. If the policy requires the use of our armed forces, we must carefully assess their capacity to carry out their mission, especially if it involves the multiyear peacekeeping and nation-building operations that are the central focus of the Bush administration.

Over the long term, more open, tolerant, and democratic societies and governments in the Arab world would certainly mark a significant improvement for the people of the region and an important step forward for the national security interests of the United States. But the key policy issue is to what extent democracy may be imposed on the governments in the region rather than encouraged in a more gradualist, incremental approach toward that goal. As a recent article in *The National Interest* noted:

> Development of democracy in the Arab world will depend more on internal and political developments than what happens in Iraq. Indeed, instability in Iraq could encourage a reaction against democratization in some Arab states. Fortunately, serious if incremental change can be expected from governments throughout the region. Ferment has already begun and will expand, given the vast changes in the availability of communications and media and the workings of globalization. . . . There is a good chance over time that we will see better and more reformist Arab governments. But to assert that the occupation of Iraq will produce democracy in Iraq, which will then spread like a virus to other countries in the Middle East, is more prayer than analysis.[30]

Conclusion

As the world's only superpower, America has a military with unprecedented capabilities. While our economy has many problems, it is still the envy of every other country in the world. America has reached a historic pinnacle of military and economic power, but our leadership and our citizenry must recognize that we do not have an unlimited ability to influence global events. Our position as the world's only superpower must be kept in perspective.

- America represents slightly less than 5 percent of the world's population.
- Our military is currently overstretched.

- There are unprecedented budget deficits.
- The cost of the "regime change" in Iraq thus far is $150 billion—a sum larger than the combined defense budgets of France, Germany, the United Kingdom, and Italy.
- The cost to our enemies in Iraq to spread havoc and attempt to engender a civil war to counter America's massive financial and manpower commitment is low. Although there is clear evidence of outside powers funding fanatics to attack coalition troops, that cost is minimal. In terms of the Iraqi factions opposing the coalition, their costs are nominal—mortar rounds, rocket-propelled grenades, explosives placed in an old used car, and the free labor of fanatical suicide bombers.
- There is no support in the American populace or the Congress for further large-scale military deployments or invasions unless they should involve operations absolutely essential to our national security.

As of this writing, the Bush administration is making some encouraging adjustments to its foreign policy in terms of setting priorities and reaching out to the international community. Two years after the defeat of the Taliban in Afghanistan, a policy to pursue Osama bin Laden aggressively is finally being implemented. The administration has also called upon the United Nations to play a larger role in Iraq's future.

I believe that there must be a "regression to the mean" in our foreign policy. We must reject a unilateral policy and return to one that depends more on the cooperation and participation of other countries and our allies. We must be increasingly selective as to where, when, and why we deploy American troops in the future.

I have raised my concerns about many aspects of the administration's Iraq policy—using poor intelligence, improperly equipping our troops, overstretching our military, and ignoring the extensive warnings of its own experts on the challenge of the postwar environment. Nevertheless, a war initiated on faulty intelligence must not be followed by a premature withdrawal of our troops based on a political timetable. An untimely exit could rapidly devolve into a civil war, which would leave America's foreign policy in disarray as countries question not only America's judgment but also its perseverance.

Let me end on a personal note. American citizens must aggressively maintain a support system—financially and emotionally—for the stateside families of those serving abroad and the families of those who have been killed and wounded. As a member of Congress, I have made many trips to the Army's Walter Reed Hospital and the Navy's Bethesda Hospital to visit the wounded. I am always impressed with how upbeat they are despite their injuries. Most soldiers are of very modest means and joined the military to better themselves. Six soldiers from the district I represent have paid the ultimate price.

The widows of two soldiers killed in Iraq visited my office while they were in Washington, D.C. Both women were in their early twenties, had small babies, and had paid their own way to come to Washington to meet with wounded war veterans. They had brought gifts for the wounded at Walter Reed Hospital. They told me that their conversations with the patients helped them deal with their own losses. The injured shared their stories of how they were wounded, and the young widows shared their stories of their losses as well. During their visit to my office, one of them said, "I was married, got pregnant, lost my husband and had my baby all in the same year. I shouldn't have had to live my whole life in one year."

UPDATE 2006

When I was advised that another printing of *From Vietnam to 9/11* was going to take place, I felt that it was appropriate to include an update. Since the last printing, I had become increasingly disillusioned with the administration's Iraq policy. I decided to offer a resolution in the House of Representatives that called for an immediate redeployment of American forces from Iraq, establishing a strong "over the horizon" military presence in the region, and pursuing security and stability in Iraq through diplomatic efforts. I gave a speech in the House explaining the resolution. I also sent a "Dear Colleague" letter to each member of the House and Senate to elaborate on my views, and in February 2006, I sent a letter to the President of the United States. The speech and both letters follow.

Speech in the House of Representatives, November 15, 2005

The war in Iraq is not going as advertised. It is a flawed policy wrapped in illusion. The American public is way ahead of us. The United States and coalition troops have done all they can in Iraq, but it is time for a change in direction. Our military is suffering. The future of our country is at risk. We cannot continue on the present course. It is evident that continued military action in Iraq is not in the best interest of the United States of America, the Iraqi people, or the Persian Gulf region.

General Casey said in a September 2005 hearing, "The perception of occupation in Iraq is a major driving force behind the insurgency." General

Abizaid said, on the same date, "Reducing the size and visibility of the coalition forces in Iraq is a part of our counterinsurgency strategy."

For two and a half years I have been concerned about the U.S. policy and the plan in Iraq. I have addressed my concerns with the administration and the Pentagon and have spoken out in public about my concerns. The main reason for going to war has been discredited. A few days before the start of the war, I was in Kuwait—the military drew a red line around Baghdad and said when U.S. forces cross that line, they will be attacked by the Iraqis with weapons of mass destruction—but the U.S. forces said they were prepared. They had well-trained forces with the appropriate protective gear.

We spend more money on intelligence than all the countries in the world together, and more on intelligence than most countries' GDP. But the intelligence concerning Iraq was wrong. It is not a world intelligence failure. It is a U.S. intelligence failure and the way that intelligence was misused.

I have been visiting our wounded troops at Bethesda and Walter Reed hospitals almost every week since the beginning of the war. And what demoralizes them is going to war with not enough troops and equipment to make the transition to peace; the devastation caused by IEDs; being deployed to Iraq when their homes have been ravaged by hurricanes; being on their second or third deployment and leaving their families behind without a network of support.

The threat posed by terrorism is real, but we have other threats that cannot be ignored. We must be prepared to face all threats. The future of our military is at risk. Our military and their families are stretched thin. Many say that the Army is broken. Some of our troops are on their third deployment. Recruitment is down, even as our military has lowered its standards. Defense budgets are being cut. Personnel costs are skyrocketing, particularly in health care. Choices will have to be made. We cannot allow promises we have made to our military families in terms of service benefits, in terms of their health care, to be negotiated away. Procurement programs that ensure our military dominance cannot be negotiated away. We must be prepared. The war in Iraq has caused huge shortfalls at our bases in the U.S.

Much of our ground equipment is worn out and in need of either serious overhaul or replacement. George Washington said, "To be prepared for war is one of the most effective means of preserving peace." We must rebuild our Army. Our deficit is growing out of control. The director of the Congressional Budget Office recently admitted to being "terrified" about the budget deficit in the coming decades. This is the first prolonged war we have fought with three years of tax cuts, without full mobilization of American industry, and without a draft. The burden of this war has not been shared equally; the military and their families are shouldering this burden.

Our military has been fighting a war in Iraq for over two and a half years. Our military has accomplished its mission and done its duty. Our military captured Saddam Hussein and captured or killed his closest associates. But the war continues to intensify. Deaths and injuries are growing, with over 2,079 confirmed American deaths. Over 15,500 have been seriously injured, and it is estimated that over 50,000 will suffer from battle fatigue. There have been reports of at least 30,000 Iraqi civilian deaths.

I just recently visited Anbar Province, Iraq, in order to assess the conditions on the ground. Last May 2005, as part of the Emergency Supplemental Spending Bill, the House included the Moran Amendment, which was accepted in conference, and which required the Secretary of Defense to submit quarterly reports to Congress in order to more accurately measure stability and security in Iraq. We have now received two reports. I am disturbed by the findings in key indicator areas. Oil production and energy production are below prewar levels. Our reconstruction efforts have been crippled by the security situation. Only $9 billion of the $18 billion appropriated for reconstruction has been spent. Unemployment remains at about 60 percent. Clean water is scarce. Only $500 million of the $2.2 billion appropriated for water projects has been spent. And most importantly, insurgent incidents have increased from about 150 per week to over 700 in the last year. Instead of attacks going down over time and with the addition of more troops, attacks have grown dramatically. Since the revelations at Abu Ghraib, American casualties have doubled. An annual State Department report in 2004 indicated a sharp increase in global terrorism.

I said over a year ago, and now the military and the administration agrees, Iraq cannot be won "militarily." I said two years ago, the key to progress in Iraq is to Iraqitize, Internationalize, and Energize. I believe the same today. But I have concluded that the presence of U.S. troops in Iraq is impeding this progress.

Our troops have become the primary target of the insurgency. They are united against U.S. forces and we have become a catalyst for violence. U.S. troops are the common enemy of the Sunnis, Saddamists, and foreign jihadists. I believe with U.S. troop redeployment, the Iraqi security forces will be incentivized to take control. A poll recently conducted shows that over 80 percent of Iraqis are strongly opposed to the presence of coalition troops, and about 45 percent of the Iraqi population believe attacks against American troops are justified. I believe we need to turn Iraq over to the Iraqis.

I believe before the Iraqi elections, scheduled for mid-December, the Iraqi people and the emerging government must be put on notice that the United States will immediately redeploy. All of Iraq must know that Iraq is free—free from United States occupation. I believe this will send a signal to the Sunnis to join the political process for the good of a "free" Iraq.

My plan calls:

- To immediately redeploy U.S. troops consistent with the safety of U.S. forces.
- To create a quick reaction force in the region.
- To create an over-the-horizon presence of Marines.
- To diplomatically pursue security and stability in Iraq.

This war needs to be personalized. As I said before, I have visited with the severely wounded of this war. They are suffering.

Because we in Congress are charged with sending our sons and daughters into battle, it is our responsibility, our *obligation*, to speak out for them. That's why I am speaking out.

Our military has done everything that has been asked of them; the U.S. cannot accomplish anything further in Iraq militarily. *It is time to bring them home.*

"Dear Colleague" Letter to House and Senate Members, December 15, 2005

Dear Colleague:

I am writing you this letter because many have asked me to spell out more completely how I arrived at my decision to introduce a resolution calling for the immediate redeployment of our troops in Iraq and their withdrawal at the earliest practicable time and an emphasis on diplomacy.

From a military perspective, our forces have accomplished an important mission. They have deposed an evil dictator and defeated his army.

The war in Iraq is approaching the end of its third year.

It is time for Iraqi leaders to take control of the future of their country.

It is time that the over 200,000 Iraqis who have received military and police training over the past three years take over the hard job of providing domestic security themselves and stop using American forces as a crutch to lean on.

It is time for U.S. forces to redeploy out of the country in an orderly but rapid way, soon after the Iraqi government is elected on December 15.

It is time that our military "footprint" in the area is converted from a pervasive presence inside Iraq to a powerful quick reaction force outside of Iraq.

It is time for a vigorous and engaged debate on the administration's Iraq policy based on substance and facts, not political hyperbole.

The American people are ahead of the politicians in Washington and are demanding a change of course. They are deeply disturbed by the high level of ongoing violence, the ever-changing explanations of why we are in Iraq, the lack of progress in achieving the war's poorly articulated goals, and the utterly confusing and conflicting messages from the administration telling the American people we plan to "stay the course" while at the same time planning a rapid drawdown of our troops.

In engaging in the debate about how to proceed, let's stick to the facts. It is a disservice to substitute personal and political attacks for reasoned debate about a deadly serious topic, especially when such prominent Americans as the following have spoken out:

—General Brent Scowcroft (Army Ret.), who served as President George H. W. Bush's National Security Advisor, has said that the war in Iraq is *"feeding"* terrorism.

—General George Casey Jr., Commanding General, Multi-National Force Iraq, said in a September 2005 hearing, "The perception of occupation in Iraq is a major driving force behind the insurgency."

—General John Abizaid, Commander, U.S. Central Command, said on the same date, "Reducing the size and visibility of the coalition forces in Iraq is a part of our counterinsurgency strategy."

It is also a disservice to our fine young men and women in uniform to argue that leaders in Washington and elsewhere must refrain from debating this issue for fear of hurting the morale of the troops in the field. Our troops know that diversity of opinion and honorable debate over matters of war and peace are integral and essential parts of America's democratic system. A system they have pledged to defend. A vigorous debate based on facts and not political hyperbole helps to hold our leaders accountable and keeps our country strong. Our troops expect their political leaders to come to these decisions that can affect their lives with much deliberation and a sense of putting the interests of our nation ahead of personal political gain.

Our military forces today are one of the finest in our history. They are loyally and faithfully fulfilling their duty and carrying out their orders. *What is demoralizing to them is not a debate in Washington, but the many missteps by the civilian leadership that have led to a situation where the vast majority of the Iraqi people now view them as occupiers, not as liberators.*

My own views have evolved and taken shape after making a number of inspection trips to Iraq, participating in numerous Congressional hearings on the war, holding untold numbers of private conversations with members of the military and Middle East specialists, and visiting hundreds of the wounded at our military hospitals around the world.

Ultimately, my decision to recommend an immediate redeployment of our troops came down to the answers to three basic questions:

(1) Are the Bush administration's stated goals of the war achievable and are they worth the cost in lives and treasure?
(2) To what extent, if any, is the war in Iraq contributing toward winning the War Against Terrorism?
(3) Would the security of the United States of America be strengthened or weakened by a continued open-ended military presence in Iraq?

Iraqi War Goals Are a Moving Target

It is next to impossible to say America's war goals for Iraq are achievable because they shift and change so often. I believe this is one of the main reasons why the American people are turning against this war. They have not been given a clear and convincing set of reasons as to why the continued sacrifice of brave young Americans is vital to our national security interest.

The administration is currently on its sixth different explanation as to why this war is necessary. The rationale for conducting the war began with emphatic and unequivocal claims that Saddam Hussein and his regime constituted an imminent threat to America. Over time the rationale morphed to the assertion that the war was necessary to remove a vile dictator and free the Iraqi people. It changed again to "if we don't fight them in the streets and back alleys of Baghdad and Tikrit, they'll be here in America wreaking havoc and destruction." It then shifted to the need to spread democracy in the Middle East, followed by the need to prevent a civil war. We are now told that Iraq is the central front of the War on Terror and we can't depart until Iraqi forces are fully and completely trained to take over our mission and not until "complete victory" is achieved.

At the time of our invasion, it was portrayed that Saddam Hussein was a clear and present danger and an "imminent threat" to America and must be removed before a "mushroom cloud" appeared over American soil. It was also implied that Hussein was somehow linked to Osama bin Laden and al-Qaeda. Of course, as we now know, Saddam had no nuclear weapons and there was no proven link to al-Qaeda.

After no nuclear weapons or biological weapons of mass destruction were found, the justification for the war changed to the argument that we have removed a despicable dictator and freed the Iraqi people from oppression and suffering. While this in itself was a significant achievement, the reality is that there are many evil, dictatorial regimes around the world. The American people rarely have been supportive of a policy of using the American military for regime change simply because we could potentially better the lives of the oppressed in other countries. There also must be an overriding national security interest.

The Iraq war rationale then morphed once again into an argument that it was better to fight the terrorists in Iraq than on the streets of Washington, D.C., or Los Angeles. At first glance, this may seem to be a logical argument. A closer look reveals this argument to be based more on emotion and domestic political concerns than on analysis and reason. Every credible analyst believes that the majority of Iraqi insurgents are not al-Qaeda members, but disaffected Sunni Baathists left over from the Saddam regime who perceive no real hope for their future. They are fighting because they lost power and privilege and need to gain a seat at the bargaining table when the future government is put together. They have little need to export their violence to other lands. They want to share power in Iraq.

When it became apparent that the American public was accepting none of these justifications, the administration turned to a policy rationale that involved a sort of Wilsonian construct, saying our goal really has been to make Iraq the centerpiece of our efforts to spread democracy across the Middle East.

I agree with the administration that the upcoming Iraqi election on December 15th is a very important step toward establishing a democratic style of governance. I commend the Iraqi people for the courage they have shown by participating in past elections and no doubt will show again in the upcoming election. It is gratifying to see the citizens of Iraq go to the voting booths, defy the insurgents, dip their fingers in indelible ink, and vote. The "birth throes" of democracy are taking place. American soldiers, Marines, sailors, and airmen who have served in Iraq should feel especially proud of this achievement.

However, this unfolding milestone must be kept in perspective. *Holding a free election is not equivalent to having a functioning democracy.* Without the robust institutions of a free press, an effective police force, a fair judicial system, and an impartial system of laws and regulations that guarantee equal rights and privileges for all, a nation can't truly function as a vibrant democracy.

Unfortunately, this administration has been seen as inconsistent when it comes to setting a good example for the establishment of these democratic institutions, which has set back our objective immensely. We are widely seen around the world as hypocritical, pursuing a policy in Iraq of "do as I say, not as I do." The disaster at Abu Ghraib, sending incoherent messages from the very top of the American government regarding the use of torture, paying for favorable Iraqi news stories, running secret prisons, instituting inconsistent practices on giving prisoners due process rights, and running what many people are beginning to see as a circus trial of Saddam Hussein all hurt U.S. credibility around the world, making it more difficult to achieve this worthy goal.

I agree that our foreign policy should support the opening up of Arab societies—culturally, economically, and politically. This is very important for the long-term peace and stability of the Middle East. But our policy must be guided by an achievable plan that has a realistic timetable and a full appreciation of the limitations of encouraging radical change for nations with cultures and traditions far different from ours.

The administration simply has run out of both time and American soldiers to install a democracy in Iraq in the way it had planned. Instead, the next steps toward achieving this difficult transition rest with the Iraqis themselves, with the role of America reverting to the traditional approach of providing strong and consistent leadership through steady statesmanship, economic aid, and technical assistance. Keeping our troops in Iraq will be a hindrance toward reaching this goal, not a benefit.

We are also hearing yet another new justification for "staying the course"—i.e., if we leave, a civil war will ensue. I would make three brief observations. First, this position is the ultimate in circular logic. The proponents of this view are saying, in effect, "Our invasion and pervasive military presence have created a highly unstable environment in which a civil war may occur in Iraq, and therefore we can't leave Iraq because a civil war may occur."

Second, the ethnic and religious strife in the area of what is now the country of Iraq can be measured not in decades or centuries but in millennia. Those potentially explosive hatreds and tensions will be there if our troops leave in six months, six years, or six decades. The answer to stability in Iraq is not based in military power; it is based in a new political structure that gives all people an effective voice and hope for a brighter economic future.

Third, let's face it: a civil war is already going on, at least to some extent, in the central portion of Iraq—in the four provinces where 50 percent of the Iraqis reside. Would it expand if American troops withdrew in a relatively short time frame?

> *Probably so* if the Iraqis establish a governmental system in the coming months that excludes meaningful participation from major portions of the population (such as the Sunnis).

> *Probably not* if all major stakeholders are given a voice and have a sense of participation in the new government.

The War in Iraq and the War on Terror

The Bush administration's most recent rationale for the war is that Iraq has become the "central front" in the War on Terror, and American troops cannot depart until an Iraqi army and police force is fully trained and equipped to provide stability and contain or eradicate these terrorists.

If the war in Iraq and our continued large military presence was actually succeeding in driving a stake into the heart of al-Qaeda, the terrible loss of life and limb and the quarter of a trillion dollars we have spent in Iraq to date would be worth it. But I believe that President George H. W. Bush's National Security Advisor, General Brent Scowcroft, was right when he observed that the way we are handling the war in Iraq is "feeding" terrorism, not eliminating it. Our heavy military presence in Iraq is the single most important reason our radical enemies have been able to recruit fresh new suicide bombers and terrorists and garner a measure of support from the Iraqi people. Even by the administration's own numbers, our current policy is creating as many or more terrorists than it is eliminating. It is simply not working.

Recent polls now show that 80 percent of the Iraqi people view us as occupiers and want us to leave. In a recent conference in Cairo, Iraqi leaders who are friendly to U.S. interests and are under the constant threat of death from radical terrorists called for a timetable for the withdrawal of American forces. They know what our administration refuses to acknowledge, that our military presence is adding to instability in Iraq, not contributing to peace.

I also have to question the way we have decided to fight this war from a military strategy perspective. From the beginning of the invasion, our civilian war planners in the Pentagon and the White House have badly miscalculated and made gross errors. They have no effective political strategy to this day to win the hearts and minds of the Iraqis.

Instead they have adopted a strategy of military attrition in which they assume the terrorists (or "dead enders," as they were first called) had no base of support, only limited numbers, and no recruiting capability for new fighters. Therefore our policy has been to kill or capture them with U.S. troops (and eventually Iraqi troops) until they are effectively wiped out or neutralized. But we have found this to be a much tougher fight that requires a far more sophisticated approach.

The war in Iraq is the ultimate case of "asymmetrical warfare"—i.e., one side has overwhelming superiority in weapon systems, tactics, and training, and the other has a very limited conventional military capability but uses other strengths such as knowledge of the local neighborhoods, language, and culture, a strong nationalistic sense of resistance to any foreign intervention among the population, religious zealotry, and an abundance of weapons left over from Saddam Hussein (that we have been unable to secure) that will supply them for years to come.

Does the United States have the staying power to fight this type of war of attrition as designed by the civilian Pentagon planners? We have proved we can do amazing things when our nation is committed to doing so. But it is a different question when our leaders have not convinced the country of the need for an all-out commitment. That is certainly the case for Iraq even though the American people overwhelmingly support a true War on Terrorism.

Let us compare, for a moment, the staying power of the two sides in terms of sustainability of their logistics base and their ability to provide sufficient manpower. We have an 8,000-mile supply chain to sustain our forces costing about $1.5 billion dollars a week. The total cost thus far has been a quarter of a trillion dollars. The complexity of this logistics "tail" is as enormous as its length. As just one example, we must supply fourteen different grades of gasoline for our various vehicles and aircraft in the region. At a bare minimum, to sustain our forces, there must be two long truck convoys coming out of Kuwait every day to distribution points near Baghdad, each consisting of roughly one hundred Army trucks the size of eighteen-wheelers that must travel a gauntlet of 700 miles round trip, or the distance between Washington, D.C., and Canton, Ohio. The routes of these long convoys are known by many Iraqis, as are the general schedules. They are regularly attacked. On the personnel side, we have an Army and Guard and Reserves stretched so thin that many soldiers are preparing for their fourth tour in Iraq. This has caused grave concern about our ability to recruit quality men and women into the Army, the Marine Corps, and our Guard and Reserve units, which has grave consequences for our armed forces for many years to come.

For the insurgents to maintain their battle, they need only to hire from what seems to be an inexhaustible supply of apolitical locals for a nominal fee to imbed cheap explosive devices in the roadbed, or to convince young religious zealots to drive an old car filled with explosives into an American convoy.

Without the resolve of the American people, our current strategy for Iraq is bound to fail over time and we must change course.

On the other hand, the American people know we need to be fully engaged in the War on Terror. The administration has tried to make the case that the war in Iraq is the central front in the War on Terror. I simply do not concur that these are one and the same. I believe the American people have reached the same conclusion.

There should be two "central fronts" in the War on Terror. For military purposes, it should be focused on where the leadership and main strength of al-Qaeda and related organizations exist. To me, that is clearly in the area of Afghanistan, Pakistan, and Saudi Arabia, not Iraq. We do not have unlimited intelligence and military assets to cover both theaters, and unfortunately the priority of Iraq has hurt our ability in the true fight, which is currently in Afghanistan and surrounding areas.

The second and perhaps more important "front" in the War on Terror is the long-term battle for the hearts and minds of the Muslim world. This is not a battle for the Department of Defense, but for the Department of State. It is a battle we should be able to win resoundingly because we share so many values with common Muslims and stand for the principles of freedom and equality. Yet by any measure, our efforts have been a dismal failure so far. We simply have not put the emphasis on articulating our common purpose, values, and intentions with the general Muslim population that we should. This is the area that deserves the most attention in the coming years.

America Needs a National Strategy to Win the War Against Terrorism

In setting a national security strategy, communicating that strategy to the public, and analyzing alternative proposals, America's leaders must, first and foremost, view matters through the lens of the threat. What is the primary threat to America's national security? How do we best protect ourselves from that threat? What resources should we allocate to which programs in order to counter the threat in the most cost-effective manner? This administration has become so deeply engrossed and invested in the politics of the Iraqi war that they have lost this bigger and more important perspective.

The $1.5 billion-a-week cost of the war in Iraq is astronomical. Funds appropriated for the war and related nation building are quickly approaching $300 billion. In constant dollars, that total is almost three-quarters of the cost of the Korean War and one-half of the cost of the Vietnam War.

The annual expenditures for the war on Iraq dwarf those of the combined budgets of all other programs in place to fight terrorism. That is a gross misallocation of resources and has important consequences for making our population safer from terrorist attack. The dollars used to pay for an 8,000-mile logistical pipeline to Iraq could be reapplied to fixing our many vulnerabilities at home in the transportation sector, or at chemical plants, river levees, or nuclear power plants.

Just in the last two weeks the bipartisan National Commission on Terrorist Attacks Upon the United States, chaired by Gov. Thomas Kean, issued a failing report card on the administration's leadership to improve our counter-terrorist defenses. Of the forty-one commission recommendations made seventeen months ago, progress was judged to be "unacceptable," with many more grades of Fs than As being issued by the commission (5 Fs, 12 Ds, and 1 A-). Basic recommendations, such as the coordination of fire and police communication lines, still have not been accomplished.

Conclusion

The administration has spelled out its "Strategy for Victory in Iraq." Instead, I believe we must have a "Strategy for Victory Against Global Terrorism."

We should be conducting a war against the terrorists in which America's borders are effectively guarded to keep out terrorists, and programs are in place to ensure that none of the millions of cargo containers that enter American ports contain explosives that could render one or more of our great ports inoperable and debilitate our economy, not a "War on Terror" where our finest young people are sacrificing their lives and limbs to implement the visions of "intellectual geopolitical strategists" who fantasize about Jeffersonian democracies being installed in Middle East cultures that have had authoritarian regimes during their entire two millennia of existence.

A "War on Terror" should be waged in which respect for America's policies and America's principles enables our country to count heavily on the cooperation and action of the intelligence, military, and law enforcement agencies of countries around the world to achieve ultimate victory against the terrorists.

Ever since the invasion of Iraq, each major event has been described by the administration as an important turning point toward achieving its goals in Iraq. Those events include Saddam Hussein's sons being killed in a firefight, the agreement to transfer power to an interim government, the capture of Saddam Hussein, the Iraqi Council signing an interim constitution, replacement of the Iraqi Governing Council with a caretaker government, Ayad Allawi being designated Prime Minister of the Iraqi interim government, and October 15th elections to approve a Constitution.

Yet the violence is as widespread as ever. The killed in action and wounded soldiers, those who have lost limbs, have been maimed and dis-figured, those with traumatic head injuries, those whose bodies are embed-ded with shrapnel and the thousands who are suffering from battle fatigue are returning home every day.

As I noted earlier, if the war in Iraq was actually driving a stake through the heart of al-Qaeda, the cost of the war and loss of life and limb could be justified. But I believe the opposite is true—the war in Iraq is not enhancing the War Against Terrorism, it is hurting the prospects for winning it.

It is time to "change the course" of our Iraqi policy. It is time to wage an effective war against international terrorism. The American people know it. It is time for the administration and the Congress to catch up with them.

JOHN P. MURTHA
Member of Congress

Letter to President George W. Bush, February 1, 2006

Wednesday, February 1, 2006

The Honorable George W. Bush
President of the United States of America
1600 Pennsylvania Avenue
Washington, D.C. 20500

Dear Mr. President,

This March will mark the beginning of the fourth year of the war in Iraq. In contrast, U.S. involvement in WWI came to an end after nineteen months. Victory in Europe was declared in WWII after three years, five months. In the Korean War, a cease-fire was signed after three years and one month. But after more than three and a half years into the war in Iraq, your administration finally produced what is called a "Plan for Victory" in Iraq.

Iraq is not the center for the global war on terrorism. I believe Iraq has diverted our attention away from the fight against global terrorism and has depleted the required resources needed to wage an effective war. It is esti-mated that there are only about 750 to 1,000 al-Qaeda in Iraq. I believe the

Iraqis will force them out or kill them after U.S. troops are gone. In fact, there is now evidence that Iraqi insurgent groups are increasingly turning against al-Qaeda and other foreign terrorists.

Our country needs a vigorous and comprehensive strategy for victory against global terrorism. The architect of 9/11 is still out there but now has an international microphone. We must get back to the real issue at hand—we have to root out and destroy al-Qaeda's worldwide network.

There are four key elements that I recommend to reinvigorate our global anti-terrorism effort: Redeploy, Replace, Reallocate, and Reconstitute.

Redeploy

The war in Iraq is fueling terrorism, not eliminating it. Our continued military presence feeds the strong anti-foreigner fervor that has existed in this part of the world for centuries. A vast majority of the Iraqi people now view American troops as occupiers, not liberators. Over 80 percent of Iraqis want U.S. forces to leave Iraq, and 47 percent think it is justified to attack Americans. Seventy percent of Iraqis favor a timetable for withdrawal of U.S. forces, with half favoring a withdrawal in the next six months. In fact, 67 percent of Iraqis expect day-to-day security for Iraqi citizens will improve if U.S. forces withdraw in six months and over 60 percent believe violent attacks, including those that are ethnically motivated, will decrease. Our military presence is the single most important reason why the Iraqis have tolerated the foreign terrorists, who account for less than 7 percent of the insurgency. Ninety-three percent of the insurgency is made up of Iraqis. Once our troops are redeployed, the Iraqis will reject the terrorists and deny them a safe haven in Iraq. The Iraqis are against a foreign presence in Iraq of any kind.

The steadfast and valiant efforts of the United States military and coalition partners have provided the Iraqi people with the framework needed to self-govern. The Iraqis held elections that have been touted as highly successful, based primarily on the accounts of Iraqis who went to the polls. But our continued military presence in Iraq, regardless of the motives behind it, is seen by Iraqis as interfering in Iraq's democratic process and undercuts the chances for the newly elected government to be successful. Recently, Iraq's National Security Adviser accused U.S. negotiators of going behind the back of the Iraqi government on talks with insurgents, saying the process could encourage more violence. He said, "Americans are making a huge and fatal mistake in their policy for appeasement and they should not do this. They should leave the Iraqi government to deal with it. . . . The United States should allow the new Iraqi government to decide on how to quell the insurgency."

In December 2005, an ABC News poll in Iraq produced some noteworthy results. Fifty-seven percent of Iraqis identified national security as the country's top priority. When asked to rate the confidence in public institutions, they gave Iraqi police a 68 percent confidence level, the Iraqi army 67 percent, religious leaders 67 percent. But the U.S./U.K. forces scored the lowest, a mere 18 percent.

The longer our military stays in Iraq, the more unwelcome we will be. We will be increasingly entangled in an open-ended nation-building mission, one that our military cannot accomplish amidst a civil war. Our troops will continue to be the targets of Iraqis who see them as interfering occupiers.

Redeploying our forces from Iraq and stationing a mobile force outside of the country removes a major antagonizing factor. I believe we will see a swift demise of foreign terrorist groups in Iraq if we redeploy outside of the country. Further, our troops will no longer be the targets of bloody attacks.

Replace

The ever-changing justifications of the war in Iraq, combined with tragic missteps, have resulted in a worldwide collapse of support for U.S. policies in Iraq.

The credibility of the United States of America will not be restored if we continue down the path of saying one thing and doing another. We must not lower our standards and tactics to those of the terrorists. In order to keep our homeland secure, we must hold true to the values that molded our American democracy, even in the face of adversity. Former Secretary of Homeland Security Tom Ridge said it best during a speech in March 2004 to the Institute of Defense and Strategic Studies: "America knows we cannot seek a double standard. And America knows we get what we give. And so we must and will always be careful to respect people's privacy, civil liberties and reputations. To suggest that there is a tradeoff between security and individual freedoms—that we must discard one protection for the other—is a false choice. You do not defend liberty to forsake it."

Restoring the world's confidence in America as a competent and morally superior world leader is essential to winning the war on global terrorism.

A recent pubic opinion poll, conducted jointly with Zogby International and taken in Jordan, Lebanon, Morocco, Saudi Arabia, Egypt, and the United Arab Emirates, found that 81 percent said the war in Iraq had brought less peace to the Middle East. A majority of the respondents said they view the United States as the biggest threat to their nations.

Mr. President, I believe in order to restore our credibility, you must hold accountable those responsible for so many missteps and install a fresh team that demonstrates true diplomatic skill, knowledge of cultural differences, and a willingness to earnestly engage other leaders in a respectful and constructive way. This would do much to reinvigorate international participation in a truly effective war on global terrorism.

Reallocate

The Department of Defense has been allocated $238 billion for the war in Iraq, with average monthly costs growing significantly since the beginning of the war.* In 2003 the average monthly war cost was $4.4 billion; by 2005 the average monthly cost had reached $6.1 billion.

Despite the urgent homeland security needs of our country, the bipartisan 9/11 Commission issued a dismal report card on the efforts to improve our counterterrorist defenses. Even the most basic of recommendations, such as the coordination of fire and police communication lines, still have not been accomplished.

In the face of threats from international terrorists, we need to reallocate funds from the war in Iraq to protecting the United States against attack. A safe and swift redeployment from Iraq will allow us to do just that.

Reconstitute

The U.S. Army is the smallest it's been since 1941. It is highly capable. But this drawn-out conflict has put tremendous stress on our military, particularly on our Army and Marine Corps, whose operations tempo has increased substantially since 9/11.

The Government Accountability Office issued a report in November

---

*After this letter was sent, I was advised that additional supplemental requests for fiscal year 2006, totaling approximately $120 billion, will be submitted.

2005 addressing the challenges of military personnel recruitment and retention and noted that the Department of Defense had been unable to fill over 112,000 positions in critical occupational specialties. This shortfall includes intelligence analysts, special forces, interpreters, and demolition experts—those on whom we rely so heavily in today's asymmetric battlefield.

Some of our troops have been deployed four times over the last three years. Enlistment for the regular forces as well as the Guard and Reserves is well below recruitment goals. In 2005, the Army missed its recruitment goal for the first time since 1999, even after offering enlistment bonuses and incentives, lowering its monthly goals, and lowering its recruitment standards. As retired Army officer Andrew Krepinevich recently warned in a report to the Pentagon, the Army is "in a race against time" to adjust to the demands of war "or risk 'breaking' the force in the form of a catastrophic decline" in recruitment and reenlistment.

The harsh environment in which we are operating our equipment in Iraq, combined with the equipment usage rate (ten times greater than peacetime levels), is taking a heavy toll on our ground equipment. It is currently estimated that $50 billion will be required to refurbish this equipment.

Further, in its response to Hurricane Katrina, the National Guard realized that it had over $1.3 billion in equipment shortfalls. This has created a tremendous burden on nondeployed Guard units on whom this country depends so heavily to respond to domestic disasters and possible terrorist attacks. Without relief, Army Guard units will face growing equipment shortages and challenges in regaining operational readiness for future missions at home and overseas.

Since 9/11, Congress has appropriated about $334 billion for military operations in Iraq and Afghanistan, while the insurgents have spent hundreds of thousands. We have seen reports estimating that the total cost of the wars may reach as high as $1 trillion. These estimates are said to include such costs as providing long-term disability benefits and care for injured service members. It is estimated today that over 16,000 U.S. troops have been wounded in Iraq, 10,481 of whom have been wounded by "weaponry explosive devices."

But while war costs continue to climb, cuts are being made to the defense budget. As soon as the war is over, there will be pressure to cut even more. This year, even while we are at war, 8 billion dollars were cut from the base defense spending bill. You ordered another $32 billion in cuts to the defense budget over the next five years, with $11.6 billion coming from the Army.

The Pentagon told Congress only last year that it needed seventy-seven combat brigades to fulfill its missions, but now insists it only needs seventy. In fact, six of the seven combat brigades will be cut from the National Guard, reducing its combat units from thirty-four to twenty-eight. Even though all of the National Guard combat brigades have been deployed overseas since 9/11, your administration has determined that because of funding shortfalls, our combat ground forces can be reduced. Not only will these cuts diminish our combat power, but our ability to respond to natural disasters and terrorist threats to our homeland will be adversely affected. It is obvious that the cost of the war, in conjunction with the Army's inability to meet recruitment goals, has impacted this estimate. My concern is that instead of our force structure being based on the future threat, it is now being based on the number of troops and level of funding available.

I am concerned that costly program cuts will lead to costly mistakes and we will be unable to sustain another deployment even if there is a real threat. The future of our military and the future of our country could very well be at stake. The high dollar forecasts of our future military weapons systems and military health care add pressure to cut costs on the backs of these programs. As our weapons systems age, the concern becomes even greater.

During a time of war, we are cutting our combat force, we have not mobilized industry, and have never fully mobilized our military. On our current path, I believe that we are not only in danger of breaking our military, but that we are increasing the chances of a major miscalculation by our future enemies, who may perceive us as vulnerable.

Sincerely,

JOHN P. MURTHA
Member of Congress

NOTES

1. Service in Vietnam, 1966-1967

1. Norman Schwarzkopf, *It Doesn't Take a Hero* (New York: Bantam, 1992), 157.
2. Richard Cohen, "Tunnel War," *Washington Post*, May 2, 2000, A26.
3. Colin Powell, *My American Journey* (New York: Random House, 1995), 146–47.
4. Quoted in Bernard B. Fall, *Last Reflections on a War* (New York: Schocken, 1972), 180.

2. Election to Congress and Return to Vietnam

1. "An Unclear Gauge," *Time*, February 18, 1974, p. 13.
2. Lewis Sorley, *A Better War: The Unexamined Victories and Final Tragedy of America's Last Years in Vietnam* (New York: Harcourt Brace, 1999), 119.
3. Stephen Morris, "Don't Blame America for the Killing Fields," *Wall Street Journal*, May 3, 2000, A26.
4. Ben Kiernan, *The Pol Pot Regime* (New Haven: Yale University Press, 1996), 8.
5. Russell R. Rose, ed., *Cambodia: A Country Study* (Washington, D.C.: Federal Research Division, Library of Congress, 1990), 51.

3. Tragedy in Lebanon

1. Federal Research Division, Library of Congress, *Lebanon: A Country Study* (Washington D.C., 1989), 59, 21.
2. Sandra Mackey, *Lebanon: Death of a Nation* (New York: Congdon & Weed, 1989), 11.
3. Ibid., 224.
4. *Department of Defense Commission on Beirut International Airport Terrorist Attack* (Washington, D.C.: Navy Library Department, 1983), 29.
5. Eric Hammel, *The Root: The Marines in Beirut* (New York: Harcourt Brace Jovanovich, 1985), 53.

6. Ibid., 52.

7. Ibid., 53.

8. Caspar Weinberger, *Fighting for Peace: Seven Critical Years in the Pentagon* (New York: Warner, 1990), 151.

9. Colin Powell, *My American Journey* (New York: Random House, 1995), 291.

10. Report of Department of Defense Commission on Beirut International Airport Terrorist Attack (Navy Library Department, 1983), 32; Clyde Mark, "Lebanon: The Internal Conflict," issue brief (Congressional Research Service, 1983), 8.

11. Federal Research Division, *Lebanon*, 5.

12. Report of Department of Defense Commission, 41.

13. James Wright, *Balance of Power* (Atlanta: Turner, 1996), 393.

14. Powell, *My American Journey*, 291–92.

15. Gideon Rose, "The Exit Strategy Delusion," *Foreign Affairs*, January/February 1998, p. 56.

4. The Soviet Union's Defeat in Afghanistan

1. Milton Bearden, "Afghanistan, Graveyard of Empires," *Foreign Affairs*, November/December 2001, p. 17.

2. Sandy Gall, *Afghanistan: Agony of a Nation* (New York: Random House, 1988), 4.

3. American University, *Afghanistan: A Country Study*, Foreign Affairs Studies (Washington, D.C., 1986), xxiii.

4. Gall, *Afghanistan*, 5–6.

5. Oleg Sarin and Lev Dvoretsky, *The Afghan Syndrome: The Soviet Union's Vietnam* (Novato, Calif.: Presidio Press, 1993), 177.

6. American University, *Afghanistan*, xxi, 29.

7. Ibid., xxi.

8. Robert Pear, "Arming Afghan Guerrillas: A Huge Effort Led by U.S.," *New York Times*, April 18, 1988, p. 1.

9. "Stingers That Backfire," *Boston Globe*, September 1, 1988, p. 20.

10. David B. Ottoway, "Big Losses of Soviet Planes Cited; Afghan Rebels Said to Down One a Day," *Washington Post*, December 17, 1986, A32.

11. Gabriel Schoenfeld, "Twenty-four Lies About the Cold War," *Commentary*, March 1999, p. 28.

12. James Dale Davidson and Lord William Rees-Mogg, *The Great Reckoning* (New York: Simon & Schuster, 1993), 186.

13. Ibid., 185.

5. High-Drama Election in the Philippines

1. Stanley Karnow, *In Our Image* (New York: Ballantine, 1989), 398.

2. Bryan Johnson, *Four Days of Courage* (New York: Free Press, 1987), 16.

3. Pico Ayer and David Aikman, "Woman of the Year," *Time*, January 5, 1987, p. 18.

4. International Observer Delegation, *A Path to Democratic Renewal* (Washington, D.C.: National Democratic Institute for International Affairs and National Republican Institute for International Affairs, 1986), 10.

5. Lewis Simons, *Worth Dying For* (New York: Morrow, 1987), 224.

6. Richard Lugar, *Letters to the Next President* (New York: Simon & Schuster, 1988), 97.

7. *Economist,* World Politics and Current Affairs sec., U.S. ed., February 15, 1986, p. 31.

8. International Observer Delegation, *Path to Democratic Renewals,* 122.

9. Johnson, *Four Days of Courage,* 82.

10. George Shultz, *Turmoil and Triumph: My Years as Secretary of State* (New York: Scribner, 1993), 624.

11. Ayer and Aikman, "Woman of the Year," 18.

12. Shultz, *Turmoil and Triumph,* 636.

13. Quoted in Lawrence Knutson, "Washington Dateline," Associated Press, Lexis-Nexis, February 14, 1986.

14. International Observer Delegation, *Path to Democratic Renewal,* 127.

15. *Los Angeles Times,* February 27, 1986.

16. Ayer and Aikman, "Woman of the Year," 20.

17. George de Lama and Dorothy Collin, "U. S. Offers Asylum to Old Friend," *Chicago Tribune,* February 26, 1986, p. 1.

18. Fox Butterfield, "In Manila Palace, Silk Dresses, 6000 Shoes," *New York Times,* March 9, 1986, p. 1.

19. Simons, *Worth Dying For,* 6.

20. Karnow, *In Our Image,* 6.

21. Ibid., 7.

22. Frank Murkowski, "Observations on Recent Events in the Philippines," in *The Fletcher Forum,* Summer 1986, pp. 189–90.

6. A Stolen Election and U.S. Intervention in Panama

1. David McCullough, *The Path Between the Seas* (New York: Simon & Schuster, 1977), 147.

2. Ibid., 151.

3. Walter LaFeber, *The Panama Canal: The Crisis in Historical Perspective* (New York: Oxford University Press, 1989), 47, 48.

4. Ibid., 198.

5. Bob Woodward, *The Commanders* (New York: Simon & Schuster, 1991), 120.

6. Malcolm McConnell, *Just Cause* (New York: St. Martin's Press, 1991), 12.

7. Ibid., 17, 18.

8. Ibid., 95.

9. "The Dictator and the Diplomat," *Newsweek,* January 15, 1990, p. 27.

10. Larry Rother, "Papal Envoy Asserts Psychology, Not Ultimatum, Turned Noriega," *New York Times,* January 6, 1990, A1, A9.

11. Colin Powell, *My American Journey* (New York: Random House, 1995), 434.

7. Operations Desert Shield and Desert Storm

1. Mortimer Zuckerman, "The Most Dangerous Addict," *U.S. News & World Report,* February 16, 1998, p. 8.

2. Adel Darwish and Gregory Alexander, *Unholy Babylon: The Secret History of Saddam's War* (New York: St. Martin's Press, 1991), 201.

3. Barbara Crossette, "1,500 Executions Cited for Iraq in Past Years, Mostly for Politics," *New York Times,* April 14, 1998, A1.

4. Judith Miller and Laurie Mylroie, *Saddam Hussein and the Crisis in the Gulf* (New York: Times Books, 1990), 9.

5. "Kuwait: How the West Blundered," *Economist,* September 19, 1990, p. 8.

6. Ibid., 7.

7. Miller and Mylroie, *Saddam Hussein,* 227.

8. H. Norman Schwarzkopf with Peter Petre, *It Doesn't Take a Hero* (New York: Bantam, 1992), 342.

9. George Bush and Brent Scowcroft, *A World Transformed* (New York: Knopf, 1998), 391.

10. Schwarzkopf, *It Doesn't Take a Hero,* 342.

11. John B. Conaway and Jeff Neligar, *Call Out the Guard* (Paducah, Ky.: Turner, 1997), 56.

12. Harry Summers, *On Strategy: A Critical Analysis of the Vietnam War* (New York: Dell, 1984), 47.

13. Stephen Solarz, "The Stakes in the Gulf," *New Republic,* June 7, 1991, p. 24.

14. *Triumph without Victory: The Unreported History of the Persian Gulf War/U.S. News & World Report* (New York: Times Books, 1992), 5–6.

15. Bush and Scowcroft, *World Transformed,* 489.

8. Humanitarian Mission Turns to Manhunt in Somalia

1. Russell Watson, "Troops to Somalia," *Newsweek,* December 7, 1992, p. 17.

2. Federal Book Division, Congressional Research Service, *Somalia: A National Profile* (Washington, D.C.: Library of Congress, 1993), xxi.

3. Donald M. Snow, "Peacekeeping, Peacemaking, and Peace Enforcement: The U.S. Role in the New International Order," paper published by the Strategic Studies Institute, U.S. Army War College, Carlisle, Pa., February 1993, p. 17.

4. William Shawcross, *Deliver Us from Evil* (New York: Simon & Schuster, 2000), 86.

5. Vernon Loeb, "Warlords, Peacekeepers, and Spies," *Washington Post Magazine,* February 27, 2000, p. 12.

6. Keith Richburg, *Out of America* (New York: New Republic Book, Basic Books, 1997), 78.

7. Loeb, "Warlords, Peacekeepers, and Spies," 11.

8. Michael Maren, *The Road to Hell* (New York: Free Press, 1997), 228.

9. Ibid., 230.

10. John R. Murphy, "Memories of Somalia," *Marine Corps Gazette,* April 1998, p. 20.

11. Mark Bowden, *Black Hawk Down: A Story of Modern War* (New York: Atlantic Monthly Press, 1999), 12.

12. Ibid., 111.

13. Edward N. Luttwak, "Toward Post-Heroic Warfare," *Foreign Affairs,* May/June 1995, p. 11.

9. War in the Balkans

1. David Fromkin, *Kosovo Crossing: American Ideals Meet Reality on the Balkan Battlefields* (New York: Free Press, 1999), 89.

2. Federal Research Division, Library of Congress, *Yugoslavia: A Country Study* (Washington, D.C., 1992), 69–70.

3. Robert Kaplan, *Balkan Ghosts: A Journey through History* (New York: Vintage Books, 1993), 57–58.

4. William Shawcross, *Deliver Us from Evil* (New York: Simon & Schuster, 2000), 15.

5. Ibid., 154.

6. Ibid., 158.

7. Ibid., 166.

8. Richard Holbrooke, *To End a War* (New York: Random House, 1998), 72–73.

9. Shawcross, *Deliver Us from Evil,* 187.

10. Julie Kim and Steven Woehrel, *Kosovo and U.S. Policy* (Washington, D.C.: Congressional Research Service, 1999), 2–3.

11. Julie Kim, *Kosovo Conflict Chronology: September 1998–March 1999* (Washington, D.C.: Congressional Research Service, 1999), 11.

12. Javier Solana, "NATO's Success in Kosovo," *Foreign Affairs,* November/December 1999, p. 114.

13. Steve Bowman, *Kosovo: U.S. and Allied Military Operations* (Washington, D.C.: Congressional Research Service, 2000), 4.

14. Michael Ignatieff, *Virtual War: Kosovo and Beyond* (New York: Henry Holt, 2000), 96.

15. Ivo Daalder and Michael O'Hanlon, "Unlearning the Lessons of Kosovo," *Foreign Policy,* Fall 1999, p. 133.

16. U.S. House of Representatives, Committee on Armed Services, Subcommittee Professional Staff, "Operations in Kosovo: Problems Encountered, Lessons Learned, and Reconstitution," memorandum for Military Readiness Subcommittee, October 22, 1999, p. 3.

17. General John P. Jumper, Commander, U.S. Air Force in Europe, testimony before Committee on Armed Services, Subcommittee on Military Readiness, U.S. House of Representatives, 106th Cong., 1st sess., October 26, 1999.

18. Dana Priest, "A Decisive Battle That Never Was," *Washington Post,* September 19, 1999, A1.

19. Kosovo Task Force, Foreign Affairs, Defense, and Trade Division, Congressional Research Service, *Kosovo Situation Reports,* April 1999, p. 31.

20. Daalder and O'Hanlon, "Unlearning the Lessons of Kosovo," 134.

21. Ignatieff, *Virtual War,* 108.

22. Ibid., 108–9.

23. Albert Speer, *Inside the Third Reich* (New York: Simon & Schuster, 1970), 280.

24. Richard J. Newman, "The Bombs That Failed in Kosovo," *U.S. News & World Report,* September 20, 1999, p. 29.

25. Testimony of General John P. Jumper, House Committee on Armed Services, Subcommittee on Military Readiness, October 26, 1999.

26. Steven Lee Myers, "Chinese Embassy Bombing: A Wide Net of Blame," *New York Times,* April 17, 2000, A10.

27. Newman, "Bombs That Failed," 29.

28. Ignatieff, *Virtual War,* 106.

29. Department of Defense, *Kosovo/Operation Allied Force after Action Report* (Washington, D.C.: GPO, 2000), 141.

30. Wesley K. Clark, *Waging Modern War: Bosnia, Kosovo, and the Future of Combat* (New York: Public Affairs, 2001), 238.

31. Miranda Vickers, "Kosovo, One Year Later," *Wall Street Journal,* Mar. 24, 2000.

32. Jeffrey Smith and Peter Smith, "How Milošević Lost His Grip; Leader Was Isolated in Final Days," *Washington Post,* October 15, 2000, A1.

10. September 11, 2001

1. U.S. Commission on National Security/21st Century, *Road Map for National Security: Imperative for Change* (Washington, D.C.: February 15, 2001), 10.
2. David Kennedy, "Fighting an Elusive Enemy," *New York Times,* September 16, 2001, sec. 4, p. 11.
3. Thomas G. Donlan, "What's in a Box?" *Barron's,* January 14, 2002, p. 35.

11. Reflecting on the Past/Looking to the Future

1. Robert Gates, "The Global Challenge to American Intelligence," speech delivered on December 15, 1992, Los Angeles, Calif.
2. Vernon Loeb, "Warlords, Peacekeepers, and Spies," *Washington Post Magazine,* February 27, 2000, p. 11.
3. Joseph S. Nye Jr., "Redefining the National Interest," *Foreign Affairs,* July/August 1999, p. 24.
4. Michael O'Hanlon, "Saving Lives with Force," *New Republic,* July 12, 1999, p. 23.
5. David Fromkin, *Kosovo Crossing: American Ideals Meet Reality on the Balkan Battlefields* (New York: Free Press, 1999), 79–80.
6. Quoted in James Traub, "The Ambitions of Richard Holbrooke," *New York Times Magazine,* March 26, 2000, p. 81.
7. William Langewiesche, "Peace Is Hell," *Atlantic Monthly,* October 2001, p. 51.
8. Nina Serafino, *Military Interventions by U.S. Forces from Vietnam to Bosnia: Background, Outcomes, and Lessons Learned for Kosovo* (Washington, D.C.: Congressional Research Service, 2000), 14.
9. Karl Mueller, "Flexible Power Projection for a Dynamic World: Exploiting the Potential of Air Power," in *Holding the Line: U.S. Defense Alternatives for the Early 21st Century,* ed. Cindy Williams (Cambridge: MIT Press, 2001), 236.
10. John Keegan, "The Changing Face of War," *Wall Street Journal,* Nov. 27, 2001, 22.
11. Ivo Daalder and Michael O'Hanlon, "Unlearning the Lessons of Kosovo," *Foreign Policy,* Fall 1999, pp. 132, 139.
12. William Shawcross, *Deliver Us from Evil* (New York: Simon & Schuster, 2000), 166.
13. Quoted in Traub, "Ambitions of Richard Holbrooke," 81.
14. Martin Wolf, "Ascent towards an Open Future," *Financial Times,* December 22, 1999, p. 26.
15. Richard Hart Sinnreich, "Delusions of a Superpower," *Washington Post,* November 22, 2000, A25.
16. Loren Thompson, "Military Supremacy and How We Keep It," *Policy Review,* October/November 1999, F20.

Epilogue

1. President George W. Bush, remarks on Iraq in television address to the nation, Cincinnati, Ohio, October 7, 2002.

2. Condoleezza Rice, interview by Wolf Blitzer, *Late Edition,* CNN, September 8, 2002.

3. David Kay, testimony before Senate Armed Services Committee, Washington, D.C., January 28, 2004.

4. David Kay, interview by Jim Lehrer, *Newshour with Jim Lehrer,* PBS, January 29, 2004.

5. Paul Wolfowitz, testimony before House Appropriations Committee, Washington, D.C., March 27, 2003.

6. James Fallows, "Blind into Baghdad," *Atlantic Monthly,* February 2004, p. 43.

7. David Reiff, "Blueprint for a Mess," *New York Times Magazine,* November 2, 2003, p. 22.

8. Fallows, "Blind into Baghdad," p. 43.

9. Kay, interview by Lehrer, January 29, 2004.

10. Carl Bildt, "We Must Build States and Not Nations," *Financial Times,* January 16, 2004, p. 15.

11. Paul Wolfowitz, remarks in town hall meeting with Iraqi-American community, Dearborn, Mich., February 23, 2003.

12. Rajiv Chandrasekaran, "The Final Word on Iraq's Future: Bremer Consults and Cajoles, But in the End, He's the Boss," *Washington Post,* June 18, 2003, A1.

13. Gregg Zoroya, "Citizen Soldiers Report Long Tour, Little Support," *USA Today,* January 16, 2003, A1.

14. Ibid.

15. Lee Hockstader, "Army Stops Many Soldiers from Quitting: Orders Extend Enlistments to Curtail Troop Shortages," *Washington Post,* December 29, 2003, A1.

16. Joseph L. Galloway, "Longer Stay Takes a Toll on Army's Equipment," *Miami Herald,* September 23, 2003, p. 1.

17. Ibid.

18. Ibid.

19. White House, *The National Security Strategy of the United States of America* (Washington, D.C.: GPO, 2002), 1.

20. President George W. Bush and Tony Blair, joint news conference, Washington, D.C., January 31, 2003.

21. Barry Renfrew, "Al Qaeda Ranks Boosted by War on Terror, Iraq," *Washington Times,* May 26, 2004, A13.

22. President George W. Bush, remarks at photo opportunity with President Alvaro Uribe of Colombia, Washington, D.C., September 25, 2002.

23. "The Moral of Saddam Hussein," *Economist,* December 20, 2003, p. 11.

24. Michael Ignatieff, "Why America Must Know Its Limits," *Financial Times,* December 24, 2003, p. 11.

25. Fareed Zakaria, *The Future of Freedom* (New York: W. W. Norton, 2003), 120.

26. "They Say We're Getting a Democracy," *Economist,* November 15, 2003, p. 9.

27. Susan Sachs, "The Cleric Spoiling U.S. Plans," *New York Times,* January 18, 2004, sec. 4, p. 1.

28. Quentin Peel, "No Democracy Is Immune to Extremism," *Financial Times,* January 8, 2004, p. 13.

29. Georgie Anne Geyer, "Dysfunctional Democracy," *Washington Times,* March 8, 2004, A17.

30. Morton Abramowitz, "Does Iraq Matter?" *The National Interest,* Spring 2004, p. 44.

INDEX

Page numbers in italics refer to illustrations.

Index

Index

Index